In Our Own Words

A Guide with Readings for Student Writers

SECOND EDITION

REBECCA MLYNARCZYK

*Kingsborough Community College
of the City University of New York*

STEVEN B. HABER

Jersey City State College

 **CAMBRIDGE**
UNIVERSITY PRESS

For Ruth Adams
and Frank, Susanna, and Alex Mlynarczyk

R.M.

For Ruth and Martin Haber and Xiao-Lan Gao

S.H.

PUBLISHED BY THE PRESS SYNDICATE OF THE UNIVERSITY OF CAMBRIDGE
The Pitt Building, Trumpington Street, Cambridge, United Kingdom

CAMBRIDGE UNIVERSITY PRESS
The Edinburgh Building, Cambridge CB2 2RU, UK   www.cup.cam.ac.uk
40 West 20th Street, New York, NY 10011–4211, USA   www.cup.org
10 Stamford Road, Oakleigh, Melbourne 3166, Australia
Ruiz de Alarcón 13, 28014 Madrid, Spain

First published by St. Martin's Press, Inc. 1996

Reprinted 1998
Second printing 1999

Printed in the United States of America

Library of Congress Cataloging-in-Publication Data Available

ISBN 0 521 65764 4 Student's Book
ISBN 0 521 65763 6 Instructor's Manual

Acknowledgments are given on pages 330–331.

Contents

Part II Writing   33

HOW TO USE PART II *35*

PERSONAL WRITING *36*

Preface

The idea for *In Our Own Words: A Guide with Readings for Student Writers* originated with the discovery that when we used writing by student authors in our college courses, students responded differently than when we assigned works by better-known, published authors. While the prose of famous writers excited the imagination of some students, many found it difficult to become engaged in words and worlds so different from their own. We saw student writing as a way to bring more voices into the literary conversation.

The positive responses from students and teachers who have used the first edition of this book have amply rewarded our belief in the importance of highlighting student writing. Students who never before thought of themselves as writers have been inspired by reading the student essays and have responded by producing equally engaging pieces.

The accessibility of student writing is based on a simple principle: People are interested in that which they hold in common. The students in our classes share the experience of living or having lived in two cultures, the challenge of learning a new language, and the exhilaration and frustration of cultural surprise. Those who share so much are naturally curious about the observations, sensitivities, tensions, and successes of their peers.

Yet beyond multiculturalism, another shared experience is the recent arrival of these students into the arena of writing in an academic context. For those who find being in a writing class unfamiliar or threatening, the presentation of student writing sends a clear message: You are welcome here; your writing is welcome here.

Selecting the readings for the second edition was exciting because it gave us a chance to introduce new student writers to an audience beyond the writing classroom. These new writers come from a variety of countries, cultures, and social backgrounds. Their essays made us smile, laugh out loud, shake our heads in amazement, and feel the deepest respect. They are the artifacts of wonderful hidden worlds that lie within each of our students; we felt privileged to be allowed inside.

GUIDING PRINCIPLES

In Our Own Words, second edition, motivates students to take themselves seriously as writers and actively engage in writing as a communicative process. The book accomplishes these goals in five ways:

- *Engaging the students' interest through reading selections by other students on high-interest themes.* Students read essays by student writers on such topics as cultural differences and the challenges of learning English, subjects that are of immediate relevance to multicultural college students.
- *Increasing students' motivation to write by featuring the writing of their peers.* It is our belief that good writing is contagious. A student reads another student's reminiscence about a childhood home, and similar memories are automatically summoned. One writer's description of a first encounter with a new culture inspires others to relate their own stories of cultural surprise.
- *Including well-designed classroom activities that encourage students to see writing as a social process.* These activities, all of which have been successful in our own classes, encourage discussion and social interaction among students as they work on their writing. Students are helped to provide meaningful response to the writing of their classmates through activities that teach the techniques of constructive criticism and through the Peer Response Sheets included at the end of each of the writing chapters.
- *Providing a framework of support as students move from personal to more formal writing.* The book begins with personal writing and ends with the more formal writing required for many content-area courses. In the transitional chapters, students are encouraged to see their own experience and that of their peers as valid sources of ideas for formal analysis. The chapter on research encourages students to use personal interviews as well as traditional library work to explore topics and generate ideas for writing.
- *Encouraging students to reflect on their own writing.* The book includes three Self-Evaluation Surveys, which students complete at the beginning, middle, and end of the course. These questionnaires encourage students to reflect on their attitudes and to take an active role in assessing their progress in writing.

NEW IN THE SECOND EDITION

Benefitting from the suggestions of reviewers and instructors who have used the first edition, we have made several changes that we hope will make *In Our Own Words* even more useful for students and teachers.

- *Sixteen new reading selections by student writers.* For teachers who have used the book before, the new readings offer variety. For students, these readings stimulate an even higher level of engagement. New essays include "The Experiences of an Illegal Alien," based on a student-conducted interview, and "The Coldest Winter of Beijing," a poetic description of a Chinese student's disillusionment after the Tiananmen Square massacre.
- *Six new reading selections by professional writers.* Like the new student essays, these pieces provide variety and updated content. For example, in "Teacher, It's Nice to Meet You, Too," Ruby Ibañez, who taught English as a Second Language at a Cambodian refugee camp in the Philippines, writes from the

perspective of one of her students who is preparing to emigrate to the United States. This powerful essay causes students and teachers to take a closer look at the struggles and the courage of ESL students.

- *Updated writing topics.* New topics such as immigrant perspectives on the American Dream and coping with the language barrier encourage students to approach more formal writing from the solid base of their own experience.
- *Expanded and contextualized grammar activities.* The revised edition includes many new activities and exercises on form, mechanics, vocabulary, and spelling. These activities are designed to complement specific chapters and are placed conveniently within those chapters.
- *Expanded coverage of library research.* Chapter 10 has been enlarged to include more support for the complex processes involved in library research. New activities give students an opportunity to practice summarizing, paraphrasing, and quoting from published sources. The chapter includes an expanded guide to documentation, with examples of in-text citation and bibliographic listings for both APA and MLA styles.

STRUCTURE OF THE BOOK

We hope that teachers and students will feel free to move back and forth among the different sections of the book, using those parts that suit their own interests and needs.

Part I: Starting Out asks students to reflect on the writing process.

- *Chapter 1, Attitudes toward Writing,* asks students to focus on the crucial importance of their feelings about writing and to articulate their goals for the course.
- *Chapter 2, Strategies for Getting Words on Paper,* suggests ways to warm up by writing in a variety of informal situations.
- *Chapter 3, Coping with Common Writing Problems,* deals with such challenges as choosing a topic and overcoming writer's block.

Part II: Writing, the core of the book, is organized thematically. In Chapters 4 through 10, students are asked to

- Read and respond to some or all of the readings at the beginning of the chapter. The readings are intended as invitations for reflection and discussion rather than as models to imitate.
- Do an activity or practice a writing strategy to facilitate the type of writing called for in the chapter.
- Do one or more of the grammar-in-context activities. These activities encourage experimentation with some of the specialized structures and vocabulary required for the chapter's writing assignment.

- Write a draft of an essay on the general theme of the chapter.
- Discuss the draft with a partner or group using the Peer Response Sheet at the end of the chapter.
- Hand in the draft to the instructor and revise it as needed.

Part III: Rethinking/Rewriting is concerned with the final stages of the writing process.

- *Chapter 11, Revising,* suggests practical strategies for refining a rough first draft into a polished final draft. It also helps students learn to comment effectively on the writing of their classmates through activities on providing useful peer feedback.
- *Chapter 12, Editing,* deals with the final part of the writing process: correcting grammar, spelling, and punctuation. Students are encouraged to take an active approach to improving grammar and usage by keeping an individualized grammar correction notebook. The chapter includes new reference materials on spelling, irregular verbs, and capitalization as well as strategies for effective proofreading.

The title of this book, *In Our Own Words,* emphasizes our belief that students write best when they are free to write about subjects that engage them in a voice that is their own. We realize, however, that good writing does not just happen. Carefully designed activities, suggestions, and assignments are necessary to provide the structure that enables developing writers to explore their own thoughts and find their own words. We hope that the second edition of this book will continue to inspire new writers and new writing.

ACKNOWLEDGMENTS

We have been energized throughout the revision process by the enthusiastic responses of teachers and students who have used the first edition of *In Our Own Words.* We have also been sustained by the collaborative nature of our work, which has made the writing and revising of this book one of the most satisfying experiences of our professional lives.

We are especially indebted to the professors who reviewed the book and suggested ways in which we could improve it. We would like to thank Larry Berking, Monroe Community College; Susan El Rayess, Monroe Community College; Thomas Ferruci, Southern Connecticut State University; Jim Lambrinos, El Paso Community College; Bernard B. Marshall, Community College of Philadelphia; Mark McTague, Edinboro University of Pennsylvania; Susan Roberts, University of Connecticut at Hartford; and Catherine Sagan, Santa Rosa Jr. College.

Many people at St. Martin's Press have helped *In Our Own Words* to become a reality. Instrumental in the first edition were Susan Anker, our acquiring editor, and Kathleen Keller, who saw the project through to completion. For the second edition, we have been privileged to work with ESL editor Naomi Silverman, a fine editor and a good friend, and Steven Kutz, associate development editor, who provided invaluable conceptual and logistical help. We also wish to thank Carl Whithaus, Nick

Webb, Jennifer Valentine, Scott Lavelle, and Rod Hernandez for helping manage the book through the production process.

We would like to thank our colleagues at the three colleges where we have taught during the evolution of this book. The first edition was written during our years of teaching in the Developmental English Program at Hunter College. We are grateful to Karen Greenberg, coordinator of the program; Ann Raimes, former coordinator; and Allan Brick, chair of the Department of English, for creating the supportive atmosphere in which a book like this could be developed. Rebecca, now at Kingsborough Community College, is pleased to be part of an English Department that is actively exploring new and more effective approaches to teaching reading and writing. She particularly acknowledges the support of Stephen Weidenborner, chair; Bonne August, director of freshman English; and Robert Viscount, director of ESL. She would also like to thank ESL instructor Rachelle Maltzman, whose student Rose-Laure Lamothe contributed two new pieces of writing to the second edition. At Jersey City State College, Steve would like to thank Dr. Anne Mabry, coordinator of the ESL program; Dr. Dorothy Harris, former dean of the School of Arts and Sciences; and Dr. Ansley La Mar, dean of the School of Arts and Sciences. The essays by Sha Sha Chen, Hikaru Takahashi, and Naresh Kumar were originally published in *Second Stories*, a magazine of student writing published at Jersey City State College.

Our own teachers have led us to a deeper understanding of the complexities of teaching writing, which has contributed to this book in important ways. Rebecca thanks her professors in the Department of Teaching and Learning at New York University, particularly John Mayher, Barbara Danish, and Margot Ely. She also wishes to thank the members of her writing group—Susan Babinski, Jane Isenberg, and Pat Juell—who regularly demonstrate the immense value of honest and supportive peer response. Steve thanks his professors at Teachers College, Columbia University, particularly John Fanselow, Lucy McCormick Calkins, Bob Oprandy, and Gay Brookes.

We are grateful to our families for their constant love and support throughout the writing and revising of this book. Rebecca offers heartfelt thanks to Frank, Susanna, Alex, and Stephanie Mlynarczyk, Ruth Adams, Carol Williams, and Robert Asher. Steve would especially like to thank Xiao-Lan Gao, Jonathan Rui Haber, and Maya Lin Haber for their help and support.

Finally, we extend our deepest thanks to the students whose writing appears in this book and to the hundreds of others we have taught over the years. They have been our most important teachers.

Rebecca Mlynarczyk
Steven B. Haber

To the Student

This book is based on a very simple idea: People write better and learn more when they write about things that are important to them.

Most of the reading selections in this book are written by students like yourselves. The energy in these pieces comes from the fact that the students were truly interested in what they were writing about. But the essays didn't start out in the polished and correct versions that you will be reading. All of them have been revised by the student writers, often several times. Any remaining errors in grammar, spelling, and punctuation have been corrected, as is done for all published writing. However, the ideas, organization, and wording of these essays came entirely from their authors, the students.

We hope that you will enjoy the reading selections and that they, in turn, will make *you* feel like writing. We will suggest some topics for writing, but we also hope that you will discover some topics of your own as you move through the book.

It is important to understand that different people learn in different ways. What helps the student sitting next to you may not help you at all. Try to figure out what activities work best for you.

Finally, a word of caution about the book's arrangement: Textbooks, by their very nature, must be organized in a linear way, with a beginning, a middle, and an end. But the writing process does not necessarily work this way. As writers, we may begin by writing, then observing and taking notes, writing some more, then editing what we have written so far, going back and taking more notes, and so on. Sometimes we decide to throw out everything we have done and start over on a new subject. We hope that you will use this book in a way that suits your own writing process, flipping back and forth between the different sections as you need them.

But let's not spend any more time talking about writing. Let's simply start out.

Part I

Starting Out

1
Attitudes toward Writing

Most writing textbooks start with introductions that few people ever read. The introduction to this book is different because you, the student, are going to help to write it.

In this chapter you will find a number of questions that may help you and your teacher to understand your thoughts and feelings about writing. In addition, the questions can be used to establish your goals as a writer. Remember that you should not try to answer all of them during the first week but should return to them from time to time during the course.

The following statements describe three different attitudes toward writing. Read the statements carefully and compare them to your own feelings.

1. I like to write. I think writing is important for me both in school and in my personal life. I believe that if I work hard, I can become a good writer.

2. I feel that writing is important, and I would like to write well, but in my case it's just not possible. English is not my native language, and I don't feel that I will ever be a good writer, no matter how hard I try.

3. I don't like to write. I don't feel that writing is important to me in school or in my chosen career. I will never be a good writer; I just want to pass this course with a satisfactory grade.

Do any of these statements describe your feelings? Write a statement describing your feelings, telling as much as you can about your attitude toward writing.

Examples

Before or after you have written your description, read these statements by other students. Underline any sentences that remind you of your own feelings about writing

I like to write. I believe that writing is helpful to me both in school and for the rest of my life.

Writing for me is very fun. My habit is to write poems, and when I start writing, it's hard for me to stop. Writing makes me think, and it helps me to develop my ideas and put them into words.

I have mixed feelings about writing. Sometimes I like to write to my friends. It seems to be that I have a million things to write about. But sometimes I hate to write, and those times are usually when I'm writing an essay or something for work.

When I want to write something, I have trouble getting my thoughts together and putting them down on paper. When I know I have to write something for school, I always get nervous and put it off until the last possible minute. Then I sit down and write very fast and try to get all my ideas out of my head before I lose them. After I hand it in, I try not to think about it. I think it's much easier to speak. I never seem to have any trouble thinking up ideas and organizing them when I'm speaking. But when I write, I have to think about so many things, it makes me feel like giving up halfway through.

I realize that English is important in school and in my later life. I want to learn good English so that I can be successful in my future. However, when people criticize my English writing, I get angry. Criticism makes me ugly. I know this is my shortcoming, and I intend to change it for good. If I don't change the way I feel about criticism, I will hurt myself in the long run.

My attitude toward writing in English? Well, the good thing is that attitudes can be changed as a person gets older; otherwise I wouldn't be here to write for you. I remember the way I used to feel about writing; I thought it was impossible for me to learn how to write. Now it is obvious to me that it takes patience but I can be a good writer.

Activities for Getting Feedback

Once you have written about your attitude toward writing, do one or more of the following activities.

1. Choose another student in your class to work with. Exchange papers and read each other's answers. Then discuss your papers. In what ways are your attitudes toward writing similar? In what ways are they different?

2. Exchange papers with another student. Write a letter to your partner responding to what he or she wrote. In your letter, discuss how your attitudes toward writing are similar and how they are different. After you have finished, exchange letters with your partner and discuss them.

3. Give your paper to your teacher, who may respond in writing, in a conference, or by reading some of the answers aloud in class.

PAST EXPERIENCE WITH WRITING

One of the most important factors in your present attitude toward writing is how writing has affected you in the past. Whether your experiences have been positive or negative, it is useful to take an honest look at them and to think about how they have influenced your feelings. We would like you to recall your past experience in detail, so choose only *three* of the following questions, and try to write as much as possible in response.

1. What are your earliest memories related to writing?

2. Write about a pleasant experience you have had with writing. Did this experience affect your attitude toward writing? Explain.

3. Write about a bad experience you once had with writing. How did this experience affect your attitude toward writing?

4. Describe how writing was taught in your previous schooling by answering some or all of these questions:

- How often did you have to write?
- What kinds of topics did you write about? Give one or two examples.
- What kinds of comments did the teacher make on your papers?
- What was considered more important: the content of your papers (what you said) or correct grammar and spelling (how you said it)?

5. How do you feel about writing in your native language compared to writing in English?

6. When you are writing a paper for a class, do you try to please yourself or the teacher?

7. Have you ever done any writing for yourself only—letters, journals, diaries, poems? If so, explain how this writing was different from the writing you did for school assignments.

Examples

Before or after you answer these questions, read the following answers given by other students. How are their experiences similar to or different from your own?

1. What are your earliest memories related to writing?

It was the first grade of my elementary school years. My first experience in writing was a story about the day when I climbed a mountain with my family. Nobody told me to write it, but I wanted to write like my older sister did. Since I didn't have any writing paper, I used some pieces of advertising paper which were all blank on the reverse side. I just put down the words as they came to me about the great mountain climbing. When my father read it, he said, "It's so nice. I am proud of you." I was proud of myself, too.

2. Write about a pleasant experience you have had with writing.

Writing is one of my hobbies and I enjoy it a lot. It started when I was about fifteen and was in love. (Ordinary, isn't it?) I wrote a couple of very bad poems for that girl, without any intention of sending them to her. For the first time I was writing for myself, without any rational reason. Just for fun, just to express my feelings. Later I forgot about the girl entirely, but I never stopped writing poems. There was always something to express, relations between people, usual events, even politics and caricaturing of other people's mistakes. I am still writing for myself, for fun and to document my opinions for the future. Someday I guess I will laugh at my present thoughts in the same way I now smile about my past.

3. Write about a bad experience you once had with writing.

The moment that I have to write something, I feel a tingle that starts at the back of my head and goes down my spinal cord through my arms and fingers and ends in my nails. As I move the pen to draw each letter, I remember when I was a child in third grade. My teacher, a middle-aged woman, would make us copy a long paragraph from a magazine into our notebooks.

The paragraph probably was ten or twelve lines long, but for me it seemed an eternity. By the time I finished my assignment, I had a strong headache. I think I felt that way because I was just starting to learn how to write. The same feeling that I had when I was learning to write in Spanish, I have now in English.

4. *Describe how writing was taught in your previous schooling.*

In my elementary school, writing instruction was started in the third grade. I don't recall that I had any grammar or vocabulary problems at that time, at least not very serious problems. The most difficult thing was to find something to say. The subjects usually were about a person whom we love, a holiday, or a trip. Before a holiday, the teacher always said, "We will have an essay about the holiday. So don't play too much and forget to study." During the whole holiday, I was in the shadow of the essay.

5. *How do you feel about writing in your native language compared to writing in English?*

Picking up this pen to start writing in English, I feel as if I were a fish being forced to walk on the land. I feel just like an old grandma, knitting in a rocking chair, being dragged into the gymnasium and asked to lift weights. I have been learning this new language for just a few years, and my vocabulary is not more than that of a second-grade American student. Certainly, one cannot ask a second grader to write an essay on nuclear war.

6. *When you are writing a paper for a class, do you try to please yourself or the teacher?*

I have done both kinds of writing—for myself and for the teacher. When I'm writing for myself, I find it easier and more carefree, maybe because I don't worry about the criticism and I'm not under pressure. Another thing is I don't have to worry about the grammar, punctuation, etc. I just write whatever I want without worrying. When I'm writing for the teacher, it is totally the inverse of writing for myself. I have to worry about the criticism and correction. I have to watch out for my grammar and be sure my information is correct. I'm under pressure when writing for the teacher and that makes it worse.

7. *Have you ever done any writing for yourself only—letters, journals, diaries, poems?*

Once in my life, during the night, I took my pen and started to write to my dead father. I wanted to tell him how much I loved him, for when he was alive I never did this. When I was doing this freewriting, I felt that it was much simpler than the essays given by my writing teachers; words came to me just like rays in my mind.

Reactions

After you have finished writing your own answers to three of these questions, share your results in a small group with three or four other students. Take turns reading one of your answers. After everyone has had a chance to read, discuss what you learned. Were any of the experiences similar? How were they different?

SELF-EVALUATION OF WRITING PROGRESS

The previous activities should have helped you to clarify some of your attitudes and past experiences related to writing. As you continue to work in this book, you will probably notice some changes in these attitudes as well as in your writing itself.

We encourage you to think about these changes and to evaluate your own progress in writing. While grades and examination scores are certainly important, they are not the only way of measuring student progress. It is equally important for students to evaluate their own writing and to examine which activities, strategies, and readings were useful in helping them to improve their writing skill.

We have included three forms for student self-evaluation of writing progress to be used at different times in the course. The first of these forms, entitled "Goals for This Course: A Beginning Survey" (pages 30–31), asks you to think about your hopes and expectations for this writing course.

After you have filled out the Beginning Survey, share your results by doing the following activity. Be sure to save the Beginning Survey so that you can refer to it later.

In-Class Activity

1. Work in a small group with three or four other students. Choose one student to act as recorder and take notes about what group members say.
2. Have each person in the group read his or her answers out loud.
3. After everyone has finished reading, discuss the answers. Do you find the same things about writing easy and difficult? Are your attitudes similar or different? How would you compare your approaches to writing assignments? What suggestions would you make to help the other students achieve their goals?
4. After all the groups have finished, each recorder should give a brief report of what happened in his or her group.

CONCLUSION

Congratulations! For many people the most difficult thing about writing is getting started; if you have reached this point in the book, you have already done some writing and are therefore ahead of the game.

Once you have begun to write, what next? On the following pages we will offer some suggestions.

2
Strategies for Getting Words on Paper

One of the most difficult things for any writer to do is to get started on a piece of writing. You sit there at your desk and think, "I have nothing to say, no ideas. My mind is totally blank." The truth is, however, that there are always plenty of ideas floating around in your mind. The problem is finding a way to get those ideas onto a sheet of paper.

In this chapter we will suggest some ways to do this. First, we invite you to try one or more writing experiments, which are like games that end with writing. Next, we offer some suggestions for writing letters. This is a familiar form of writing that most people find easier than more formal writing, perhaps because they know exactly who the reader will be. Finally, we recommend that you start keeping a journal, which you will use throughout this writing course. Much of what you write in your journal will remain strictly private, but some of the ideas can later be developed into more formal pieces of writing.

WHERE DO I START? TRY SOME WRITING EXPERIMENTS

GETTING ACQUAINTED

As you work in this book, you will often be asked to work with a partner or small group. This activity encourages you to get acquainted with the other students in your class by conducting an informal survey.

Instructions

Move around the room and try to locate as many of the following types of people as possible. Write down their names in the blanks. Try to get at least one name for each blank, but list additional names if you find them. Later you will be asked to write up the results of your survey.

1. Find someone who is majoring in the same area that you are.

   _____

2. Find someone who is working at a job you would like to have. What sort of job is it?

   _____

3. Find someone who speaks more than two languages.

   _____

4. Find someone who has done a lot of writing in his or her native language.

   _____

5. Find someone who likes to draw or paint.

   _____

6. Find someone who knows how to use a computer or word processor.

   _____

7. Find someone who is a good cook.

   _____

8. Find someone who likes the same kind of music you like.

   _____

9. Find someone who likes to play a sport you like to play.

   _____

10. Find someone you can call if you need to get homework assignments. Write down the name and phone number.

   _____

Writing Assignment

After you have finished, write up the results of your survey. Imagine your reader to be a classmate who was absent on the day of the survey. Do not try to include everything, just the most important parts. For example: What did you learn about other members of the class that was interesting or surprising? What might be useful to you? What might be useful to others? What do you think was the purpose of this activity?

WRITING WITH AND WITHOUT A DICTIONARY

In most of the writing activities in this book, we ask that you not use a dictionary, at least not in the beginning. The reason for this is that we have found people spend more time looking up words than they do writing, and by the time they have found the one word they were looking for, they have lost track of the larger idea they were trying to express.

Here are some suggestions for writing without a dictionary:

- If you need the English translation for a word or sentence, write it in your own language and look it up or ask someone later, after you have finished the writing.
- Leave a blank space for a word you cannot think of and fill it in later.
- Write down the word, even if you are not sure it is the right one. Put a small question mark above it and check it later.
- For spelling, write down your best guess as to how the word is spelled, and mark it with a question mark. Then look it up or ask later.

To compare writing with a dictionary to writing without one, try the following experiment.

In-Class Activity

1. Write for five minutes about a person you know well. Use a dictionary (either in your native language or in English) to look up any words that you do not know or that you are unsure of.

2. Pick another person and again write for five minutes, but without the dictionary. At the end of the second writing, count how many lines you wrote in the first five minutes and how many you wrote in the second five minutes.

3. After you have counted the lines, open your dictionary and look up any words or spellings you were unsure of in the second writing. Time yourself. How long did it take to look up all the words you needed?

4. Discuss your reactions with others in your class. How was writing with the dictionary different from writing without it? List as many differences as possible.

SILENT CONVERSATIONS

This is an experiment to get you to think about the difference between spoken and written communication.

Instructions

1. With a partner, talk for two or three minutes about any topic that is of interest to both of you—for example, what you did over the weekend, what happened this morning, something strange or unusual.

2. During the next five minutes, continue your conversation in writing on a sheet of paper without talking to your partner.

3. Exchange papers with your partner and read each other's writing carefully.

4. Write down any differences you observed between spoken and written communication. Which was easier? Which took longer? What advantages does writing have over speaking? What are the disadvantages? What do you think the purpose of this exercise was?

5. Read your answers to these questions to your partner. Discuss how your answers were similar and different.

Example

Here is an example of a silent conversation. Two women had been having an oral conversation about hiring a math tutor. Zyary Hurtado continued the conversation in writing this way:

> Sophia, as I told you before, the chemistry between people has to be positive in order to do something together. The first meeting you are going to have with your tutor should be like an interview. This is the moment when you analyze the person, see if there is anything in common between you, and also ask for her credentials. By doing this you save time and maybe future misunderstandings.

Her partner, Sophia Grendly, wrote:

> You are quite right about the chemistry between two people. As I told you before, the first section of math is doing much better than our own, and one of the reasons is that we have not developed a rapport, a special chemistry that connects the students with their professor.
>
> So back to the drawing board. Should I hire the independent tutor? Or should I just struggle with my course for the next few months?

Responding to the question about the differences between spoken and written communication, Hurtado explained:

> Oral communication is much easier because there is an interaction. I have feedback from the other person. At the same time it is faster. Thoughts come easily into my mind and the exchanging of ideas makes it more fruitful.
>
> Written communication is more formal. I have to think about how I am going to express my thoughts so that the other person understands their meaning, and avoids misunderstandings. Writing has the advantage that one can carefully organize the ideas and make them worthy. On the other hand, oral communication can provoke many mistakes that sometimes are impossible to correct due to lack of time to analyze what we are talking about.

THINGS WE HAVE IN COMMON

In classes where collaborative learning is encouraged, students learn as much from other students as they do from their teachers. For this reason, it's important for students to start learning about one another and working together from the beginning of the course. This activity asks you to interview a student partner and later to develop generalizations based on what you learned.

Instructions

Working with a partner, answer each of the following questions:

1. When you receive a bill, do you pay it right away, or do you put it off until the last minute?

2. When you use toothpaste, do you squeeze the tube from the middle or from the end?

3. When you cook, do you follow the recipe exactly, or do you like to improvise?

4. When you are eating, do you like to save the most delicious food for last, or do you eat it right away?

5. When you go shopping, do you like to find things by yourself, or do you ask for help from the sales clerk?

6. When eating at a restaurant or going to a movie, do you prefer to go alone, with one person, or with a group?

7. When you get a new piece of electronic equipment such as a VCR or a CD player, do you read the instructions before connecting it, or do you like to figure things out for yourself?

8. When you draw or paint, do you prefer to copy a picture or make one up yourself?

9. When you study, do you prefer to work alone or with someone else?

In-Class Activity

1. After you have answered each of these questions, look at them again. Try to classify the type of information they ask for.

- Put an <u>O</u> next to any questions that have to do with whether someone is well-organized.
- Put a <u>C</u> next to any questions that have to do with creativity.
- Put an <u>I</u> next to any questions that have to do with independence.

2. Based on the information you learned about your partner while answering the questions, write out three guesses about that person's personality compared to yours.

Examples: Chen seems more organized than I am.
I may be more independent than Chen.
Chen seems to be more creative than I am.

Writing Assignment

Write a brief essay comparing your partner to yourself. Try to form at least two generalizations about your partner that you can support with details from the questions you discussed. For example, "Although I may be more independent than Chen, she seems to be more creative than I am. . . ."

WHO'S LISTENING? WRITE A LETTER

While letters are not a substitute for more formal types of writing such as essays, they are a useful way of loosening up and getting comfortable with writing. In this section we offer some suggestions for writing letters to people inside and outside your class. Feel free to adapt these suggestions or invent some totally new ones.

Suggestion 1

Work with a partner. Take about ten to fifteen minutes to write a letter to your partner in which you discuss your feelings about living in this country. In your letter you may want to answer some of the following questions: Where do you come from? How long have you been in the United States? Do you intend to stay here or go back to your own country when you complete your education? What are your plans for the future?

Be sure to finish your letter when the time limit is up. One thing that makes letters easier to write than essays is that no one expects them to be perfect. Most letters end with a hurried closing phrase such as "I have to go now. It's time to leave for class."

Exchange letters and spend another ten to fifteen minutes writing a reply to your partner.

Suggestion 2

Write a letter to your partner in which you describe a problem that has been bothering you lately—a difficult class, a problem at work or home, a language problem, a problem with a friend, or some other type of problem. (Remember that you can make your letter personal or impersonal depending on what type of problem you choose to discuss. If you have not had any problems recently, write about a problem from the past.) Describe the problem in as much detail as possible. Tell your partner what you have done to solve the problem or what you plan to do. Ask your partner to offer some advice or suggestions.

Exchange letters and read your partner's letter carefully. Then write a short reply.

Suggestion 3

Write a letter to your teacher about something you have read recently. It could be a newspaper or magazine article, a book, an essay written by someone in your class, or an essay from this book.

Tell your teacher the main idea of the reading and your personal reaction to it. You may want to answer one or more of the following questions: How long did it take you to read it? Did you find it difficult or easy to read? What did you like most about the reading? Were there any things you did not like? What did it make you think about? Did you have any questions about it? Did it make you want to write something yourself? Ask for a reply to your letter.

Before you start your letter, find out the correct spelling of your teacher's name and begin with either a formal or an informal greeting. Ask your teacher which type he or she prefers.

Suggestion 4

Write a letter to the editor of your college newspaper or to the president of your college explaining your opinion on some issue of importance in your institution. For example, you might write a letter of complaint about the food in the cafeteria or a letter criticizing or supporting your school's system of English language requirements. If your letter is critical, be sure to give suggestions about how to improve the situation. Ask for a reply.

DO I HAVE TO KEEP A JOURNAL?

Many professional and student writers keep journals. These are personal diaries and may contain writing on any subject imaginable. Here is a list of possible things to write about in a journal:

descriptions of daily events
memories
dreams
secrets
plans for the future
travel notes
notes about work
beginnings of essays, poems, or stories
beginnings of letters, memos, or speeches
reactions to readings
ideas from other courses

The journal is the place to experiment with writing, to be as silly or as serious as you want. You never have to worry about making mistakes because no one will ever see your journal except those people you choose to show it to. Some teachers collect their students' journals. If this is the case, you may choose to remove or cover up those pages you do not want anyone else to see.

Since the journal is more for you than for anyone else, choose a notebook that reflects your own taste; it can be a simple spiral notebook or something fancier. Just be sure it is used only as a journal and not for anything else.

You should try to write in your journal once a day for at least ten to fifteen minutes. You do not have to write a lot each day. Some days you may write only a sentence or two. Other days you will write more. The important thing is to get into the habit of writing regularly. If you write a little each day, you will be amazed at how much you have written by the time you have finished this course.

One thing that may surprise you if your teacher collects your journal is that he or she will respond only to the ideas you are expressing and will not correct errors in grammar or spelling. Actually, teacher correction of errors in student journals would defeat the purpose of this type of writing, which is to write as quickly as possible and to focus on content instead of mechanics. Also, teacher correction of errors does not usually mean that students will never make the same errors again. In fact, it is much more helpful for students to correct their own errors rather than to rely on the teacher to serve as an editor. If your previous instruction in English emphasized correctness above all else, loosening up to write in a journal may feel strange or even uncomfortable at first. But we are convinced that if you continue to write regularly in your journal, eventually your writing will become more fluent—and more correct.

FREEWRITING

Freewriting is the technique that most people use when writing in their journals. It is a way of getting thoughts down on paper when you want to write but are not sure exactly what you want to say or how to say it. The purpose of freewriting is not to turn out a finished piece, but rather to discover a place to begin.

Instructions

Take about five to eight minutes. Without stopping, write down as many words as you can about any subject that comes into your mind. For example, you might describe all the different sounds that you hear as you are writing or discuss a problem that has been on your mind lately. Do not use a dictionary; do not worry about grammar or spelling. Ideas do not have to be connected or written out in complete sentences. They do not even have to make sense. The important thing is to keep writing. If you can't think of anything, just repeat, "I can't think of anything to say. I can't think of anything to say." Soon a new idea will come to you. The object is simply to see how many words you can put down on paper.

Example

Here are excerpts from one student's journal:

1–10–95

I compare myself to a flower which grows and becomes more beautiful everyday. My color is made with a "pinch" of the color of each flower surrounding me. This way I always change, becoming more beautiful every day, but keeping my uniqueness.

Tomorrow, for the first time I will give blood. Just the thought of it frightens me. I wonder how much the needle will hurt when it is put in my arm. Eck. Ooo. My heart is in my throat. My stomach is tight at the thought of it. Oh! Well, I know that it is a good action. Who knows? I know that I am a rare blood type and maybe someone will need it.

2–8–95

I am studying the great philosophers (ancient and medieval). I learned that a movement of intellectual change started to happen around 600–500 B.C. A few people, the philosophers, started to move away from the mythological explanation of nature.

The causes for this change may vary. There was a growth in freedom of thought, a beginning in literacy. But one reason strikes me especially. This was the contacts of people from different cultures.

Now if we take a look around us, with the technology revolution, with the speed at which communication can travel from one part of the world to another, with the mix of cultures in the big cities—if we are not moving toward a big change, or refuse to believe in it: it is because we are blind.

CONCLUSION

We hope that the ideas in this chapter have helped you to get some words on paper. Take some time now to assess your progress so far. Freewrite your answers to the questions that follow. Then share them with a partner or small group. Your teacher may also ask to read your answers.

1. What activities that you tried in this chapter have been useful to you?
2. What activities did not help?
3. Do you think your approach to writing has changed at all as a result of doing the activities in this chapter? Explain.

3

Coping with Common Writing Problems

In the previous chapter most of the writing you did was informal. Much of it was read only by yourself or perhaps a small group of classmates. You knew that you would not be evaluated or graded on what you wrote. The sole purpose was to get some words down on paper.

But when students move into more formal situations, such as writing a paper for a class assignment, problems sometimes arise. In this chapter we will discuss several common writing problems and suggest ways of dealing with them.

WHAT DO I WRITE ABOUT? CHOOSING A TOPIC

Often teachers assign the topic for writing. There may be times, however, when you need to choose a topic of your own. At first this freedom of choice sounds wonderful. But students often discover that finding a good topic to write about can be difficult. The following activity will help you to choose an appropriate topic.

Topic-Choice Activity (In Class)

1. Take about five minutes to write down four or five topics that you might want to write about. They can be anything that interests you. Here are some topics that other students have chosen:

My First Day in the United States
Teenage Pregnancy
A Person I Miss
The Problem of Drugs

2. After you have written down some topics, show them to a partner. Discuss the topics and talk about what thoughts led you to each one. Which topic is most interesting to you? Which one seems most interesting to your partner? Choose the topic that you think will be best and start writing about it. Remember, if the topic does not work well or proves to be too difficult, you can always change it later. The important thing is to get started.

3. Before or after you begin, you may need to narrow your topic down to make it more manageable and easier to develop. The following are some examples of general topics that were narrowed down to more specific ones:

    a. Crime
       Crime in My City
       Crime in My Neighborhood
       The Fear of Crime in My Neighborhood
    b. My Trip to California
       The Things I Like Best about California
       Three Things I Don't Like about California
       San Francisco vs. New York: Which Place Would You Choose?
    c. Immigration in the United States
       The New Asian Immigrants
       Korean Immigration in the United States

Korean Immigration: Advantages and Disadvantages

Five Korean Immigrants: How Do They Feel about America?

4. If you think you need to narrow down your subject, write a list in which you make your topic more specific, as was done in the previous examples. Discuss with a partner or your teacher which of these narrower topics seems most appropriate. Note that the narrowing process may result in two or more equally good but different topics.

5. Once you have chosen your topic and narrowed it down, you are ready to begin writing. Take about fifteen to twenty minutes to write as much as you can about the topic you chose. If you discover that after a few minutes you have nothing more to say, pick another topic from your list and try again.

6. After you have written for fifteen or twenty minutes, stop writing even if you have not finished. You are now ready for your first peer conference.

HOW CAN I GET HELP WITH MY WRITING? PEER CONFERENCES

Students often feel terribly alone when they are working on a writing assignment. However, every writing class contains a valuable resource to help you with your writing—the other students in your class.

Peer is an Old English word meaning one who is of equal standing with another. A peer conference is a discussion among two or more students in which they give and receive comments about their writing. We have found that students can get valuable suggestions from their peers and that some students feel more comfortable talking with a classmate than with their teacher. Of course, teachers can give valuable feedback too, and the peer conference is not designed to replace the teacher. Peer conferences can, however, do many things that an individual teacher cannot. For example:

- One teacher cannot give immediate feedback to a whole class.
- A teacher can give you only one point of view. Peer conferences can give you many.
- In most classes a few people do most of the talking. Peer conferences give everyone a chance to participate.

Once you start working on conferences, we think you will see that they can be an efficient and useful way of working on writing. However, they require discipline and responsibility to your fellow students.

Instructions

1. Work in groups of three or four. One person should be selected by either the group or the teacher to be the reporter. When appropriate, this person can report the results of the peer conference to the rest of the class.

2. One of the students begins by reading his or her writing aloud.

3. The group members take about five minutes to write their reactions by answering the following questions:

    a. What did you understand from this writing?

    b. What did you like about it?

    c. What do you want to know more about?

4. Each group member reads his or her reactions aloud.

5. Repeat the process until each person has had a chance to read and get reactions.

6. Each group should then answer these questions for the whole class:

    a. What happened in your group?

    b. What worked well?

    c. What problems did you encounter?

    d. What did you learn from the peer conference?

7. Based on your own feelings and the feedback you got from your classmates in the peer conference, you may decide to work on your writing again. Or you may choose to put the paper aside for a while and come back to it later. You may decide that you want to change your topic completely. It would be a good idea to consult with your teacher for suggestions at this point.

ON GIVING CONSTRUCTIVE CRITICISM

In this course you will do a great deal of writing, and often you will be asked to let others in the class read and comment on what you have written. Thus, it is important to establish some ground rules for responding to student writing.

First of all, we might as well admit that writing is a very personal thing. What we write is part of us—perhaps even more than the clothes we wear or the friends we choose. All of us are sensitive when our writing is being discussed.

The other people in your class can be an invaluable resource for getting feedback on your writing and ideas for improving it. However, you need to be able to trust them, to feel that you can take risks with your writing without the fear of being ridiculed. Think of how we treat a baby who is learning to walk. We give a lot of praise even when a new step leads to a fall. Learning to write in a second language is, in its own way, just as difficult as learning to walk, and the learners need support, not ridicule.

All criticism of student writing should be constructive—that is, it should focus on the positive and should be offered in a helpful spirit. There is a practical aspect to this advice as well. If your classmates tell you what they like about your writing, you can use this strength in other writing; if you did something once, you can do it again. On the other hand, if your classmates focus only on what they think you did wrong, you may feel confused the next time you write; you know what you *should not* do, but not what you *should* do.

Read the following ground rules and discuss them with your class. Decide if you would like to add any additional rules.

GROUND RULES FOR RESPONDING TO STUDENT WRITING

1. No student should be forced to share a piece of writing that he or she considers too personal.

2. Positive aspects should be discussed first, unless the writer specifically asks for help with problem areas.

3. The writer should tell the other students what specific aspects of the writing to respond to—for example, the first paragraph or the conclusion.

4. Students should never write on other students' papers without first getting the writer's permission. All comments should be given orally or written on a separate piece of paper.

5. All comments offered by others are only suggestions. The writer remains in charge of his or her writing and decides whether or not to take the advice that was offered.

By following these rules from the beginning, you should gradually develop a feeling of community in your writing class—a sense that you are working together and helping each other with something important. Responding to other people's writing is a skill that takes practice. As the course progresses, you should find yourself getting better at giving and receiving constructive criticism.

HOW CAN I DO WELL ON OUT-OF-CLASS WRITING ASSIGNMENTS?

Unfortunately, there is no set of foolproof rules to follow to get high grades on all your papers. How you approach a writing assignment depends very much on the specific course, the specific teacher, and the purpose of the assignment.

In order to understand the problems students face on out-of-class writing assignments, we interviewed four students who were working on papers for different courses. After listening to what they had to say, we came to the conclusion that if you want to do well on a paper, you must take an active approach. You have to start early and work hard to make it happen. Although each paper you write will be different, several general suggestions apply to most college writing assignments.

1. *Be sure you understand the assignment.* This is probably the single most important piece of advice we have to offer. When you are doing an academic assignment, it is essential to be clear about what the instructor wants. For example, one of the students we interviewed decided to change the subject for her research paper after talking to her professor and learning that her original topic was not what the professor had in mind. Whenever you are writing on an assigned topic, you should take the teacher's advice into account. It is *always* a good idea to schedule a conference with your instructor to discuss the upcoming paper. Be sure that you know the desired length, proper format (typed or handwritten, preferred footnote style, and so on), and the date the paper is due. If you plan to vary your approach from what was stated in the assignment, be sure to get your instructor's approval.

2. *Acquaint yourself with the special vocabulary and style of the subject area you are writing about.* It is important to recognize that what is considered good writing may vary from one discipline to another. Each subject area has its own specialized vocabulary and preferred style of writing. Let's say that you are interested in art and are taking a course in Egyptian archaeology. It is to your advantage to become familiar with the type of writing that is called for in this field. Obviously, this takes time, but you can start by noting the instructor's corrections on your writing and by asking the instructor to recommend some books or journals that could serve as models for your own writing. Once you are able to use the vocabulary and style of a particular subject area, the instructor will respond more favorably to your papers.

3. *Be imaginative in your approach to the assignment.* Once you are sure what the instructor expects from a particular assignment, try to use your imagination. If you are doing a research paper, look for unusual sources of information. For example, one of the students we interviewed was asked to write an informative paper for her political science class. She was to pretend that she was a member of the U. S. State Department writing a memorandum to the newly elected president about recent events in the Middle East. Many of the other students in the class probably headed to the *Reader's Guide to Periodical Literature* in the library—but not Sophia Grendly. First, she contacted the State Department and the Russian Mission to the United Nations to get their official statements on the Middle East. In order to get the opinions of the American Jewish population, she went to a large newsstand and looked through the different magazines until she found several Jewish publications. She subsequently went to a meeting of one of the groups and subscribed to three of the publications (one that was liberal, one that was middle-of-the-road, and one that was conservative) and noted their opinions on the Middle East.

Obviously, this was a time-consuming and fairly expensive process, but Sophia explained, "Following foreign affairs is my hobby, so I enjoyed all of this." Also, she took advantage of living in New York City, where she had easy access to information from countries all over the world. If you do not live in a large city, however, you can still find unusual sources, through e-mail, by writing letters requesting information, or by consulting your college librarians. The important thing is to use your imagination to think of authoritative and up-to-date sources that may be available to you.

4. *Look up the information you need and take notes on it.* Most college writing assignments involve getting information from books, articles, or other sources. In addition, computers are becoming more important in our information network, as demonstrated by the fact that two of the four students we interviewed had to get some of their information from computers. Whether you are getting your information from a book or a computer, you cannot go very far in planning your paper until you know what that information is. You need to preview the information before you can decide what you want to say in your paper. Be sure to take notes to refresh your memory later. (For more guidance on giving credit to sources, see pages 259–72.)

5. *Allow yourself plenty of time for the writing process.* As you can tell from the experience of the students we interviewed, doing well on a writing assignment requires much time and effort. Yet most of us tend to put off writing as long as possible. The more difficult the assignment, the longer we put it off. Unfortunately, this natural tendency to procrastinate may lead to additional pressure as the deadline approaches.

Instead, try to face up to the task. As soon as you get the assignment, write out a schedule showing how you can best budget your time, and check off the different activities as they are completed. If you fall behind, revise your schedule so that you can still turn in the paper on time. Build in enough extra time so that you can meet your deadline even if you get sick for a few days or have an unexpected visitor.

The sample schedule that follows can be adapted to fit your own situation. Notice that the writer plans to write two drafts before typing the final essay; this type of careful revision is a key to success in any kind of writing. Professional writers usually revise their work many times before it is published. (You may find it helpful to write on a word processor. That way, you can make changes easily later without retyping the whole paper.)

March 15   Ten-page history paper assigned, due on May 15
March 15–22   Think about topic and talk it over with friends
March 23   Meet with instructor to clarify assignment and discuss possible approaches
March 23–30   Look up information in library and take notes
March 31–April 6   Work on prewriting activities: freewriting, brainstorming, etc.
April 7–30   Write first draft
May 10   Complete second draft
May 11–13   Type and proofread second draft, correct typing errors
May 15   Turn in paper

Writing a paper is hard work. But if you take an active approach to the assignment and allow yourself plenty of time, you may discover that the work has been rewarding and that you have learned a great deal.

HOW CAN I ADAPT MY WRITING FOR DIFFERENT PURPOSES AND AUDIENCES?

Purpose and audience, two factors that often are not mentioned when you are asked to write something, can greatly influence what you say and how you say it.

Purpose refers to the reason for writing—what you want the readers to do or think after they have finished reading. For example, the purpose of a letter of complaint to a department store might be to *convince* the store that they made a mistake on your bill. The purpose of a personal essay describing an important experience in your life might be to *describe* the experience clearly and *entertain* the reader. The purpose of a lab report on your dissection of a rat might be to *inform* the reader of the procedures you used and the findings you made. The purpose of an essay for a literature class might be to *analyze* the psychological motivation of one of the characters in a short story.

Audience means the intended readers for a piece of writing. In the first example in the preceding paragraph, the audience would be the person who handles complaints for the department store. For the other examples, the audience would most likely be the instructor and interested classmates.

Activity

This activity will give you an idea of how audience and purpose influence what you write. You will be asked to do four short pieces of writing. The *subject* of each of them is the same—yourself. But the different audiences and purposes will influence what you say and how you say it.

1. Spend ten to fifteen minutes doing each of the following:
   a. Write a letter to a girlfriend or boyfriend (real or imagined) explaining what kind of person you are. (You will not be asked to show this letter to anyone else.)
   b. Write a short description of yourself to share with your writing class.
   c. Write a one-page description of your personal background as part of a job application for a position as a computer programmer.
   d. Write a one-page description of your personal background as part of a job application for a position as a social worker.

2. Before your next writing class, read over all four pieces. How did the different audiences influence what you wrote? What was your purpose for each piece? In other words, what did you want the reader to do or think after reading it?

3. Write your intended purpose at the bottom of each piece. For example, the purpose for the first piece might be "to reveal my deepest personal qualities." For the second piece, it might be "to introduce myself to the class and explain personal information that relates to our concerns as a class."

Reactions

With a small group of students from your writing class, discuss some or all of these questions:

1. How did the different audiences influence what you said in each of the four pieces of writing?

2. Which one was the hardest to write? Which was the easiest?

3. Compare the purposes you wrote at the bottom of the page with those written by others in your group. Were your purposes basically the same or different?

4. Have each student choose one of the four pieces to read to the group. Then discuss how effective it would be at achieving the purpose stated at the bottom of the page.

We will have more to say about purpose and audience later in the book. But for now remember that these two factors can play a major role in your approach to any piece of writing.

WHAT IF I CAN'T WRITE? WAYS OF DEALING WITH WRITER'S BLOCK

Writer's block is a peculiar thing. Simply put, it is the inability to get your thoughts down on paper. Sooner or later, all writers—professionals as well as students—are faced with this troublesome problem.

What keeps people from writing? Fear is part of the problem. What if my writing isn't good? What if I make mistakes? What if I fail? These kinds of fears can be distracting and stop you from doing your work. If you can figure out what it is that worries you, you may be able to overcome the fear and start writing again.

Sometimes personal problems interfere with writing. The end of a love affair, an illness or death in the family, too much work and not enough sleep can all contribute to writer's block.

The one good thing about writer's block is that it is almost always temporary. Sooner or later, you will find yourself writing again. It is important to recognize that these ups and downs are a normal part of writing.

We talked to some writing teachers, writing students, and professional writers to find out what they do when they have difficulty writing.

Steven Haber, writing instructor and co-author of this textbook:

> I am probably the world's worst procrastinator. As much as I love writing, if I have to write something with a deadline, I almost always put it off until the last minute. I think the reason this happens is that before I start, every writing job seems enormous, impossible. I don't know where to begin. So before I start to write, I do other things, such as clean up my room, clear off my desk, drink a cup of coffee, turn on some soft music on the radio. Then, when I feel relaxed, I sit down at my desk and take a look at what I have to do.
>
> I tell myself, I only have to write a few pages. Surely I can write a few pages. Once I get started, it seems so much easier than I thought. Then I begin to enjoy it again.

Maria F. Barrueto, a student from Peru:

> Sometimes having my blank page and pen ready to start what I expected to be an adventure or at least a trip is like being in front of a wall, a huge, tall, dark wall without any door or window to see through.

First, the sensation of being so small takes me, but as I think of what is waiting for me on the other side, and the great panorama that I can enjoy once I see it, that feeling changes. I start growing and growing and without me realizing it, the wall has disappeared.

Pikwah Chan, a student from China:

If I can't think of something to write, I will just not write, just take a break. I put my pen down and take a walk outdoors or just do something else. I may totally forget what I am writing, or I may think about my subject in my leisure time, almost 90 percent sure that when I sit at my desk again, I can easily continue my writing.

Sometimes the thinking is there, but it is subconscious. You should not ignore these kinds of impressions or feelings. They usually are important. They are just not really formed yet. When you give yourself time or release yourself from pressures, you will catch them easily.

Susan Sackett, novelist:

Writer's block. My fingers tremble at the mere sound of the words.

My first reaction is denial, just as in any other crisis of life. I think that if I turn my back on the typewriter, maybe the whole problem will go away.

All writers have their own cures, but mine is basic stubbornness. I do not allow myself the freedom of not writing until I start to get some ideas. If I did that, I'd never finish a book.

So instead of giving up, I sit there, staring at the typewriter keys, even if it means I have nothing to show for that day's effort. My mind is free to wander, and eventually it takes a course along the lines of my work.

I never aim for perfection, especially on a first draft. I don't allow myself to agonize over a word that is lurking at the edge of my consciousness, nor do I bother with spelling or grammar. Details, I find, only get in the way of the story I'm writing, and they can always be taken care of later.

All I've really been saying is that writing requires work. After all, it's a craft, like any other, and if you don't allow yourself to give up on it, sooner or later you begin to see results.

Reactions

Which of these descriptions seems most similar to your own methods of dealing with writer's block? What do you do that is similar or different? Write for ten to fifteen minutes about your own experiences with writer's block, and then discuss your ideas with others in your group or class.

CONCLUSION

Everyone who writes faces problems at one time or another. As you move into the next part of this book and begin to write essays, there will undoubtedly be times when you, too, will have problems. The important thing to remember is that most writing problems have solutions.

If you haven't filled out the questionnaire entitled "Goals for This Course: A Beginning Survey" (on the following pages), this would be a good time to do so.

GOALS FOR THIS COURSE:
A BEGINNING SURVEY

Instructions: Write your answers to these questions in the spaces provided. Be sure to save this survey so that you can refer to it later.

1. What are your strengths as a writer: creativity, good ideas, ability to organize ideas, ability to express ideas clearly, correct grammar, other (explain)? List your strengths below, starting with the most important one:

a. _____

b. _____

c. _____

d. _____

e. _____

2. What do you find most difficult about writing: getting ideas, putting the first words down on paper, not having enough background knowledge about the writing topics, finding the right words to express your ideas, organizing ideas, finding the correct grammar and spelling, writing in class with a time limit? List your problems below, starting with the most serious:

a. _____

b. _____

c. _____

d. _____

e. _____

3. Briefly, how would you describe your attitude toward writing in English—positive, negative, or somewhere in between? Explain. If English is not your first language, do you have a different attitude about writing in your native language?

_____

_____

_____

_____

_____

_____

_____

4. How do you usually approach an out-of-class writing assignment? Do you start early or put it off until the last minute? Do you write only one draft or revise your essay one or more times? Where do you go for help if you find a writing assignment to be difficult?

_____

_____

_____

5. In what ways do you hope your writing will improve by the end of this course: confidence in writing, more ideas for writing, better organization of ideas, ability to develop ideas in more detail, ability to write more quickly, ability to write more correctly, a larger English vocabulary, other (explain)?

a. _____

b. _____

c. _____

6. What do you feel will help you most to improve your writing: writing practice, getting advice from other students (peer conferences), grammar drills, freewriting, reading in English, speaking English outside of class, conferences with your teacher, revising papers after seeing the teacher's comments, other (explain)?

a. _____

b. _____

c. _____

d. _____

Part II

Writing

——HOW TO USE PART II——

Part II begins with personal writing and ends with the more formal type of writing required for many college courses. The skills you develop in the earlier chapters should be helpful as you move into the more abstract writing needed in the later chapters. However, it is not necessary to use all of the chapters or to use them in the exact order in which they are presented.

For each of the chapters in Part II you will be asked to:

1. Read and respond to some of the essays that appear at the beginning of the chapter.
2. Do one or more of the writing activities.
3. Do some of the Grammar in Context activities.
4. Write a draft of an essay on the general theme of the chapter.
5. Discuss your draft with a partner or group, using the Peer Response Sheets at the end of the chapters to guide your discussion.
6. Hand in the draft for response from your teacher.
7. Revise your essay as needed.

Personal Writing

There are many different kinds of writing, having different purposes and intended for different audiences. Some writing is very informal. For example, freewriting in a journal is intended just for yourself, to work out a problem, gather your thoughts, or develop an idea in your mind. A letter to a close friend may also be quite informal.

Other writing is more formal. For instance, in school you often write to reveal your knowledge about a particular subject or to demonstrate your writing skill. A letter applying for a job or a memo to your boss will usually be quite formal as well.

Personal writing falls somewhere in between. When you write a personal essay, it is based on your own experience—an incident that occurred when you were a child, something that happened to you on the way to school, a job you once loved or hated. However, it is not written for you alone but for others as well—your classmates, friends, teachers, or anyone who is interested in learning more about you, where you come from, what you care about.

Many students enjoy doing this kind of writing because it allows them to write about what they know best, their own lives. Others feel less comfortable doing personal writing; they see it as an invasion of their privacy. We respect such feelings and agree that no one should force you to write about something you choose not to reveal. However, the writing activities in the following chapters are structured in such a way that you can reveal as much about yourself as is comfortable for you. The student essays included in each chapter demonstrate the wide range of possibilities.

Many students wonder if personal writing will help them with the writing they will need to do in their other courses or to pass writing proficiency tests. We feel that the answer to this question is yes. Our belief is based on a very simple observation: if you want to be a good cook, you have to cook; if you want to be a skilled auto mechanic, you have to fix cars; and if you want to write well, you have to write often.

The skills involved in personal writing—attention to detail, organization, description, dialogue, and drawing conclusions—are all skills that are needed for more formal writing. In addition, grammatical fluency, sentence structure, and vocabulary can also be developed by doing personal writing.

Even more important, as you think and write about your own life, you may come to a better understanding of yourself and the world around you.

4
Experiences

In some ways, all writing is about experience. It can be the experience of learning something new or remembering something from the past. It can be about a painful or frightening or dangerous moment. Or it can be about something very simple and ordinary.

Writing, especially writing about experience, gives us a chance to recall moments, both large and small. And in the process of thinking about them and writing about them, we can discover how these moments fit into the larger patterns of our lives.

The reading selections in this chapter are mostly about ordinary life—a child's pride in learning how to cook rice, another's excitement about a Christmas present, the daily routine of a taxi driver. It is not the experiences themselves that make this writing interesting. Rather, it is the way the writers have been able to show us how these moments were meaningful to them. By recording their experiences, these writers have opened up the private worlds of their lives.

READINGS

Learning How to Cook
by Florence Cheung

In this simple story, Florence Cheung, a student from Hong Kong, tells of an ordinary childhood experience—learning to cook rice. Yet by her careful choice of details, Cheung also paints a picture of family respect and togetherness. Before you read, think of a time in your own childhood when you learned a new skill.

"Kit Wah! Kit Wah!" my mother was calling me. I was her eldest daughter. 1 She was a thirty-three-year-old married woman, with four children, six, four, three, and two years old.

In the 1960s, every Chinese had to work very hard in order to earn his living 2 in Hong Kong. My father worked twelve hours a day but his salary was scanty. Thus, my mother had to bring up four of us and sew trousers at home.

"Mama, Mama!" 3

I came back from outside. The house was dark. For a moment, I could not 4 see anything. Then, I saw my mother sitting in front of her sewing machine. The spot lamp shone on the left side of her face. She picked up the unfinished pair of trousers and examined them carefully under the light. As I was four feet in height and fifty pounds in weight, I leaned onto the table of the sewing machine and talked to my mother. "Mama, did you hear me? Why did you call me?"

My mother moved her eyes away from the sewing machine and said, "It's 5 time to cook. Switch the light on first." She yawned and stretched her arms.

Though people might think a child should play around, I started making 6 beds in the morning at the age of four. Thus, I lifted a stool towards the wall and climbed on top of it to reach the switch, and put the light on. Now, I could see my mother's whole figure in the middle of the parlor. She responded to the light.

"Listen! I have to finish this piece of work tonight. You have to cook."   7

She rolled my sleeves up and tied the apron around my abdomen. I was so   8
small that the apron covered my back as well. It looked like a long blue skirt.

"Put one full cup of rice into the inner pot of the electric rice cooker. Then,   9
wash the rice with water. Be careful!"

I followed her instructions. Her voice was still in my ears, "Be careful!" I   10
crashed the pot into the sink. "Ah!" I cried out. All the rice was in the sink and
the pot was empty.

I went back to my mother with the empty pot. My head was down. Instead   11
of scolding me, my mother patted me on the back for admitting the fault.

"I heard what happened. Remove the dirty rice and try again! There is noth-   12
ing that you cannot do. Even a rod of iron, you can make it into a fine, small needle!" my mother told me as she reached into her bottomless supply of Chinese
maxims.

This time, I held the pot as tightly as possible. I washed the rice and poured   13
the water out carefully. This procedure was repeated several times. Then, I mea-
sured the depth of the rice with my middle finger, a trick that I had learned from
my mother, and put the same amount of water into the pot. I brought the pot back
to my mother. She did the same thing to measure the depth of the water.

"That's right! You're a smart girl. Remember to switch the electric cooker   14
on." She smiled for the first time that evening.

I checked to see that the small red light of the electric cooker was on. My   15
heart was lightened.

Later, my mother got up from her seat and went into the kitchen. When she   16
saw the steam coming out from the rice cooker, she was satisfied. Then, she taught
me how to wash the white Chinese cabbage leaf by leaf and inspect for any
worms. I was told to wash them at least four times. My mother steamed the fish
with some ginger and spring onions. Then, she fried the vegetable while I set the
table.

"Mama, we smell something good! We're hungry!" My sister and brothers   17
came back from playing.

"Wash your hands first," my mother said. "Your sister cooked the rice   18
tonight."

My three-year-old brother rolled his sleeves up and pretended to wash the   19
rice with his hands. "Mama, I know how to cook."

When my mother saw the performance, she burst into laughter. We laughed,   20
too. "Next time, it will be your turn." She smiled down at him.

Lord, how I loved the first time that I cooked.   21

Personal Connections

1. When Florence Cheung was six years old, she was already doing quite a
bit of work around the house. How do you feel about this? Should children be free
to play all day, or should they be expected to help out from an early age?

2. We learn from the ending that Cheung was very proud of her accomplishment the first time she cooked the rice for the family's supper. Think of a time in your own childhood when you were proud of something you did. Freewrite about your memories of this accomplishment.

Content and Writing Techniques

1. Although this essay focuses on learning how to cook rice, we also learn a lot about the relationship between Cheung and her mother. Go back through the essay and underline three details that reveal the mother's attitude toward her daughter. Try to explain what you learn about their relationship from each of these details.

2. Do you think Cheung is telling this story from a child's or an adult's point of view? Underline the evidence you find in the essay to support your opinion.

3. There is quite a bit of dialogue (direct quotations of a person's exact words) in this essay. Look back through the essay and underline five examples of dialogue. Why do you think Cheung decided to use so much dialogue? How would the essay be different if she had presented this information without using direct quotations?

4. Look back at the last paragraph of the essay. Why do you think Cheung decided to end this way? Do you like the ending? Why or why not?

What Is It Like to Have an Empty Stomach?
by Youssef Rami

In this essay, Youssef Rami, a student from Morocco, describes an important event in his spiritual life—his first experience of fasting. Before you read, think back to your own childhood. Can you remember a time when you decided to act like an adult? What were your reasons for this decision?

Ramadan is the holiest month in the Muslim year. In fact, it's the fourth pillar of Islam. All adult Muslims must fast from dawn to sunset every day of Ramadan. This means abstaining from eating, drinking, smoking, and conjugal relations during the hours of fasting. Travelers, the sick, and pregnant women can defer fasting during Ramadan and make up for it later. Fasting in a hot climate such as Morocco is quite difficult. Nevertheless, those who have to fast have developed a great deal of patience and self-control.

Going back to my childhood's best memories, I still recall my first day of fasting when I was only six years old. Of course, I was not supposed to fast since most children usually start fasting at the age of thirteen; however, since I was the only one among all my brothers and sisters who did not have to fast, I was very anxious and curious to experience the feeling of fasting for at least one day, so I decided to fast the following day.

"It is a great decision, Son," my father said. I smiled and promised to keep my word. At the same time, I ignored my mother's exhortation that I was too young to fast.   3

It was about 2:30 A.M. when my mother woke me up to eat our last repast that we could have before the sunrise. After I washed my hands and face, I sat at the table next to my father with a great feeling, knowing that I was allowed to eat as much as I could without being interrupted by my mother as usual, claiming that I eat too much.   4

After I finished my last meal, my father gave me some good advice. He said, "Kid, I want you to understand something very important." I looked at him and said, "What is it, Dad?" He replied, "Tomorrow is your first day of fasting. If you feel incapable of finishing the day, eat and break your fast and be honest about it, but never cheat because Allah is always watching you." I nodded my head and headed to bed.   5

The next morning, which was my first fasting day, was so terribly hot that I felt thirsty as soon as I got up. Yet I remembered that I could only rinse my mouth without letting a drop of water get into my throat. An hour later I was in school; of course, none of my friends was fasting, and that made it worse. They kept eating all kinds of fruits, candies, and cookies in front of me. At first I didn't care, but later, at lunch time, when everybody was enjoying his meal and I was the only one left with an empty stomach, so many ridiculous ideas came to my mind. Fortunately, I remembered my father's last words, "Allah is watching you." So I found the courage to defeat all crazy and silly ideas.   6

During lunch time, I felt what it was like to have an empty stomach and not be able to eat while food was next to me. I then knew how a poor person would feel if he was hungry and could not afford to feed himself or his family. I said to myself, "Maybe one of the many reasons why people have to fast is to experience what others feel."   7

My school sessions ended at 3 P.M., so I had about four and a half hours to finish my day. I was very hungry, thirsty, and tired. As soon as I got home, I went to sleep. Honestly, the last hours of that day were the most difficult time I ever experienced in my childhood, and only now do I understand why I remained unruffled the whole day. During that day I learned how to resist my selfish desires, and I understood that self-control is very important for human beings.   8

The time of breaking our fast was 7:45. I was delighted that I had made it successfully. The first thing that got to my mouth was a glass of water followed by some dates. This has been a traditional way to break the fasting throughout the Muslim world since the time of the prophet Muhammad.[1] The first glass of water really rejuvenated me, and I felt refreshed. I was in a great bliss.   9

Now, when I go back to this childhood memory, I feel proud that I knew so much.   10

---

[1] Peace be upon him.

Personal Connections

1. For Muslims, fasting during Ramadan is an important part of their spiritual lives. Even people who do not believe in organized religion usually have something they regard as special or sacred. Write about an experience in your own life that was special in the way that this experience was for Rami.

2. In many religions the concept of self-denial (for example, by fasting or giving money to the poor) is considered important. How do you feel about this idea? Do we become better human beings by doing without material things? Why or why not?

Content and Writing Techniques

1. In paragraphs 3 and 4, Rami hints at the different ways his mother and father reacted to his decision to fast. How would you describe each of the parents' reactions? Why do you think the parents greeted his decision differently?

2. Notice the use of direct quotations in this essay. Put a *Q* in the margin next to each of these quotations and write down who is speaking. Why do you think Rami chose to include these quotations?

3. The conclusion to this essay consists of only one sentence: "Now, when I go back to this childhood memory, I feel proud that I knew so much." What was it that Rami knew as a child? Freewrite about this question for about ten minutes. Compare your answer with that of a partner. Do you think Rami should have expanded his conclusion by explaining what he knew? Or do you agree with his decision to let the readers of his essay supply this missing information?

The Photograph
by Sha Sha Chen

> *In the following selection, Sha Sha Chen, a student from Taiwan, recalls a painful memory from her childhood in this story about a missing photograph. Was there ever a moment in your own childhood when you were disappointed by someone you loved or trusted?*

"Little Sister, Little Sister," my big sister whispers into my ear.   1

"Mn . . . ," I answer.   2

"I need to go to the bathroom," she whispers again.   3

"Go by yourself." I do not want to leave my sleep.   4

"I can't. It's so dark and quiet. I'm scared. Please get up and come with me. Please!"   5

Her voice is like a frightened little kitty. I wait for her outside the bathroom,   6 which is on the same floor as my parents' bedroom and ours. As soon as she finishes, we walk quietly back to our room and right away I'm asleep again.

* * *

"Don't be ridiculous! There is no ghost in our house," I say to my big sister. [7]
We are on our way home from school.

"Then how would you explain the missing photo of our father?" She is looking at me; she seems puzzled. [8]

"What's such a big deal about that?" I wince a little. [9]

"Don't you think it's strange that the photo disappeared all by itself? Nobody [10]
knows where it went."

"Well, it may be strange, but still, what has this got to do with a ghost?" [11]

I move my eyes down to the sidewalk to avoid her eyes. [12]

"I think it was a ghost who stole the photo of our father." [13]

"Why would a ghost want a picture of our father?" I say, moving my eyes to [14]
take a peep at my sister.

"I don't know, but Mother is very worried. She has gone to pray in a temple [15]
this morning."

When my mother hears the rumbling sound of my father's motorcycle approaching the door, she gives us a relieved smile. And I, as usual, take out the pair of slippers which my father wears at home from the shoe cabinet and lay them on the floor by the living room door. [16]

"Put this on and keep it with you all the time," my mother says, showing my [17]
father a red string with a square of red cloth hanging from the center. It is called a *fu sen fu* in Chinese.

"What do I need this for?" my father frowns, refusing to take the *fu sen fu*. [18]

My father is a man who doesn't believe in superstitions. He told us there are [19]
no such things as ghosts. When he was in the military, his commander made him stay overnight in a graveyard, and he did not see any ghosts.

"It is to protect you. Please wear it. Otherwise I can't rest for a minute," my [20]
mother says.

"Nonsense, " my father refuses firmly. [21]

"Father, please wear it. Don't let us worry!" The voice comes from my big [22]
sister.

"Don't be so superstitious. A missing photo doesn't mean I'm going to die." [23]
My father is lighting up a cigarette.

A moment of silence follows. Neither my mother nor my sister utters a [24]
sound. It seems to deepen their worry each time the missing photo is mentioned. And I pretend to watch TV all through it.

* * *

It was a week before the photo had disappeared. I was at school one morning. My best friend Shu Yi told me that my father had a girlfriend and she had seen them together in a restaurant. [25]

"You lie," I said, and made a face at her. [26]

"I'm not. It was just last night. Didn't I tell you it was my mom's birthday, so [27]
my dad was going to take us out to dinner?"

What Shu Yi said was true, but I still couldn't believe what she was telling me. [28]

"I saw your father's girlfriend. She was crying in the restaurant. They talked   29
and talked, and she cried."

My heart began to sink. For three nights I had not seen my father at the din-   30
ner table. My mother said he was working late. Poor Mother.

That day, after school, I went home and asked my mother if Father was com-   31
ing home for dinner that night.

"No, he is working late again."   32

"When is Big Sister coming back?" I asked. My sister was on a school trip to   33
Taipei for a week.

"The day after tomorrow."   34

I left the kitchen, where my mother was cooking, and went into the living   35
room. I sat there angrily, not knowing what to do. Suddenly my eyes met my father in the photo, which was framed and displayed behind a glass door of a wall
cabinet. I stood up on the sofa and let my hand reach for the photo. I separated
the photo from its frame and put the frame back in place. I came down from the
sofa, holding the picture in my hand, and went upstairs to my room. In my room,
I took up a big ink brush lying on the desk and wrote *wan ba dan*[1] on the face of
my father in the photograph.

The doorbell rang the next morning, and there was my aunt's husband stand-   36
ing at the door, asking to see my father. I let him in and went back to my breakfast. In the meanwhile, from the conversation between my father and my uncle, I
realized that my aunt had run away from her husband and was living in a hotel.
My father had been seeing her after work for four days.

*   *   *

Twenty years have passed since the photo of my father disappeared, and still,   37
my father keeps the *fu sen fu* in his wallet.

Personal Connections

1. Look up the word *superstition* in the dictionary. What are some superstitions from your own country or culture? How are they similar to or different from
those described in this story?

2. The fear of ghosts, monsters, and other scary things may seem silly to
adults, but to children, they are very real. Some psychologists believe that fears of
such imaginary things are related to more realistic fears or problems in daily life.
Think of some of the fears you had as a child, or that you have observed in young
children. How might these fears be related to real life problems?

Content and Writing Techniques

1. This essay consists mostly of dialogue in direct speech: that is, quotes of
what each person in the story said. Look at the first six paragraphs, and rewrite all
the examples of direct speech, using indirect (or reported) speech. For example:

---

[1]*Wan ba dan* is an insulting curse in Chinese.

Direct speech: "I need to go to the bathroom," she whispers again.
Indirect speech: She whispered that she needed to go to the bathroom.

How is direct speech different from indirect? Why do you think the writer chose to use so much direct speech in this story?

2. The little piece of cloth called a *fu sen fu* seems to be an important symbol in this story. Which of the following reasons might explain why the father kept it in his wallet for twenty years?

    a. He kept it because it reminded him of the love his family felt for him.
    b. He kept it to remind him to be faithful to his wife.
    c. He kept it because he believed it would protect him from harm.
    d. He kept it because it reminded him of his girlfriend.

Discuss your answer with a partner or small group.

3. The writer never tells us whether or not her father was actually having an affair with her aunt. Find three details from the story that suggest he *might have been* having an affair. Find three details that suggest he *might not have been* having an affair.

From *Growing Up*
by Russell Baker

> *In this excerpt from his autobiography, Russell Baker, the well-known American newspaper columnist, tells what happened when he discovered a wonderful surprise his mother had planned for him. Before you begin to read, write about a time when you had a pleasant surprise.*

She was a magician at stretching a dollar. That December, with Christmas approaching, she was out at work and Doris was in the kitchen when I barged into her bedroom one afternoon in search of a safety pin. Since her bedroom opened onto a community hallway, she kept the door locked, but needing the pin, I took the key from its hiding place, unlocked the door, and stepped in. Standing against the wall was a big, black bicycle with balloon tires. I recognized it instantly. It was the same second-hand bike I'd been admiring in a Baltimore Street shop window. I'd even asked about the price. It was horrendous. Something like $15. Somehow my mother had scraped together enough for a down payment and meant to surprise me with the bicycle on Christmas morning. 1

I was overwhelmed by the discovery that she had squandered such money on me and sickened by the knowledge that, bursting into her room like this, I had robbed her of the pleasure of seeing me astonished and delighted on Christmas day. I hadn't wanted to know her lovely secret; still, stumbling upon it like this made me feel as though I'd struck a blow against her happiness. I backed out, put the key back in its hiding place, and brooded privately. 2

I resolved that between now and Christmas I must do nothing, absolutely   3
nothing, to reveal the slightest hint of my terrible knowledge. I must avoid the
least word, the faintest intonation, the weakest gesture that might reveal my possession of her secret. Nothing must deny her the happiness of seeing me stunned
with amazement on Christmas day.

In the privacy of my bedroom I began composing and testing exclamations   4
of delight: "Wow!" "A bike with balloon tires! I don't believe it!" "I'm the luckiest
boy alive!" And so on. They all owed a lot to movies in which boys like Mickey
Rooney had seen their wildest dreams come true, and I realized that, with my lack
of acting talent, all of them were going to sound false at the critical moment when
I wanted to cry out my love spontaneously from the heart. Maybe it would be better to say nothing but appear to be shocked into such deep pleasure that speech
had escaped me. I wasn't sure, though. I'd seen speechless gratitude in the movies
too, and it never really worked until the actors managed to cry a few quiet tears. I
doubted I could cry on cue, so I began thinking about other expressions of
speechless amazement. In front of a hand-held mirror in my bedroom I tried the
whole range of expressions; mouth agape and eyes wide; hands slapped firmly
against both cheeks to keep the jaw from falling off; ear-to-ear grin with all teeth
fully exposed while hugging the torso with both arms. These and more I practiced
for several days without acquiring confidence in any of them. I decided to wait
until Christmas morning and see if anything came naturally. . . .

That Christmas morning she roused us early, "to see what Santa Claus   5
brought," she said with just the right tone of irony to indicate we were all old
enough to know who Santa Claus was. I came out of my bedroom with my presents for her and Doris, and Doris came with hers. My mother's had been placed
under the tree during the night. There were a few small glittering packages, a big
doll for Doris, but no bicycle. I must have looked disappointed.

"It looks like Santa Claus didn't do too well by you this year, Buddy," she   6
said, as I opened packages. A shirt. A necktie. I said something halfhearted like,
"It's the thought that counts," but what I felt was bitter disappointment. I supposed she'd found the bike intolerably expensive and sent it back.

"Wait a minute!" she cried, snapping her fingers. "There's something in my   7
bedroom I forgot all about."

She beckoned to Doris, the two of them went out, and a moment later came   8
back wheeling between them the big black two-wheeler with balloon tires. I didn't
have to fake my delight, after all. The three of us—Doris, my mother, and I—
were people bred to repress the emotional expressions of love, but I did something
that startled both my mother and me. I threw my arms around her spontaneously
and kissed her.

"All right now, don't carry on about it. It's only a bicycle," she said.   9

Still, I knew that she was as happy as I was to see her so happy.   10

Personal Connections

1. Baker could simply have told his mother the truth about discovering the
bicycle. Yet he decided to protect her feelings by pretending that he had not seen

the bike. Have you ever faced a similar dilemma? Freewrite about those awkward situations in which a "white lie" seems kinder than the truth.

2. What do you think Baker means when he says, in paragraph 8, that his family members were "bred to repress the emotional expressions of love"? How does your family feel about openly expressing affection? Do you think that the way in which you express your feelings is determined by your family alone, or is it influenced by the culture of which your family is a part?

Content and Writing Techniques

1. What do you think Baker means when he says, in the first sentence, that his mother "was a magician at stretching a dollar"? What visual image do you get from the words "stretching a dollar"?

2. How does Baker build up suspense in the reader's mind as he tells this story? What was your own reaction when the bicycle was not under the tree on Christmas morning?

3. After Baker hugged and kissed his mother, she said, "All right now, don't carry on about it. It's only a bicycle." Why do you think she acted this way?

A Hard Life
by Peter Kisfaludi

> *In this essay Peter Kisfaludi, a student who was born in Hungary, gives us an insider's view of the life of a New York City taxi driver. It's a grim life relieved by occasional moments of excitement or good fortune. Have you ever held a job that was demanding—either physically or emotionally?*

It's 4 A.M. My wristwatch alarm is gently beeping. I can't use the regular clock because I don't want to wake up anyone else. I get up, stagger to the kitchen, put up the coffee. My cat is impatiently pacing up and down crying for her breakfast. I give it to her. I turn on the radio, listen to the news, waiting for the weather to come on. The weather is very important in my job. It can make or break a day.   1

I'm a taxi driver. Now that I'm going to school, I'm driving part-time. Three times a week I take the A train downtown to pick up my cab. It's six o'clock when I get off at Times Square. The city is quiet except for the trucks delivering milk and newspapers and picking up garbage. A few lonely prostitutes are lurking around the dark street corners.   2

The line slowly starts forming inside the trailer that serves as the office of the Kafka Taxi Management Company. The first owner was an admirer of Franz Kafka, hence the name. There used to be quotations from his novels hanging all over the walls, proclaiming such virtues as patience, thoroughness, and earnestness. That owner and his signs are long gone; we have other signs now about payments for   3 the shifts, the quality of gasoline to be used, and what to do in case of an accident. There is also a no-smoking sign, largely ignored by the men.

The night drivers are bringing in their taxi meters and ignition keys, their   4
eyes squinting from being up all night—I guess one can never quite get used to that. There is a conversation going on in several languages. Creole, Spanish, Chinese, Arabic, Polish, Southern drawl, and many more can be heard.

Behind the glass window, Jack, the dispatcher, is working slowly. If he   5
likes you, and you are a steady, safe driver, he'll give you a good car; otherwise you might get a heap that'll break down, or has to go for inspection, or who knows what. Some drivers try to avert these inconveniences by giving Jack an extra buck or two. In my experience that doesn't do much at this company. Get your car fixed when it's needed, always gas up in full, show up for work when you are scheduled, and most of all, have no accidents; then you're assured a good car.

Jack has got a no-nonsense approach to his job.   6

"Where were you Saturday? You were on schedule for that day."   7

"Jack, I had the flu."   8

"I don't run a clinic here. I run a business. You owe me sixty-three dollars.   9
You gonna give me five extra dollars a day until you paid up."

"But Jack . . . "   10

"No but. It's either that or you aren't going to work."   11

By this time there are some impatient voices taunting the unlucky fellow.   12

Finally I get ahead in the line, pay my sixty-three dollars, and get my car   13
keys and taxi meter. The next step is to find the car. That isn't easy when it's raining or snowing. Then I check the tires, the lights, see if the vehicle is fully gassed up. The working day is about to begin.

The traffic is very light, mostly the competition. Did you know there are   14
11,200 taxis in New York? It looks like a lot less in the morning, a lot more at midday, then there aren't enough again in the evenings. Some of the taxis—about 35 percent of them—are individually owned. One-third of these owners are Haitians. A yellow taxi medallion is valued at one hundred and five thousand dollars now, the car costs twelve thousand, the insurance is another three thousand, the meter, the installation, and the fees are two more thousand. One can see this is a serious investment. It is possible to find a broker who will let you buy it with a ten thousand dollar down payment. The catch is that they expect you to come up with five hundred dollars a week for five years! You end up paying more than double the money you borrowed. That can go even higher in the likely case that one has an accident, or the car just simply "dies" of exhaustion. In these cases the only way out is to refinance it, which means more money to the unscrupulous broker. Some drivers must work eighteen, twenty hours a day, six, seven days a week. Deplorable working conditions, I think. However, there is light at the end of the tunnel. Once the medallion is paid for, one only has to contend with the unfriendly traffic agents, Taxi and Limousine Commission inspectors (the much despised Commission), abrasive passengers, mounting insurance bills, and rising repair costs, consequently a shrinking real income. Not very appealing, is it?

Don't despair! There are other ways; you can go drive for the big fleets if you   15
don't want to own a small business. There aren't many fleets left. Only about 20
percent of the taxis belong to the fleets. (In this essay I'm not going to discuss the
reasons for the fluctuations amongst the modes of operations.) The fleets are
unionized. That means, you have to give money to the union, who later can't account for it. These fees might be meager compared to a good union—sixty dollars a year plus two dollars per day—but if you consider what you are getting for
it . . . They provide you with no job protection, sparse benefits that are "maneu-
vered" around by the owners (sometimes with the consent of the union) unless
you have many years of servitude for them. The fleets used to pay on a percentage
basis, 41 percent to 49 percent of the total take, plus you keep the tips. Their system now is similar to leasing.

I am a lease driver. There are several ways to lease: by the day, by the night,   16
by the week, with the owner's car or with your own car. In any case keep in mind
that I keep one out of every two dollars I get. It is true whether you own, lease, or
drive on commission. So the only way to maximize profits is to work more. As a
lease driver you have no job protection either, not even the promise of a paid vacation or medical benefits. You could face arbitrary raises in the lease rates or be
fired.

After learning all that, one may ask why anyone would want to be a taxi   17
driver? Of course it has its good sides. There is freedom to make your own income, under certain conditions your own hours, your own days. (I work Sunday,
Monday, Wednesday from 6 A.M. to 6 P.M.) There is also the joy of competitive
driving, the zig-zagging in and out of traffic. Your income doesn't get taxed "too"
heavily. (If I make about two hundred eighty dollars, I pay about forty dollars
for taxes.)

And there are the unexpected good luck rides. Here are some excerpts from   18
my five-year career:

This is the story of the largest tip, about which even some of my colleagues   19
are skeptical. It happened two years ago around Christmas time. At the time I had
my own car, and I was having a lot of problems with it ("her" as we say in the
business). I was working eighty hours a week, and still not getting anywhere. I
picked up two young British gentlemen in midtown. They were going to Kennedy
Airport. They started asking questions about the business, and I really poured my
heart out: told them about all the troubles I was having, all the money I was
spending on repairs, insurance, and so on.

Then they wanted to hear how I got here, and all the adventures through Eu-   20
rope and in the States. By this time we had arrived at the airport, and they were
getting ready to pay me. The meter showed twenty some dollars plus the toll. One
of them handed me twenty-five dollars plus two more twenties. I looked up and
asked: "Do you know what you are doing?"

He said: "Yes." And handed me fifty more.   21

I still didn't believe what was happening, and asked: "Are you sure?"   22

His friend answered: "Yes, we are." And he handed me a hundred dollar bill.   23

Needless to say, I went home after that. Unfortunately this never happened   24
again.

My "biggest" celebrity: One morning this past February I noticed the door-   25
man of the Mayflower Hotel signaling for a taxi. I stepped on the gas, and pulled
up in front. The doorman came to my window and said: "I need you to do a favor
for me. You have to take somebody to the Western Union, wait for him, and bring
him back here." I started ranting and raving about the lost time in the prime
hours, and that I wasn't going to wait around for anyone. The doorman just about
gave up. But my passenger made his way to the cab and got in without me noticing him. Suddenly I felt a heavy hand on my shoulder and I heard a deep, calm
voice: "You're gonna do it for me, aren't you?"

I turned around surprised, and my surprise grew when I saw a round face   26
smiling like the moon, and it was the face of Muhammad Ali, the heavyweight
champion of the world. I said: "Sure, Ali, I'm gonna do it."

At the end it was very well worth it because Ali gave me about thirty extra   27
dollars and his autograph.

So, every morning I wait for these things to repeat, but mostly in vain. Life   28
as a taxi driver is hard, grueling work and I make my money by the ones, twos,
not twenties, hundreds. Maybe someday, after I finish school and have a good job,
I'll be able to relax in the back seat of a taxicab listening to stories or reading a
newspaper. And when I arrive at my destination, I'll be able to afford to "throw"
an extra five to the driver.

Personal Connections

1. While talking about the advantages of his job, Kisfaludi tells two wonderful good luck stories: the time he received a tip of almost two hundred dollars and
the time he gave a ride to the former boxing champion Muhammad Ali. Write
about a good luck story from your own life.

2. There is much talk about money in this essay. Do you agree with
Kisfaludi's decision to be so open about the financial aspects of his job? Is this information important for your understanding of this kind of work?

Content and Writing Techniques

1. Reread the first paragraph. Why do you think Kisfaludi decided to begin
his essay with the details of his waking up? Underline all the verbs in paragraph 1.
What basic verb tense is Kisfaludi using? Why do you think he chose this tense?
Select three of these verbs that you think are particularly effective.

2. In paragraphs 14 and 15 Kisfaludi explains many facts and figures about
the business aspects of driving a taxi. Which of the following statements best describes the advice you would give him regarding these two paragraphs:

   a. Too many boring business details! Eliminate these two paragraphs.
   b. Important but too long! Condense this information into about half the
      space.
   c. Interesting and essential! Keep it just the way it is.

3. Reread the last paragraph of the essay. Do you think this is a good ending? Why or why not?

4. What, in your opinion, was Kisfaludi's purpose for writing? In one or two sentences write down the main impression you received from reading the essay.

Exodus
by Xiao Mei Sun

When asked to write about an experience from her past that she still remembered clearly, Xiao Mei Sun decided to explore a painful memory — the Cultural Revolution, which severely disrupted life in China from 1966 to 1976. The result was a powerful and emotionally charged essay, which was awarded a Bedford Prize in Student Writing. Before you read, write down your own definition for the word exodus.

I was standing by my desk looking for a book. When I pulled out the last drawer and searched down to the bottom of it, a small box appeared in front of me. I opened it and saw a set of keys inside. They looked familiar, but at the same time they were so strange. Holding the keys, some long-locked memories flooded into my mind, as if they had been released by the keys. I sank slowly into the chair. It was raining outside. The room was so quiet that I could hear the rain pattering on the windowpanes. My thoughts returned to another rainy day.

There were several knocks on my bedroom door. "Wake up, my dear," Mother's soft voice floated into my ears. "We need time to get everything done." I opened my eyes and muttered some sound to let her know I was awake. It was dim outside, though it was past daybreak. I turned my body; the hard "bed" beneath suddenly reminded me that I was sleeping on the floor. The only thing between me and the hard, cold boards was a thin blanket. I looked around the empty room and remembered that the day before we had sent most of our furniture and belongings to the Nanjing Railway Station, where they would be transferred to Paoying County — a poor, rural place where we were being forced to go. I heard Mother say something again and realized that I had to get up immediately. Suddenly, I loved the "bed" so much that I didn't want to leave. It seemed softer and warmer than the bed I used to sleep in. I clung to the floor as tears rolled down my face. I wished I could sleep there for the rest of my life instead of going to that strange place. I sighed deeply, wiped my face, and got up.

It was very cloudy as if it would rain at any minute. "I hope it's not going to rain today," Mother addressed my father and me when she saw us step into the dining room. I joined my parents for breakfast around the small table — the only furniture left in the house. The air above the table was as heavy as the sky. "The cave men would never imagine that people in the twentieth century would sit on the floor to eat, would they?" Father said, with a grin to me. He had a sense of humor at all times, which had never failed to make me laugh. But today the joke had no charm and tore my heart into pieces. Mother saw my despair and warned, "Mei, I'm superstitious. It's bad luck to see any water when we are going to have a long journey. I hope you understand that." I blinked my tears away and managed a smile. "There is just something in my eyes," said I. Then I left the room to pack my things.

As our bus was arriving at the railway station, some strange noises could be   4
heard in the distance. I was wondering what they could be when the bus suddenly halted in front of the station. I got off and saw a band playing music. Surrounding the band, there were quite a few people holding some colorful banners with slogans on them which read: "Long Live the Cultural Revolution!" "Go to the Rural Areas and Receive Re-education from the Peasants!" "Carry Out Chairman Mao's Revolutionary Ideas Firmly!" Another crowd was also nearby chanting frantically with their arms in the air and their faces full of excitement.

Looking at these people, I suddenly felt angry. Since earlier this year—two   5
years after the Great Cultural Revolution that had begun in 1966—thousands of party bureaucrats and intellectuals, including most students and teachers of high school and college, had been banished to the countryside, to "learn from the people." After they came to the countryside, these intellectuals were ordered to do the hardest work in the fields such as picking cotton or planting rice. They had to work every day from dawn to sunset, no matter how old they were or how bad their physical condition. Some of them even collapsed in the fields. The reason the party's leader had given was that these intellectuals were open to Western ideas and criticized the government's policies. They were too dangerous to stay in the cities. If they were punished physically, perhaps then they would learn how to keep their mouths shut. Today it was my family's turn. My parents were high school teachers. They had spent their lives educating the young generation. Many times when I had awakened at midnight, I had seen them still marking their students' papers or preparing for their classes. But now all those years of hard work had become the fatal reason they were being sent away. They shouldn't have been punished like this. The truly dangerous people were those gathered around the band. They helped the government confiscate our property, humiliate the intellectuals, and beat the innocent. They were chosen to stay only because they were labeled as the so-called working class and firm followers of Mao Tse-tung revolutionary lines. Now, at this critical moment of our lives, these "chosen people" were cheering for our bad luck and for their survival of this political disaster. Where was the justice?

I turned my head away in disgust and saw at the other side of the station a   6
lot of people standing in small groups. Most of them were wiping their eyes and blowing their noses; some were hugging each other while they murmured; the young people were just looking at each other with their mouths half open, uttering no sound. The scene on the two sides of the railway station was so contradictory that if someone came from out of the country and saw this, he would be bewildered. On one side there were people, standing around the band, who were as cheerful as if they were waiting for Napoleon's Army to return in triumph, while

across from them there were others who were as sad as if they had been exiled to Siberia in the reign of the Tsar. I felt a strong pain in my heart and was almost choked by the lump in my throat, but at the same time I was glad that no relatives and friends had come to see me and my family leave the city. This was not a happy exodus.

It was about ten o'clock now. The clouds were even heavier and moved very fast. I looked up but could not see the sun. People always praised the warm sunshine in early October. Where were its charm, brightness, and warmth today? It seemed that the sun hid her face behind a cloud; she felt pain and shame at seeing the tragedy in the world. A whirlwind swept through the station and blew pieces of white paper from the ground. The paper danced in the air for a while, then dropped slowly again. A chill came through my skin and penetrated into my bones. I stood there with my mind thousands of miles away from the present, and was aware of nothing. The world around me was frozen. I thought about the happy times I had had with my teachers and friends in school; the books I had enjoyed so much in the libraries, the warm room I had spent most of my time in; the beautiful city where I had lived for all of my fourteen years. Those memories were so close to me that I could touch them and hold them. Though the world around me now was ice cold, I felt my heart begin to warm up, warm up. . . .

"Mei, get on the train." Mother's voice broke through the frozen world and woke me up. I was so deep in thought that I hadn't even noticed that people had started boarding. I moved slowly toward the train. The music and the sobs were louder. They mingled and hung in the air. The train was packed. I was standing by the door with my left foot on the platform and the other on the step of the train. It began to rain. The drops were so big and hard that they made my face hurt with each direct hit. I looked up again and prayed: "Mother said it was unlucky to see water today. Please stop, rain!" A sharp whistle pierced the air and I jumped. The sudden shrill noise silenced the whole world. People stopped sobbing and talking; the band even stopped playing. It was so quiet that I couldn't believe there were hundreds of people around. Another whistle sounded and the train started to move. The world came to life just as abruptly as it had ceased a few seconds ago. Father reached out his hand and pulled me in. The wheels moved very slowly as though a gigantic monster were dragging its huge body unwillingly to another place. I rolled the window down and put my head outside. The heavy raindrops became a downpour. Oh, the heavens could no longer hold their tears and they finally cried out against the unfairness in the world. I watched sadly as the city and the platform were left behind. I repeated silently: "Bye, my school. Bye, my libraries. Bye, my city." Water was running down my face like a stream. I didn't know whether it was my tears or the rain. I reached my hand into my pocket and held the house keys tightly. I said loudly to the receding city: "I will come back; just wait for me. . . ."

A gleam of dim, soft light came through the windows and lighted up my room. I didn't know how long I had sat there or when tears had wet my face. I put the keys into the box and sighed heavily. Since the day I left my hometown, I had never gone back. Now I was in New York and I would never use the keys again, but they were still precious to me because they linked the happy memories of my childhood and the tragedy of my country. Closing the small box, I rose and approached the windows. The rain had already stopped. I opened the windows and inhaled the fresh, clean air greedily. The lights from the lampposts along the streets, mingled with the headlights of cars, were shining in the dark. The leaves of the trees were swaying in the gentle breeze. Oh, what a beautiful city! What a sweet night in this foreign land! My heart was melted and a smile rose on my face. . . .

Personal Connections

1. In a small group, compare the definitions of *exodus* that you wrote before reading this essay. Now that you have read the essay, would you change your definition in any way? Working with your group, write down all the features you can think of that make an exodus different from an ordinary departure. For example, an exodus usually involves the movement of large numbers of people.

2. Has your own life or that of a family member ever been disrupted by some political or economic development beyond your control (for example, a war or a depression)?

3. One of the themes of this essay is injustice—how Sun, her family, and millions of other Chinese were punished although they had done nothing wrong. Have you ever felt that you were treated unjustly? What were the circumstances? Would it be a good subject for an essay?

Content and Writing Techniques

1. In paragraph 2, underline any words that refer to sight, sound, or touch. For example: "soft voice floated into my ears." Circle any words that describe a strong emotion. How do these references to the senses and to emotion affect you as a reader?

2. Paragraph 5 was not included in the first draft of this essay but was added later in response to a question from a reader. Reread this paragraph. What do you think the question was? How does the information in paragraph 5 strengthen the essay as a whole?

3. There are many references to rain in this story. Put a check mark above all the references to rain that you find. Which of the following things do you feel the rain symbolizes: (a) sadness, (b) injustice, (c) nature, or (d) bad luck? Discuss your choice(s) with a partner or small group.

4. Notice the first and last paragraphs of the essay. When and where do they take place? What would have been lost if Sun had decided just to tell the story of her childhood experience directly and had omitted the first and last paragraphs?

The Pink Fata Morgana
by Vladimir Kuchinsky

Vladimir Kuchinsky, a student from the Soviet Union, lived and worked for many years as an engineer in the coldest, most remote region of Siberia. In this essay, which combines dream and reality, Kuchinsky explores the imaginary world called "the Pink Fata Morgana," which means the pink illusion, or mirage. As you read the essay, think about your own dreams and fantasies. What can they reveal about the real world of daily life?

"Do not listen to the alarm clock if you see a good dream."

Faraway from this sinful planet, somewhere in space, is another planet—the Pink Fata Morgana. I have been up there almost every night. Every night something new has happened in the Pink Fata Morgana. There are no such things as night or afternoon. Everything is up to you. If you want to see night—you see night. If you want to see day—you see day. **1**

There are no such things as money and army, real estate and policemen. There are no such things as shame, debauchery, and corruption. There is no enemy or terrorist. There is no fascism or communism. There is no other color—except pink. **2**

It was early in the morning. I was walking down the pink field, and watching pink clouds in the pink heaven. Something unusual happened this morning. The pink clouds were flying for a while, and then they formed a beautiful pink lady, who was playing a Chopin sonata on a piano. From the first sight, I fell in love. **3**

The lady gracefully stepped down from the pink heaven to the pink field. She was walking toward me. My head was turned, and my heart went down to my feet. **4**

"My darling," she said, "I have been waiting for you in the Pink Fata Morgana almost 2,000 years. Where have you been all this time?" **5**

I felt that my heart stopped beating and my blood was leaving my body. **6**

At this time, the alarm clock woke me up. It was 5:30 in the morning. I found myself in the gray room with icy cold water in the bathroom. I had to hurry up to be on time for my class. I was walking down the gray street, in the most gray neighborhood, in gray Brooklyn, to the gray subway station. The gray people surrounded me in the gray train. When I closed my gray eyes in the gray car, I saw my Pink Fata Morgana, and my dream repeated again. **7**

Somewhere in space there is another planet, the planet called the Pink Fata Morgana. I hope in the future I'll fly there. My pink goddess will meet me up there. We will be together forever. Nobody could separate us from each other. **8**

It will be there in the beautiful pink morning. **9**

Personal Connections

1. Many psychologists claim that dreams and fantasy can help us to understand our own real-world problems. Look through paragraphs 1, 2, and 7. What do these details tell us about the problems Kuchinsky may have faced in his life?

2. Is Kuchinsky's fantasy attractive to you? Would you like to live in the world of the Pink Fata Morgana?

3. Kuchinsky uses the alarm clock to signal the transition from fantasy to reality. What is your feeling about alarm clocks? Do you use one? If so, do you get up as soon as it rings, or do you have ways of negotiating for extra time before facing the cold gray morning?

Content and Writing Techniques

1. There is a sharp contrast between fantasy and reality in this selection. Look through the essay and put an *F* by any detail that relates to fantasy and an *R* by any detail that relates to reality.

2. Kuchinsky uses the colors pink and gray to illustrate the contrast between his dream life and reality.

Choose two colors. One should be a color you like very much; the other should be one you dislike. List your feelings or associations about each of these colors. For example, you might write:

Pink: warm, friendly, love, babies, feminine, sexy
Gray: early morning, cold, sadness, funerals, concrete

ACTIVITIES

Later in this chapter, you will be asked to write an essay about an experience in your own life. As you were reading about the experiences of others, you may have gotten some ideas for subjects that you would like to write about. It not, these activities will help you to think of possible topics. The first activity is based on an experience from the past; the second is based on the present.

MEMORY CHAIN

The purpose of this activity is to help you remember stories from your own experience that can be used as material for writing.

1. Begin by writing a list of words or phrases. You may start by listing whatever objects happen to be in the room around you. Or you may just write whatever words come to your mind. Just keep writing words until an idea or story begins to form in your mind. For example, you might write: "window, glass, broken, four years old, hospital, stitches, my father's eyes, tears."

2. Show your word list to a partner or small group and discuss it. Does it seem like something you can write about? Do you think it will make interesting reading for your partner or group?

3. Begin to draft your story, concentrating on the ideas and details first, the grammar and spelling later.

4. After writing for fifteen or twenty minutes, you may want to stop and share what you have written with your group or partner. This may help you to focus your writing and recall important details that the reader will want to know.

5. When you have completed the draft, discuss it with a partner or group. You may then choose to revise the draft or hand it in to your teacher.

Example

The selection that follows shows how one student developed her memory chain into the first draft of an essay.

I Almost Died

by Rose-Laure Lamothe, Haiti

Memory Chain: 1973; Good Friday; ten years old; swimming in the river; almost drowned.

In sum, life can hold both happiness and tragedy, and there often   1
comes a moment or a day that you will never forget for the rest of your existence. I had this experience on the day I almost died.

In 1973, I was ten years old. I was living in a little town in my native   2
country, Haiti. My neighbors, who were also my best friends, were playing together with me.

The date was on a Good Friday at about 2 o'clock in the afternoon. My   3
friends and I sat together praying and singing some religious songs, as this was our custom on this holiday.

After one hour, we decided to go to the river and swim, before we went   4
to church. We enjoyed swimming, and we would often go under the water. When I came up for air, I saw my neighbor trying to save herself, but she didn't know how to swim. I went to try to save her, but I didn't know how to rescue a drowning person. The moment I got to her, she grabbed my neck, and there was nothing I could do about it. As soon as I realized what had happened, I tried to get out from under because she was dragging me down with her. All my efforts were in vain.

I must have lost consciousness then. A few minutes later, I heard some-   5
body talking to me. It was a woman's voice, and even now I can still picture her face. I saw in my mind a beautiful little town. The woman said to me, "My husband's not home. Can I help you?"

"No," I replied.   6

Again she asked, "Do you want to stay with me?"   7

"No, no," I told her.   8

"Do you want some tea?"   9

I nodded my head and said, "Yes."   10

I drank it. Then she asked, "Do you want to sit down for a moment?"   11

I said, "Yes, I am tired. I miss my mother."   12

All this time, under the water, I had been hearing my friends crying, "She's dead! She's dead!" I had only one question in my head: "Am I dead, or in a dream? Where am I?"   13

I don't know to this day how I got out of the river. I do remember that I embarrassed one of my friends when I emotionally kissed her and said, "I don't know how, but I am still here." We prayed then, and we thanked God because I believe I was saved by God.   14

Two days later I explained my near-tragedy to my mother and my friends. We wonderingly asked each other: "Are there other planets under the earth? Was it real, what I had seen?" I know that it wasn't a dream because it really happened to me. That is the story of the day I almost died.   15

TIME CHUNKS

Students are frequently asked to write about relationships, problems, or experiences. Usually these narratives are set within a limited time frame. By deliberately expanding the time frame over the course of a lifetime, we have the opportunity to identify patterns of growth and change that might otherwise be obscured. This activity asks you to trace a theme from your own life over a long period of time.

1. Choose a theme that has been important in your own life for many years— for example, smoking, homework, a sport or game, watching TV.

2. Make a time-chunk outline, using the following life stages as a guide. Write a brief summary (no more than one sentence) explaining the significance of the theme in your life at each stage.

Early childhood:

Elementary school:

High school:

Two years ago:

The present:

The future (Try to predict):

3. Use your time-chunk outline to help you write an essay tracing the theme in your life from birth until the present. If you like, you can make a prediction about the future as well.

Example

In this essay, written with the help of a time-chunk outline, a student traces her history of obesity, and in so doing, shows great personal strength in struggling with this problem over the course of her life.

Obesity: Life Problem?

by Maryla Dedza, Poland

Can you agree with me that obesity is a big problem for many people? I can see many of them every day. There are also articles in newspapers and magazines on how to lose weight. Some of those people go to doctors, eat special diets, or exercise, but this is not helpful for everyone. And this is my problem too. 1

I remember when I was a child, I was always plump. I was born a big baby, about twelve pounds. I had a good appetite too. I remember how we ate from one big plate. Our mother put a big plate on a chair and we all sat around that chair on our small chairs, took spoons, and started to eat. We ate very quickly. But at that time, I didn't feel that my being overweight was a problem. 2

When I started grammar school, my problem with overweight started too. Some of my classmates called me "thick," and I felt very bad. I remember once a boy called me "thick" so I called him "stupid." He punched me and I went home crying. The next day I complained to our teacher about him, and she punished him, keeping him one hour after school, so I had enough time to get home. 3

Later on, I was ashamed to tell the teacher if somebody was laughing at me. My classmates didn't make fun of me so often as we got older, but I still had that problem in my mind. I was very ashamed when I had to undress for gym class. I felt that everyone was looking at me and laughing. 4

When I entered high school, my overweight problem caused me to have an inferiority complex. If I saw other girls with boyfriends and I didn't 5 have one, I thought that I was not as attractive as they were because of my obesity.

I was seventeen when I decided to lose weight. I went on a serious diet. I had almost nothing to eat, and during three months of vacation, I lost almost twenty pounds. When I came back to school, I surprised my friends. Some of them asked me for a prescription for that fantastic diet. I was very proud of myself.   6

But I wasn't happy for long. In the dormitory where I lived, I started to eat regular meals. I also ate some extra food, which my mother always gave me when I came home for a weekend. Can you imagine that during one year I came back to my previous weight and gained another twenty pounds? After that I really broke down. And I stopped even thinking about a diet for the next few years.   7

Nothing changed with my overweight until two years ago. At that time I had some bad personal problems. I was very nervous, but I didn't give up. I found a new school, which I attended during the day. Some afternoons, Saturdays, and Sundays I worked. My day started at 7 A.M. and finished about midnight, sometimes later. And what happened with my weight? I lost about ten pounds in a few weeks, then more and more. And it occurred without any effort from me.   8

Then I met a really nice guy, who is now my boyfriend. He helped me very much and encouraged me to lose weight. As a result, I became a regular-size girl.   9

I have kept the same weight for about one year, but I have to pay dearly for that. Ice cream and cookies I can only look at, but I can't eat. Even at regular meals I sometimes eat only half the food on my plate. And I also have another bad habit. I smoke cigarettes.   10

My problem with obesity isn't over and will probably not be for the rest of my life. Even though I look good now, I have to think about my diet all the time. However, I feel that I am now mature enough to surmount that obstacle.   11

GRAMMAR IN CONTEXT

IDENTIFYING SUBJECTS AND VERBS

In order to understand how English grammar works, it is necessary to be able to identify the parts of a sentence, especially subjects and verbs. It works best to find the verb first; look for (1) words that express action, (2) clues such as *-ed* endings, or (3) verbs of being (*is, are, was, were, be, am, been, being*). Once you have found the main verb, ask "Who or what?" and then repeat the verb. For example, in the sentence "The children played all day long," you would first locate the verb "played," and then ask "Who or what played?" The answer, "children," is the subject of the sentence.

Activity

Using the system described above, identify the verbs and subjects in the following sentences, in which a student discusses the difference between "like" and "love." Underline the verb two times and the subject one time. Draw an arrow from the verb to the subject that goes with it.

Example: <u>Love</u> <u>is</u> a stronger emotion than like.

1. Love usually involves people and things you cannot buy with money.

2. Also, love is consistent.

3. It does not change every day or every month.

4. Things you like can change with your mood or with the season, but

   not things you love.

(See Answer Key, page 313.)

CHOOSING THE RIGHT VERB TENSE

In English, every main verb in every sentence has a *tense*. Basically, tense refers to time; in other words, it tells *when* something happened. Three of the most common tenses in English are the *simple present*, the *simple past*, and the *simple future*.

Examples

Simple Present: I *like* to write.
Simple Past: When I was younger, I *liked* to write.
Simple Future: Maybe someday I *will like* to write.

When writing about experiences that happened in the past—whether many years ago or only yesterday—most writers choose the simple past tense. But sometimes writers choose to describe past events in the present tense in order to create a sense of excitement and immediacy. The following exercise will help you to see how the choice of verb tense can affect the mood of a piece.

Activity

Working with a partner, supply the correct present tense form of each verb in parentheses. Then go back and read the passage aloud, changing the verbs to the past tense. With your partner, discuss which version you prefer for creating a mysterious mood.

It (be) _____ a cold and windy afternoon. When I first   1
(get) _____ to class, I (look) _____ out the window. There
(be) _____ many buses and cars crossing the road. Suddenly, I
(hear) _____ the teacher talking in the classroom next to mine. But I
(be) _____ not sure what she (be) _____ saying. The students in
my class (be) _____ busy writing an essay. They (do) _____ not
even know the clock (be)_____ making a noise.

Finally, I (look) _____ outside. There (be) _____ a lady   2
lying in the street. People (be) _____ looking at her. They (seem)
_____ like they (do) _____ not know what (be) _____ happening or who the murderer (be) _____ .

Later on, there (be) _____ a couple of police cars that (come)   3
_____ and (take) _____ her away.

(See Answer Key, page 313.)

USING VERB TENSES CONSISTENTLY

Within any piece of writing, you should be consistent in your use of verb
tenses; this does *not* mean that you can use only one tense in the entire piece, but it
does mean that you should have a good reason for changing tenses.

The following exercise asks you to examine the choices of verb tense made by
two of the student writers whose work appears in this chapter and to discuss with a
partner why they made these particular choices.

Activity

1. Working with a partner, analyze the choice of verb tenses in "Learning
How to Cook" on pages 38–39. Underline all of the main verbs in paragraphs
1 through 5 except for those that are included in direct quotations. What is the
basic verb tense of this essay? Why do you think the writer has chosen this tense?

2. Working with the same partner, examine the choice of verb tenses in "The
Photograph" on pages 42–44. Notice how the writer has divided her story into four
different segments, using a space with asterisks [* * *]. Fill in the chart on the
next page by answering the following questions: In your opinion, when did the
events in each of the segments take place? What basic verb tense did the writer
choose for each of these segments?

Segment	When Events Occurred	Basic Verb Tense
Paragraphs 1–6	_____	_____
Paragraphs 7–24	_____	_____
Paragraphs 25–36	_____	_____
Paragraph 37	_____	_____

3. Why do you think the writer chose different tenses for different parts of the story? Was she consistent in her use of verb tenses within the four different segments? Do you agree with the choices she made in selecting verb tenses? Why or why not?

KNOWING WHEN TO USE THE PLURAL FORM OF NOUNS

Students who are unsure about when to add *-s* to nouns are often those whose native languages or dialects do not change the endings of nouns to indicate the plural form. As an experiment, try translating these sentences into your native language:

She gave me a book.
She gave me three books.

Did you make any changes in the word for *book* in the second sentence to show that it was plural? If so, how did the word change? If not, do you think this fact causes you any problems with plural forms in English?

Activity

In the following student essay, all the *-s* endings on nouns have been removed. Add *-s* endings wherever necessary. Compare answers with a classmate, and discuss why you felt these *-s* endings were needed.

Eat Fast . . . Die Fast?
by M. K. Pun

"Good time, great taste . . . at McDonald's." "We do it like you do it at   1
Burger King." I don't think so. However, thousand of American do agree, and they
have been living on fast food like hamburger and French fry since they were born.
So, would it be possible that the more fast food you eat, the faster you will die?

According to the Surgeon General's report on nutrition and health, what you   2
eat can kill you. The U.S. population eats altogether too much, and too much of

the wrong food, especially saturated fat. In fact, American' favorite food—hamburger, hot dog, and French fry—are where the saturated fat and cholesterol are mainly from, as well as from meat and dairy product. That fat can increase the risk of obesity, heart disease, and cancer.

A lot of people believe that salty food is tasty food. And usually a lot of salt is put in fast food when it is being prepared. However, the Surgeon General also stated that American should minimize the use of salt in cooking and at the table.

Now, imagine yourself as a balloon. Whenever you eat a hamburger, the hamburger will be put in the balloon, and the balloon will explode when there are too many hamburger. The more you eat, the easier the balloon explodes. The more fast food you eat, the faster you will die. Next time, when you have a Big Mac, won't you think twice before taking a big bite?

(See Answer Key, page 314.)

SPELLING STRATEGY: USING THE SPELLING CHECKER

If you use a computer or word processor for your writing, you may already know how to use a spelling checker program. The program identifies misspelled words and then supplies a list of possible corrections from which to choose. The following exercise will help you to practice using a spelling checker.

Activity

Read the sentences below, from the essay entitled "What Is It Like to Have an Empty Stomach?" which appeared earlier in this chapter. Try to locate the misspelled word in each of these sentences. Then find the correct spelling of the word in the list below each sentence.

1. Travelers, the sick, and pregnent women can defer fasting during Ramadan.

   pregnable
   pregnancy
   pregnant
   prehensile
   preignition

2. Of course, I was not suposed to fast since most children usually start fasting at the age of thirteen.

> support
> supportive
> suppose
> supposed
> suppress

3. I was very anxious and curios to experience the feeling of fasting.

> curie
> curio
> curiosity
> curious
> curium

4. After I finished my last meal, my father gave me some good advize.

> advertise
> advice
> advise
> adviser
> advocate

5. The time of brakeing our fast was 7:45.

> braking
> breakfast
> break-in
> breaking
> breaking-point

(See Answer Key, pages 314–15.)

ASSIGNMENT

Your assignment for this chapter is to write an essay in which you describe an experience that you remember clearly and that was important to you. The purpose should be to re-create this experience in writing so that it seems almost as real to the person reading your paper as it did when it happened to you. Think of your audience as interested classmates from a different cultural background.

For all the essays you will write, we encourage you to use the process of drafting. A draft is a rough or unfinished piece of writing. Remember that your first draft is not meant to be a polished essay but rather a start toward discovering what you want to say. As you are working on the first draft, do not slow yourself down by worrying about correct grammar and spelling; it is more important just to get your ideas down on paper so you have something to work with in later drafts.

SUGGESTED TECHNIQUES

Certain specific writing techniques that you have observed in the readings earlier in this chapter may help you to achieve the goal of making your experience seem real to the reader:

1. *Try to write an opening that will capture the reader's attention.* Beginnings are very important. Usually within the first few moments, the reader forms a basic impression. Either she cannot wait to read on to see what comes next, or she is bored and may not read past the first few paragraphs. Notice how Peter Kisfaludi immediately gets his readers involved with the short opening sentences: "It's 4 A.M. My wristwatch alarm is gently beeping," Florence Cheung achieves a similar effect by beginning with a direct quotation: "'Kit Wah! Kit Wah!' my mother was calling me." Vladimir Kuchinsky gets the readers' attention by beginning with a line of poetry.

Often it is hard to write a good beginning until you know what the rest of your essay will be like. Many writers actually skip the beginning and go back and fill it in later. If you did write the beginning first, read it again after you have finished the essay, and decide if you would like to change it in any way.

2. *Include significant details to help your reader imagine the experience.* To make your experience seem real to the reader, include details that will re-create the experience. What was the weather like? How were people dressed? What did they say? For example, notice how Youssef Rami makes his first experience of fasting seem real by including this specific detail in paragraph 6: "I remembered that I could only rinse my mouth without letting a drop of water get into my throat."

3. *Use verbs effectively to describe the action.* Verbs, the action words, are important in any piece of writing, but they are especially important when you are describing an experience. Find the verbs in these sentences taken from Xiao Mei Sun's description of the scene at the railway station as she was being sent to the countryside: "A sharp whistle pierced the air and I jumped. The sudden shrill noise silenced the whole world." How do the verbs help to set the mood for this scene? How would you describe this mood?

When writing about an experience, most writers use the past tense because the experience happened in the past. Sometimes, however, writers use the present tense to make the reader feel more involved in the experience, as Peter Kisfaludi does at the beginning of his essay about the life of a taxi driver.

As you begin your first draft, think about what basic verb tense you would like to use. (For more help with verbs, see the section on Using Verb Tenses Consistently on pages 62–63.)

4. *Try to express—directly or indirectly—what you learned from this experience.* The experience you are describing may have been as simple as learning how to cook rice or as dramatic as being forced to leave your home. But for whatever reason, you remember it clearly as an important experience.

You may merely imply why the experience was significant for you. Florence Cheung uses this indirect method when she ends her essay with the sentence: "Lord, how I loved the first time that I cooked." It is up to her readers to decide why she loved it so much. Or you may state the meaning of the experience directly, as Youssef

Rami does when he ends by saying: "Now, when I go back to this childhood memory, I feel proud that I knew so much." Your essay will mean more to the reader if you express a sense of what you learned from this experience or why it was important in your life.

After completing your first draft, take some time to have a peer conference. Exchange papers with a partner, read the essay carefully, and then fill out the Peer Response Sheet located at the end of this chapter. Discuss your reactions to each other's essays. Then turn in the essay to your teacher for comment. If he or she thinks you should continue working on it, see Part III: Rethinking/Rewriting for help with revising and editing.

PEER RESPONSE SHEET:
WRITING ABOUT EXPERIENCE

Writer's Name: _____

Reader's Name: _____

Date: _____

(*Note to the reader:* As you respond to the writer's draft, try to focus on the ideas rather than the grammar and spelling. Discuss only those mistakes that interfere with understanding.)

1. What was one detail that made this experience seem real to you? _____

_____

_____

_____

2. Were there any places where you got confused? If so, what were they? _____

_____

_____

_____

3. Reread the first paragraph of the essay. Do you think this is a good beginning?
Does it make you feel like reading on? Explain. _____

_____

_____

_____

4. Select one paragraph in the essay and find all the verbs. What basic verb tense does the writer use? Does he or she use this tense consistently throughout the essay?_____

_____

_____

_____

5. What would you like to know more about when the writer revises this essay?

_____

_____

_____

5

People

Pan Qingfu, martial arts master

Nothing is quite so interesting to most people as other people, so they provide a natural subject to write about. Of course, some of the writing you do for other chapters will also be about people. When you write about an experience, it is often the people involved who make the experience memorable. Even when you are writing about a place, it is sometimes people who make that place special.

What you are asked to do in this chapter is slightly different. Here we invite you to write a character sketch. Almost as an artist makes a sketch that reveals a person's appearance, it is possible to reveal a person's character using words.

As you read the selections that follow, think about some of the important people in your own life.

READINGS

From *Iron and Silk*
by Mark Salzman

Mark Salzman, an American, first became interested in Chinese martial arts when he was thirteen years old. Later his interests expanded to include Chinese painting and calligraphy and eventually the language. He majored in Chinese literature at Yale University, and from 1982 to 1984 he taught English at Hunan Medical College in China. Salzman's book Iron and Silk *tells of the people he met and the experiences he had during his two years in the People's Republic. In this selection Salzman describes his first encounter with the famous Chinese martial arts expert Pan Qingfu.*

. . . One after the other, the athletes performed routines with spears, halberds, hooks, knives and their bare hands. My stomach hurt by now just from the excitement of watching them; I'd never seen martial arts of this quality before, nor sat so close to such tremendous athletes as they worked. Just as the last man finished a routine with the nine-section steel whip, someone clapped once, and all the athletes rushed into a line and stood at perfect attention. I turned toward the wooden doors to see who had clapped and for the first time saw Pan. 1

I recognized him immediately as one of the evil characters in *Shaolin Temple*, and I knew from magazine articles about the movie that he had choreographed and directed the martial arts scenes. . . . Pan had a massive reputation as a fighter from the days when scores were settled with blows rather than points. His nickname, "Iron Fist," was said to describe both his personality and his right hand, which he had developed by punching a fifty-pound iron plate nailed to a concrete wall one thousand to ten thousand times a day. 2

Pan walked over to where the athletes stood, looked them over, and told them to relax. They formed a half-circle around him; some leaned on one leg or crossed their arms, but most remained at stiff attention. He gave them his morning address in a voice too low for me to hear, but it was clear from the expressions on his face that he was exhorting them to push harder, always harder, otherwise where will you get? 3

He stood about five foot eight, with a medium to slight build, a deep reced- 4
ing hairline, a broad, scarred nose and upper front teeth so badly arranged that it
looked as if he had two rows of them, so that if he bit you and wrecked the first
set, the second would grow in to replace them. Most noticeable, though, were his
eyebrows. They swept up toward his temples making him look permanently angry,
as if he were wearing some sort of Peking Opera mask. At one point he gestured to
one of the athletes with his right hand, and I saw that it was strangely disfigured.
Dr. Nie, who must have known what I was thinking, leaned over and said, "That is
the iron fist."

Pan looked fearsome, but what most distinguished him was that, when he 5
talked, his face moved and changed expression. I had been in China for eight
months, but thought this was the first time I had seen a Chinese person whose
face moved. Sometimes his eyes opened wide with surprise, then narrowed with
anger, or his mouth trembled with fear and everyone laughed, then he ground his
teeth and looked ready to avenge a murder. His eyebrows, especially, were so mo-
bile that I wondered if they had been knocked loose in one of his brawls. He com-
manded such presence that, for the duration of his address, no one seemed to
breathe.

Personal Connections

1. Can you think of someone who seemed unfriendly at first but later
turned out to be quite different? Freewrite about your first meeting with that person. In what ways was it similar to Salzman's first encounter with Pan? In what
ways was it different?

2. In the next few days observe someone who is an expert in a field you are
interested in—a dancer, an athlete, a singer, a computer programmer. You can observe the individual in person or on television. What did you notice about how
this person did his or her job?

Content and Writing Techniques

1. Look carefully at the photograph of Pan, which appears at the beginning
of this chapter. Underline details in the description that you notice in the photograph.

2. Find details in the selection that suggest that Pan is:
    a. a frightening person
    b. a disciplined person
    c. a caring person

3. Underline three places in the selection that reveal the athletes' attitude toward Pan. How would you describe this attitude? Does this support the overall
impression you receive of Pan's character?

An Unforgettable Man
by Dastagir Firoz

> *In this essay Dastagir Firoz, a student from Afghanistan, explains how someone he knew only briefly made a lasting impression on him. Before you read, think about a person from your own life whom you will never forget.*

I once spent a long vacation in a mountainous region of my homeland— Afghanistan. And here I came to know an unforgettable man. 1

We had been invited to stay in a large and airy room which was in a qala[1] of a tribe; the qala was built of dry mud and stems of some of the strongest trees in the region. In fact, it was just a large ordinary-looking "mountain-house" viewed from outside. My uncle Hakim, who knew the khan (meaning chief) of the house, accompanied me on the trip. The khan's people did not call him by his formal name, Qader. They called him khan to show respect to their leader. In an Afghan family it is an offense and insult to call a leader or an elder by their first name. The khan was a member of the Pathan tribe. 2

That spring the mountains were beautiful. The blooms of trees spread a purple blanket over the mountains. The calm mountainous breeze carried the fragrance of the blooms. 3

From far away we saw a man dressed in white on a white horse with four more horsemen following him. They were coming rapidly and disturbing the dust of the bottom of the mountains. They came closer and closer. When they reached us, a few of the khan's men went forward, gave him greetings, and bowed; the rest of the men stayed back, waiting for orders. 4

The khan had just returned with a few bloody rabbits hanging on the sides of his horse. He had a thick, black moustache. His bright white turban wrapped around his high hat made of thick golden thread gave him a manly appearance. He wore a colorful Afghan vest, which matched his pair of chapli,[2] which were also hand-made. He wore a long collarless shirt with hand-embroidered silk designs and a tunban.[3] There was a strap of thick leather across his chest under the vest, which held about one hundred bullets. In addition, he had a shotgun on his shoulder and a rifle at his side. 5

As he jumped off the horse, the khan murmured to his chef, "I want the rabbits to be cooked tonight for our guests." Then he came forward rapidly with wide, stiff steps to shake hands with my uncle and me. The khan had a great deal of respect for my uncle Hakim. After all they were old-time friends. 6

The khan took us inside his complex. What unusual and beautiful primitive 7

---

[1]*qala:* a dry-mud structure surrounded by thick, high, dry-mud walls. It usually includes a large yard with a heavy wooden gate to allow caravans to enter.

[2]*chapli:* a type of footwear that is usually made by hand.

[3]*tunban:* trousers that are very wide at the top for comfort.

country furnishings he had! Most of the rooms were furnished with colorful red hand-made carpets. The lanterns were of an old type brass and burned kerosene. Lots of antique ornaments were seen all over the house. He was a man of taste. He was rich in his village. He had a lot of other men who were loyal to him. Other men and khans from nearby villages knew him.

Obviously he was living a life in which everything was in "accordance with nature." That is, there were no signs of modern inventions. If you heard a sound, it would only be the sound of leaves on the trees which were shivering from the breeze of spring, or the song of singing birds. Nowhere could we see a factory or a modern office building. All we saw were houses or camps of nomads and their herds. All we saw were purple blue skies with pieces of white clouds of spring extending far away. The skies were so clear that they seemed to be directly connected to the top of the mountains.   8

One day my uncle suggested to the khan that he should live in the city. He replied with a smile which did not approve the idea. "No sir, I am not a man of the city. I live on the land of God and I feel myself closer to him when his phenomena are visible with my own naked eyes. I would get very depressed if I had to live in the city," he continued. "I love guests and I honor them. I will support and protect the refugees regardless of the cost, and by the same token, we will attack any unwelcome strangers who try to disturb us or dispossess us of any of our God-given lives or property."   9

I was fond of this man's bravery and helping hand. We stayed there for three months. To me, it was a wonderful vacation. We talked about him with our family and took a few pictures of him that bore the memory of his Pathan way of life in our minds for many years to come.[4]   10

Personal Connections

1. By using specific details, Firoz helps us to picture a man who lives in a world quite different from our own. Underline three details indicating that the khan's way of life was very traditional. Do you think this way of life should be preserved in a modern world?

2. One of the things Firoz liked about the khan was his warm hospitality. Freewrite about what hospitality means in your culture. Try to give examples of people you know who are good hosts, and explain how they make their guests feel welcome.

---

[4]After the Soviet invasion of Afghanistan in 1979, members of the Pathan and other tribes resisted the destructive war power of the Soviet Union, fighting with practically no weapons. In 1988, after years of brutal fighting, the Soviets decided to withdraw.

Content and Writing Techniques

1. Although Firoz was writing a character sketch, he devotes much of paragraphs 3 and 8 to describing the countryside surrounding the khan's home. What is his purpose in doing this? How does this description add to our understanding of the khan?

2. Paragraph 7 ends with several short, simple sentences: "He was a man of taste. He was rich in his village. He had a lot of other men who were loyal to him. Other men and khans from nearby villages knew him." How do you feel about the shortness of these sentences? Working in a small group, try combining them into longer, more complex sentences. Which way seems better?

Rosita
by Gloria Cortes

Gloria Cortes, a student from Colombia, describes the painful relationship she had with her family's housekeeper. The two had conflicting views on religion, manners, and sexuality, creating many problems for Gloria when she was growing up. Before you begin reading, listen to the first two paragraphs of the essay read aloud. Then try to guess which of the following things will happen later in the story: (a) Rosita will come to understand Gloria better, (b) Gloria will grow to love Rosita after a while, (c) Gloria and Rosita will never understand each other, (d) Gloria will come to hate Rosita.

When my mother went away, the first person Rosita turned to after clearing away her tears was me. She was surprised that I was standing there calm and without tears. She said to me, "This girl never cries and never feels anything. She is like a rock." From that moment on, Rosita saw me as heartless and immoral. 1

Rosita built up the idea that I was a hard young girl because she couldn't understand my thoughts. I was distant from everything that happened in the house. I never paid attention to the rigid moral values that she established and by which she harshly judged me because they didn't mean anything to me, and I was too naive to understand them. But there was one thing she didn't know. The day when my mother left, I locked myself in the bathroom and cried and cried. She never noticed. 2

Rosita had worked for us for three years when my mother left. In my mother's absence, she ran the house and raised us. She was a small, frail, light brown woman. When she smiled we could see the perfectly straight, white teeth of which she was so proud. She took delight in letting everyone see how beautiful they were. We giggled at this because we knew they were not real. 3

She was so proud of her thin waist, which she seemed to exaggerate by wearing tight belts. But at the same time, she had a large stomach that flowed over her belt and made her look pregnant. When she showed off her thin waist, she somehow was able to ignore her hanging belly.

Rosita's legs were short and full of thick veins like worms burrowing under her skin. They had formed, she said, from wearing tight garters. She said that her legs were smooth and beautifully shaped when she was younger. I can still see her in front of the mirror pulling up her dress to her thighs and showing us what had been, at one time, beautiful legs.

The household that Rosita managed contained my father, my two sisters, and me. As my oldest sister, Magda, was growing up, I curiously observed the changes in her body. One day when she was changing her clothes, Rosita saw me observing her and said, "What a malicious look this girl has! What are you looking at?"

I was very confused because I didn't know what was wrong with looking at my sister. I always took showers with my sisters and we slept together. From that moment on, however, whenever my sister dressed, she hid herself from me and we no longer shared the shower. I never understood that drastic change in my sister, but at the same time, I started to hide myself from her.

We lived in the outskirts of Bogotá, Colombia, in a three-story, red-brick house with a big patio surrounded by rooms. My small, windowless room, located just off my sister's room, was like a cool, dark, moist cave. One day I woke up in my humid room and as I put my feet on the floor, I crushed a slimy slug. I screamed so loud that Rosita heard me from the kitchen. She ran into my bedroom. I was almost in tears as I told her what happened. She said, "Is that all? You yelled so loud that I thought you saw a nude man."

I didn't know what to make of her response because I always saw males as my equals and never thought there was anything to scream at if I saw one nude.

Rosita was a very religious woman who believed in a wrathful God and a ubiquitous devil. She saw the devil's work everywhere except where her stern piety kept him at bay.

Every Sunday we used to go to our neighborhood church. I never understood the purpose of it, but I knew it was a place to see my friends. It occurred to me that Sunday could be more fun if we went to the church on top of the mountain because I could climb the mountain with my friends, playing as we went.

By the time we arrived at the church, the service would be almost over, and we could resume our playing as we descended the mountain. The mountain was in the outskirts of the city. We had to take a bus at 4:00 A.M. to get to the base of the mountain, where we would begin our climb on foot. In the bus we were with a lot of poor people, many of whom got off with us and climbed the mountain on their knees to show their piety. When they arrived at the church, their knees were red with blood.

Rosita soon found out that our excursion had little to do with sacrifice and screamed at me for being evil. But again, I didn't know or understand why I was evil. I didn't see why I should make myself a martyr by climbing the mountain on my knees.

Most of my friends were little boys because young girls had the same ideas as Rosita, and with the boys I could play freely without reserve. But soon Rosita said that playing with boys was bad because they would touch me. She used to say that prostitutes were touched by men, and that I should not make myself one. I never understood what that meant because I never saw anything in the hands of my friends that would change me into a prostitute, whatever that was.   14

A few years later, when it was time for my first communion, I decided against having it because I could not bear confessing sins to a person who was just as human as I, and who had probably sinned just as much as I. Rosita attributed my refusal to the devil, who, she believed, had taken permanent hold of me.   15

A year later, Rosita left us. I did not cry.   16

Personal Connections

1. People often make unfair judgments about the behavior of others. Think of a time when someone formed such a judgment about you or someone close to you. How was that experience similar to or different from the situation described in this selection?

2. Religious beliefs and customs are valued by many people, yet others reject such traditions. Look through the essay and find places in which Cortes seems to reject a traditional belief or practice. What do you think about her rejection?

3. Do you think Rosita is someone Cortes pities, hates, or both? Find details to support your opinion. How do you feel about Rosita? Is she someone to be pitied or hated?

Content and Writing Techniques

1. Return to the guesses you made after hearing the first two paragraphs of the essay read aloud. Did you predict the correct outcome? If so, what clues helped you?

2. In paragraphs 3 to 5, find details which show that Rosita thinks herself attractive. In the same paragraphs, find details which show that Gloria thinks Rosita is ugly.

3. Put an *R* next to any statement below that applies to Rosita's views about human sexuality. Put a *G* next to those that apply to Gloria's ideas. Find the details in the essay that support your ideas.

    a. The human body is a natural and wonderful thing.

    b. The human body is sinful and must be tightly controlled.

    c. Sex is evil and should not occur except for purposes of reproduction.

    d. Sex is a beautiful and natural part of human relationships.

4. How do you react to the ending of the story? What does the last sentence, "I did not cry," mean to you?

My Grandmother
by Hikaru Takahashi

Traditional families have always had a great deal of power to influence the lives of their children, especially daughters. In this essay, a student from Japan describes her grandmother's struggle to free herself from the strictness of her family and become an independent person. Before reading, think back on some of the struggles in your own family, where a son or daughter made a decision that was in conflict with the parents' wishes.

1   She always has a little smile on her face in her portraits. Although she is smiling, there is a kind of severity and dignity about her. She passed away on a cold February morning eight years ago. When my father came to wake me up, I was seized with fear and began to shake, knowing what had happened. Yes, she had just passed away.

2   She is the one whom I respected the most. When I was a child, I was proud to show her wedding picture to my friends because everybody said that she was beautiful. However, for some reason she was keeping all the pictures of her youth away from me. She did not want me to show them to others, but I liked to look at them and always tried to find them.

3   She was from a prestigious family, and her parents were very strict with her. She went to a girls' high school in Taiwan and then returned to Japan to go to one of the most famous women's universities. She seemed to follow her parents' will and lived very happily.

4   It must have been very surprising to her parents when she told them she was going to quit school and become an actress. She chose to be a stage actress even though it would mean giving up everything she possessed: family, education, and wealth. Of course, her parents would not allow her to be an actress, but her strong will was not to be changed. Finally, she was kicked out of the family and went to acting school.

5   "I was very proud to go backstage and see her surrounded by lots of flowers from her fans," her brother told me. "She was a tall woman, so she played a lot of male roles."[1] In one of her stage pictures, her glaring eyes and tightly closed lips gave a manly impression. However, she finally did get married to my grandfather.

6   Actually, her parents arranged her marriage. At that time, nobody knew how much her marriage would change her life. She had been living a hopeful life, doing what she really wanted. But once she got married, she had to move to my grandfather's house in the countryside. She had to work in the field, a completely new experience for her. She had to get along with other women there who did not have any higher education and who devoted themselves only to hard work. She had to accustom herself to the life of the countryside. Still, she did not become a village woman who never cared about her appearance. "She always spruced herself up and was somehow different from us," one of her friends said.

---

[1]It was common for women to play male roles in the Japanese theater.

She did not tell me how hard it was for her, but I noticed it a little later when   7
I got older. I understood why she was keeping all those pictures of her youth away
from me. She did not even want to remember the time when she was really happy.
She had never shown her suffering to anyone. Her pride did not allow her to do
so.

Her last days in the hospital were too painful to look at. She could not even   8
breathe by herself because of cancer. Two small tubes were placed in her nose. She
was a mere shadow of her former beautiful and strong self. However, she still had
her pride as a stage actress and a woman from a prestigious family. Every morning
in the hospital, she put make-up on her face and groomed her hair neatly. "She did
not forget to be a woman up until her last moment," a nurse who had been taking
care of her said.

In my memory, she is still living as a beautiful woman with severity. Her life   9
was not happy all the time, but no other person knew how hard it was. Whenever
I describe her life, I use the same expression: "She lived a very short and deep life,
as many beautiful flowers do."

Personal Connections

1. Have you or someone you know ever challenged the authority of parents?
Describe the situation in writing and/or discuss it with a partner. In your opinion,
who was right, the parents or their child?

2. Which of the following statements best describes your feelings about the
grandmother's decision to become an actress? Discuss your answer with your partner, group, or class.

     a. It was a foolish decision because it offended her parents, and she suf-
        fered a lot because of that.

     b. It was the right decision because she had a great talent and needed to
        discover who she really was.

     c. The decision was neither right nor wrong. She gained as much as she
        lost.

Content and Writing Techniques

1. One of the themes of this essay is the struggle to become an independent
person. Find details in the story which suggest that the grandmother succeeded in
becoming independent. Find details which suggest she did not succeed.

2. Speaking about her grandmother, Takahashi says, "She is the one whom I
respected the most." Underline three details from the essay which show this respect.

3. Find evidence in the essay that the grandmother made the right decision to leave her family and become a stage actress. Find evidence that this
might have been the wrong decision. Discuss this evidence with a partner or
small group.

4. Throughout the essay, Takahashi uses quotations—from her great-uncle, from a village woman, and from the nurse in the hospital. Why did she choose to include these quotes in the essay? Do you feel that the quotes strengthen or weaken the essay?

My Mother
by Eileen Peng

When asked to write an essay about a person, Eileen Peng, a student from China, knew immediately that she wanted to describe her mother. As you will see, Peng's mother is a major force in her life. After you have read the first four paragraphs of this essay, stop—do not read any further for now. Based on what you learn in these paragraphs, what kind of person do you think Peng's mother is? Freewrite about this question. Then put your freewriting aside and finish reading the essay.

Her sound was usually heard before her appearance. A ten-minute walk would take her twenty minutes or more, not because she walked slowly, but because she often met so many friends on her way. 1

Once, while I played in my neighbor's home, his friend asked him about me. "Whose daughter is she?" 2

"She is hers," my neighbor said, and pointed at my house. "Her mother can ride a bicycle as if she were flying." 3

"Oh, I see. I know her," his friend said. 4

Yes, she is my mother. She is a very capable, lively woman although she has less energy now than she used to. As an accountant for a market, she could do her work fast, could even finish another accountant's work. So her boss thought that one accountant was enough and sent the other one to another branch. 5

Although she had a full-time job, she was also a very good housewife: shopping, cooking, cleaning, sewing, taking care of four children's studies and going to parents' meetings for us. My father? Except for working at the office, he usually either sat down before the TV or stayed behind the door of the bedroom. 6

My mother was the eldest daughter in her family. When she was only sixteen years old, in 1952, she was put in a sedan chair, was sent to my father's home, and became a wife. After becoming a wife, she insisted on studying in junior high school in order to finish her general education. My older sister and I were born while she was still in school. (Having children while in school was a very rare circumstance at that time in China.) 7

She had no more opportunity to take advanced study after graduating from junior high school. So she thought that her children were her hope, her future. "Study hard. Get honors for me," she often said to us. 8

My family was not living the affluent life. In many ways, my mother was   9
quite thrifty, but in buying study supplies for children, she was very generous. I
have been interested in painting since I was a child. My mother was my great supporter.

One day, she gave me a surprise. "I found a fine arts teacher for you. He is a   10
teacher of the Fine Arts Academy of Canton. Let us go to see him," she said.

She sent me to that teacher's home to have my first lesson. This teacher was   11
so important for me! He gave me a great deal of help. When I entered the Fine
Arts Academy of Canton as a freshman, my teacher said to me, "You have a great
mother. Without her, you could not be a student of this school." Indeed, he was
right.

Whenever my works appeared in newspapers or magazines, my mother was   12
proud of showing them to relatives and her friends. She was so happy that she had
such a girl. She liked to talk to those parents who felt unhappy when they had a
daughter but not a son. "Don't let it get you down. Daughters can do anything that
sons can do. Look at my daughter, how well she has done."

In my junior year of art school, I revealed to her my idea that I hoped to go   13
abroad to continue my study. "Good. Try to do it!" she said. The following year,
she helped me to do everything necessary for my application.

When I left for the United States, she gave all her possessions to me, includ-   14
ing her marriage portions—a golden necklace, earrings and wedding ring, and
money. Oh, how hard to save that money! When I received those things from her
hands, my eyes filled with tears.

I had a hard time after arriving in the United States, but I was determined to   15
"Study hard" as my mother said. I have to make a success of myself. I would never
want to see the expression of disappointment on my mother's face if I failed.

Personal Connections

1. In this essay Peng shows that education was an important value to her
mother. Think of a value you learned from your family (such as hard work, a
sense of humor, respect for other people, hospitality to guests) and freewrite about
it. Try to include specific examples to illustrate how you learned the importance of
this particular value.

2. In paragraph 12, Peng mentions the traditional Chinese belief that it is
better to have a son than a daughter—a belief her mother did not accept. Many
other cultures share this idea that it is important to have a son to carry on the family name. How do you personally feel about this? How does your family feel?

3. In paragraph 14, Peng describes how touched she was by the gifts her
mother gave her before she went to study in the United States. Write about a time
when someone gave you a special gift.

Content and Writing Techniques

1. Now that you have finished reading the essay, go back and reread the
freewriting that you did after completing paragraph 4. Were you right about the

kind of person Peng's mother would turn out to be? What clues in the first four paragraphs helped you to make a guess about her character? If your guess was not correct, would you advise Peng to change the beginning of her essay in any way?

2. In this essay Peng includes quite a few direct quotations of her mother's words. For example, in paragraph 8, Peng wrote: "'Study hard. Get honors for me,' she often said to us." If Peng had chosen to express this as an indirect quotation, she might have written: "Our mother often told us to work hard and do well in school." Underline the direct quotations in paragraphs 11 and 12, and then rewrite them as indirect quotations. For more advice about how to do this, see the section on Using Direct and Indirect Quotations on page 155.) Which do you like better — the direct or the indirect quotations? Why?

3. Reread the last paragraph of the essay. Do you think it is a good ending? Why or why not?

ACTIVITIES

Reading about the different people in the previous section probably caused you to think about some of the people in your own life. The activities suggested below will help you to focus your thinking and sharpen your perception. Even as you go about your everyday life — at the supermarket, in class, at the dinner table — try to be a careful observer of the people you see interacting all around you.

PEOPLE WATCHING

When asked to write a character sketch, most students choose to write about a person who is important in their lives, a person they know well. But this activity requires you to focus your powers of observation by writing about a stranger.

1. Go to a convenient place where there are plenty of people to observe — for instance, the waiting room of the local bus station, a park where children play, your college cafeteria.

2. For the first few minutes observe all the people you see. Then select one person to observe more carefully for ten to fifteen minutes. Try not to let the person know that you are observing him or her.

3. As soon after the observation period as possible, freewrite about what you observed. Plan to spend at least twenty to thirty minutes writing your observations. You may want to answer some or all of these questions:

- What did the person look like — size, facial expression, clothing, and so on?
- What was the person doing?
- Was there anything unusual about him or her?
- Did you hear the person say anything? If so, you might want to include some direct quotations.
- Was the person interacting with other people? If so, try to describe this interaction.

Reactions

At the next class meeting, discuss the results of this activity with a partner or small group. First read aloud from your freewriting, and then discuss what you learned. Why did you choose to observe this particular person? Did you notice things about the person that you might not have noticed if you had not been doing a writing activity? If you did this activity again, what would you do differently?

MAKING METAPHORS

The imagination is a powerful motivator for writing. Sometimes a simple metaphor such as "a woman is a book," "a tree is a home," or "a man is the brother of the rain" can inspire rich images, memories, and emotions. In this activity, you are asked to create a metaphor to describe a person you know and then to develop this metaphor into an essay.

1. Write a sentence comparing two things that are not usually compared.

Examples: My mother is a book.
My niece is an icy waterfall.
My boyfriend is a tree.

2. Discuss your sentence with a partner. Why did you think of this particular metaphor? In what ways is the person like the thing you chose?
3. Use this metaphor as the basis of an essay. Push yourself to develop the metaphor as fully as possible. When you have finished, exchange papers with your partner. Read and discuss each other's writing.

Example

In this short essay a metaphor reminded a student of a mysterious and troubling relationship with a man from her past. Like much imaginative writing, its meanings can be understood in many ways.

Rain

by Leelonghi Kwang Ja, Korea

It is the rain that forces me to think about him. This kind of weather makes me so lazy that I don't want to do anything but hold my chin up, look out at the rain, and listen to it. It is strange to say that the rain reminds me of him, but I can't help it. He is the brother of the rain.   1

He acted like the rain—for days with the same speed without any interruption, like a big shower. The rain plays a music that has a quiet harmony; he has a voice just like that. It used to make me fall asleep. The rain has the movement like him, not too fast but comfortable to walk with. Having a conversation with him while walking is the same as now, sitting in a chair next to a window by myself.   2

Sometimes he made me feel that if he was not next to me, he did not even exist. Rarely did he and I sit face to face. Mostly I was always the one who made noise and he was the one who always listened. Sometimes when he said something, he took off his glasses. 3

Well, the man with medium height and light weight with heavy, dark black-rimmed glasses did not impress me much. After all, my memory of him is not so exciting. The interesting thing is that weather like this reminds me of him for some reason. 4

But now, this rain, which reminds me of him, talks all day long and I am listening to it. It looks as if it will never stop, as if it does not care whether or not I want it to stop. Probably I will regret that there was no stop in the days of raining, just like him, who never showed me his disturbed time. 5

Questions for Discussion

1. What do you think the writer's relationship was with the person she is writing about? What line(s) in the essay support your opinion?

2. What do you think the writer means by "He is the brother of the rain"?

3. In your opinion, which of the following words best describes the writer's feelings toward this man?

    a. love

    b. hate

    c. boredom

    d. excitement

Point to specific lines in the essay to support your ideas.

4. Write down two or three questions about this story that can only be answered by "yes" or "no." Discuss these questions with a partner, a small group, or the whole class.

CHOOSING A SUBJECT

In this activity you will be asked to write a short memo (one page or less) to your teacher explaining what person you have chosen as the subject for your essay. A memo—actually a shortened form of the word *memorandum*—is a short written communication often used between the employees of a business. It is similar to a letter but with the social aspect removed; in other words, you do not have to inquire about the other person's health or comment on the weather. A memo is strictly business.

The form of memos may vary slightly, but for this activity use the following form:

      To: [your teacher's name]   Date:
    From: [your name]
  Subject: [proposed essay topic]

In your memo answer these three questions:

1. *Whom do you plan to write about, and why did you choose this person?* Explain briefly who the person is and why you are interested in writing about him or her. Remember to choose a person who is important in your life.

2. *How do you plan to focus your essay?* You cannot tell everything about a person in a short essay. You, as the writer, will have to decide what to include and what to leave out. In your memo, explain the *one* thing you would most like your readers to understand about this person.

3. *What is one important specific detail you plan to include in your paper?* A good writer, like a good painter or photographer, knows the importance of small, significant details. For example, in the essay by Gloria Cortes, it is important to know that Rosita liked to show off her small waist by wearing tight belts but seemed unaware of her large stomach (paragraph 4). What specific details come to your mind when you think of the person you plan to write about? Describe one of these details in your memo to give your teacher an idea of the kind of material you will include in your essay.

If you have any questions regarding the essay, feel free to ask them at the end of the memo. Turn in the memo to your teacher, who will respond either orally or in writing.

GRAMMAR IN CONTEXT
CLASSIFYING TYPES OF SENTENCES

To understand the four sentence patterns of English, you first need to know a few basic grammatical terms:

Clause: A group of words that contains a main verb and a subject that goes with that verb. (In the examples, which are adapted from Eileen Peng's essay, "My Mother," the main verbs are underlined twice and the subjects are underlined once.)

Examples: My <u>mother</u> <u>is</u> a very capable, lively woman.

          or

          although <u>she</u> <u>has</u> less energy now

Independent clause: A clause that can stand alone as a sentence.

Example: My <u>mother</u> <u>is</u> a very capable, lively woman.

Dependent clause: A clause that cannot stand alone as a sentence.

Example: although <u>she</u> <u>has</u> less energy now

Every English sentence is made up of these two basic types of clauses. More-over, every sentence falls into one of these four categories:

1. *Simple sentence:* One independent clause.

Example: My <u>mother</u> <u>is</u> a very capable, lively woman.

2. *Compound sentence:* An independent clause joined to another independent clause with a semicolon (;) or a comma (,) and one of the coordinating conjunctions: *and, but, or, nor, for, so, yet.* (In the examples, conjunctions are circled.)

Example: <u>I</u> <u>had</u> a hard time after arriving in the United States, (but) <u>I</u> <u>was</u> de-termined to succeed.

3. *Complex sentence:* An independent clause joined to a dependent clause. The dependent clause can come either at the beginning or the end of the sentence. A complex sentence contains either a subordinating conjunction or a relative pronoun (see lists).

Examples: (Although) my <u>mother</u> <u>had</u> a full-time job, <u>she</u> <u>was</u> also a very good housewife.

or

My <u>mother</u> <u>was</u> a very good housewife (although) <u>she</u> <u>had</u> a full-time job.

Subordinating Conjunctions

after	since
although	so that
as	such that
as if	than
as long as	though
as soon as	unless
as though	until
because	when
before	whenever
even though	where
how	wherever
if	whether
once	while

Relative Pronouns

that	who
what	whom
which	whose

4. *Compound/complex sentence:* A sentence that includes at least three clauses, one of which is joined with a coordinating conjunction and one of which contains a subordinating conjunction or a relative pronoun (see lists).

Example: I had a hard time after arriving in the United States, (but) I was determined to "Study hard" (as) my mother said.

Activity

In the following sentences, underline the main verbs two times, underline the subjects one time, and circle any conjunctions. Then, in the space provided, write whether the sentence is simple, compound, complex, or compound/complex. (Sentences are adapted from Hikaru Takahashi's essay, "My Grandmother.")

1. She always has a little smile on her face in her portraits. _____

2. Although she is smiling, there is always a kind of severity and dignity about her. _____

3. She passed away on a cold February morning eight years ago. _____

4. When my father came to wake me up, I already sensed what had happened, and I was seized with fear. _____

5. My grandmother did not like to show the pictures of her youth to others, but I liked to look at them and always tried to find them. _____

(See Answer Key, page 315.)

In-Class Activity

This activity will give you a chance to practice writing the four different types of sentences and will help you to feel more sure of yourself when you punctuate your own writing.

1. Working in a small group with three or four other students, write five sentences. Include a combination of the four basic types: simple, compound, complex, and compound/complex. Try to make your sentences interesting or funny. One group member should write down all the sentences on a piece of paper.

2. After you have completed the five sentences, decide which type each one is. If you cannot agree, underline the verbs twice and the subject once and circle any conjunctions. Consult the definitions as necessary.

3. One member from each group should write the five sentences on the board, without telling what types of sentences they are. The students in the other groups should write down what type each one is: simple, compound, complex, or compound/complex. If the class does not agree, analyze the structure by underlining subjects and verbs and circling conjunctions. Your teacher will serve as a consultant if there is any disagreement.

UNDERSTANDING SENTENCE BOUNDARIES

In speaking, we rely on nonverbal signals such as pauses and intonation to indicate where one idea ends and another one begins. In writing, we use punctuation and capital letters to show these things. Without punctuation it would be difficult, if not impossible, to understand a writer's meaning. The activity that follows will give you some idea of why punctuation is needed.

In-Class Activity

All punctuation has been removed from the first two paragraphs of an essay by Bo Sin Wong, a student writer. Have a student volunteer read the paragraphs aloud to the class.

I admired her she could repeat that exercise movement over fifty times 1 and did not seem tired I imitated it but I only could do it five times when she saw me she went over and said you dont look like a youth Im even stronger than you

This was the first time I met her at a park near Chinatown she was an old 2 healthy Chinese lady I thought she had a wealthy family and a happy life since we both spoke the same dialect we didn't have any trouble understanding each other after we had met a couple of times I learned that she got married when she was only fifteen her husband left his family in China for Singapore and then for the United States five months later they did not meet each other again until she came here twenty-eight years later when she was forty-three years old unfortunately they did not have any children she is living alone in this country now

Reactions

Working with your class or group, go through these paragraphs and try to figure out where the sentences begin and end. Add the proper punctuation and capital letters. What helped you to decide how to punctuate this passage?

(See Answer Key, page 315.)

PROOFREADING FOR SENTENCE BOUNDARIES

You can check your understanding of the basic sentence patterns in English—and how they should be punctuated—by doing the proofreading exercise that follows. For general advice about proofreading, see page 309.

Activity

The following student essay contains several errors in punctuation. Working alone or with a partner, correct these errors. If you are not sure how a particular sentence should be punctuated, underline the subject(s) once, the verb(s) twice, and circle any conjunctions. Which kind of sentence is it—simple, compound, complex, or compound/complex? Once you have analyzed the grammatical structure of the sentence, you should feel sure of how to punctuate it.

The Third Day behind the Wheel
by Wieslaw P. Zubel

When I was twenty-one, I got my first driver's license. Living in the suburbs   1
of New Orleans. I was forced to drive a car in order to get from one place to another. At the place I lived, called Violet, nobody dared to cross the street on foot.

Before I took the road test. I had driven for two hours at a shopping mall   2
parking lot. On the day after I got my license, I was already forcing my eight-year-old Ventura to fly seventy miles per hour on a two-way highway.

The next day I decided to check the Ventura's speed ability, I took her on a   3
divided highway with two lanes going each direction. In the middle was neutral ground full of potholes. On both sides along the highway were ditches filled with snakes, mud, and water. In the distance, the skeletons of dead trees greeted the haunted travelers.

It was the beginning of dusk. When I passed the Judge Perreze Bridge   4 and accelerated to ninety-six miles per hour. When the car wasn't going any faster; I had a glimmering thought of slowing down. Suddenly, the Ventura started bouncing from side to side and went off the road to the left. First I noticed the headlights of oncoming cars, so I was preparing myself mentally for a head-on collision. A second later, however, I had the panorama of eternal wetness and started subconsciously to press the brakes with all my might, the idea of dying in a swamp somehow didn't fit me. The Ventura was still turning, she made another cycle and a half and stopped, to my surprise. It took me a few deep breaths to recover my full awareness, but soon I was back on the highway again.

(See Answer Key, page 316.)

PROOFREADING FOR THE PLURAL FORM OF NOUNS

The following activity gives you a chance to practice proofreading for errors in plural forms of nouns, first discussed in Chapter 4. For general advice about proofreading, see page 309.

Activity

Locate and correct the problems with plurals in the following essay. Note that it is helpful to look for key words that always indicate the plural.

> Examples: *a few* girls
> *many* students
> *three* books

I Was a "Little Devil"

by Mai Ha Nguyen

In the summer of 1980 I had to attend a chemistry class because my father thought I was doing poorly in it. I admired karate very much at the time, but my father always gave me good reasons not to take lesson. Therefore, instead of going to chemistry class, I skipped school and took karate at a little school nearby, without my father's permission.

After I had taken a few lesson, I became one of the most annoying kid in the   2
neighborhood. I always made plan for us (our kid gang) to fight with the other
kids on the surrounding block. This was one of the game that we enjoyed most.
But as you may guess, every wild start must have an end. In my case, this was how
I ended my karate lesson.

One day when I got out of my karate lesson, two of my friend and I were all   3
excited because tomorrow would be the big contest to go a step higher in karate.
Suddenly I bumped into somebody. When I looked up, it was a guy who was
around my age, but by appearance stronger than me. However, I didn't notice that,
but stood up and started a fight with him. Even though he said "Sorry" many time
and asked me to forgive him, I didn't. We took off our slipper and started. The kid
surrounding us were cheering, and their yelling made me even more excited. I was
winning for the first several minutes, but my strength left me as the fight went on.
Finally, the guy punched me so hard that he completely knocked me down. I sat
on the ground with bruise on my body and a bloody nose. He came over, looked at
me, and asked: "Are you okay? I didn't want to fight, but you insisted. I'm sorry."
After that he left. I was sitting on the ground feeling like a total fool.

On my way home, I didn't cry out loud, but tear kept rolling down my face.   4
After crying, I began to laugh about my stupidity and decided to give up physical
fighting for the rest of my life. That was the end of my karate lesson.

Reactions

After you have completed this exercise, compare answers with a partner. Underline the clue words that helped you to decide if a noun should be singular or
plural.

(See Answer Key, pages 317 – 18.)

SPELLING STRATEGY: WHEN THE SPELLING CHECKER DOESN'T WORK

If you use a computer or word processor with a spelling checker, you will find
that the program does not find all of your spelling errors. Usually this happens when

the word you have misspelled happens to be the correct spelling of another word in the dictionary. For example, if you write *to much* instead of *too much*, the program won't catch the mistake since there is a word spelled *to* in the dictionary. The following exercise asks you to practice finding misspelled words that the spelling checker will not find.

Activity

In the following sentences, based on the story entitled "Rosita," which appeared earlier in this chapter, try to find the misspelled words and supply the correct spellings yourself.

1. She was surprise to seen me standing there calm and without tears.

2. Rosita build up the idea that I was a hard young girl cause she couldn't understood anything I though was important.

3. In my mother's absent, she ran the house and razed us.

4. When she smiled, we could see the perfectly strait white teethe of witch she was so proud.

5. One day, when she was changing her cloths, Rosita seen me observing her.

(See Answer Key, page 318.)

ASSIGNMENT

In the previous chapter you were asked to tell about an experience. In this chapter the task is to analyze a person's character. What is this person like? And why is he or she this way? These are not easy questions. Yet in understanding other people better, we often come to understand ourselves as well. Furthermore, the kind of thinking required to write a good character sketch is similar to the analytical thinking you will be asked to do for writing tasks throughout your college career. The thinking process is much the same whether you are analyzing the causes of the French Revolution or the reasons for your mother's behavior.

As you begin to work on your essay about a person, it is helpful to understand the purpose and audience for this writing. Your purpose should be to reveal some important truths about the person's character. Think of your audience as an interested and perceptive reader but one who has never met the person being described.

SUGGESTED TECHNIQUES

While working on the first draft, remember that it is better to reveal the person's character by showing, not telling, what he or she is like. You could begin your

Thur.
freewriting

essay with a straightforward assessment of the person's character: "My first-grade teacher was a domineering woman." Or you could say, "My first-grade teacher was six feet tall and had cold blue eyes and bony fingers that could grab you by the hair if you talked out of turn." You could open with an obvious statement such as "Teo was a hard-working and determined student." Or you could write, "Long after midnight, when the rest of the city was asleep, there was always one light shining from one window. That was Teo's. 'Sleep,' he said, 'is a luxury for other people.' If he could absorb another chapter of a text or solve one last math problem, why not just do it? There would be other days to sleep and dream." By providing details about what people do, think, or say, you can show rather than tell the reader who they are.

Here are some of the methods writers use to bring their characters to life:

1. *Quote what the person says.* One of the most important ways we learn about people is by listening to what they say. And good writers know that including a person's exact words in the form of direct quotations is one of the most effective ways of revealing character. When Dastagir Firoz quotes the khan as saying, "I live on the land of God and I feel myself closer to him when his phenomena are visible with my own naked eyes," we form an impression of a proud man who is at home in the natural world.

What are some of the typical sayings of the person you plan to write about?

2. *Describe what the person does.* "Actions speak louder than words," according to an old saying, and it is true that sometimes people say one thing but do another. When writing about people, we need to pay attention to what they do and describe some of their significant actions. For instance, in the third selection in this chapter, Rosita constantly talks about piety and religion but is actually cruel in her behavior toward Gloria.

You might want to list several actions that you associate with the person you will be describing. Do they reveal anything important?

3. *Tell what others say and think about the person.* The opinions of other people are also important in analyzing someone's character. Often we come to understand someone better as a result of what others say and think about that person. For example, in introducing her mother to the reader, Eileen Peng first tells how many friends her mother has and how much she is respected by the neighbors. Hikaru Takahashi quotes what other people have said about her grandmother in order to make her portrait detailed and convincing.

Think about the person you plan to describe. What can we learn about this person's character from the way other people react to him or her?

4. *Describe the person's appearance.* Often a person's outward appearance — looks, facial expression, even clothing — reflects something significant about his or her character. And many skilled writers describe a person's physical appearance as a means of revealing character. For instance, Mark Salzman writes, "Pan looked fearsome, but what most distinguished him was that, when he talked, his face moved and changed expression."

As you begin work on your first draft, try to picture the person you are writing about. Is there anything significant about the person's appearance?

You probably will not use all four of these methods in your essay, but remember that the person you are describing will seem more real to the reader if you *show* rather than *tell* what that person is like.

After you have written your first draft, exchange papers with a classmate and fill out the Peer Response Sheet located at the end of this chapter. If you decide to do another draft, refer to Part III: Rethinking/Rewriting.

PEER RESPONSE SHEET:
WRITING ABOUT PEOPLE

Writer's Name: _____

Reader's Name: _____

Date: _____

(*Note to the reader*: As you respond to the writer's draft, try to focus on the ideas rather than the grammar and spelling. Discuss only those mistakes that interfere with understanding.)

1. Write one sentence to sum up what this person is like. _____

_____

_____

_____

2. List three details from the essay that support your opinion given above. _____

_____

_____

_____

_____

_____

3. Indicate which of the following methods the writer uses to reveal the person's character. Give one example of each method used. (Most essays will probably *not* use all four methods.)

    a. What the person says _____

    _____

    b. What the person does _____

    _____

    c. What other people say and think about this person _____

    _____

    _____

    d. What the person looks like _____

    _____

4. Were there any things in this essay that you did not understand? If so, what were they? _____

_____

_____

_____

_____

5. Why do you think the writer chose to describe this particular person? _____

_____

_____

_____

_____

6. Could the writer add any new information to make the description more powerful? _____

_____

_____

_____

_____

6

Places

In this chapter you will be asked to write an essay in which you describe a place. Probably every person has an emotional attachment to some place. In the selections that follow, many of the writers reveal their love for a special place, often a place from their childhood. They also express a sense of belonging to a particular place where they feel most at home, most at peace. But in many of the selections there is a feeling of loss as well; the writers now live far away and cannot go back to visit. They can only revisit these special places in their minds by writing about them.

As you work in this chapter, we encourage you to take the time to think and write about your own places—places from the past or the present, real places or those in your imagination.

READINGS

My Garden
by Suzanne Scherzer

Although Suzanne Scherzer is German, she spent her childhood years in Africa. In this essay she describes a beloved childhood place through the eyes of an adventurous eight-year-old. Before you read, freewrite about a place that was special to you when you were young. Try to describe it, not from an adult's point of view, but as it appeared to you as a child.

My parents and I had recently moved to a new house and with it came a gar- 1 den, "my" garden. It took me, the apartment-girl, time to realize what a treasure I had gotten, and it took even longer until I had conquered every blade of grass, every flower, every stone, every little creature that lived in it.

It was an immense garden, seen in the dimensions of an eight-year-old girl, 2 larger than the area of our house. It was separated from the street and from the neighbors by a high, white brick wall that enclosed all of the property. The wall was interrupted only by an impressive iron portal that led over a stone path to our house and further on to the garage. The gate was so heavy that I could open it by myself only with great effort.

What was peculiar about the garden was that it was divided into different 3 sections. For example, one was the so-called jungle, a wild mixture of trees and bushes densely interwoven with wild lianas. It probably was a corner where the former owner never felt the need to "civilize" the plants, and I'm glad he didn't. To me it was perfect.

Another area belonged to a narrow path that led along the back side of our 4 swimming pool, close to the brick wall. The earth was hard and dry; nothing grew on it. The neighbors' trees spread the only true cool shadow in the garden. Often during the rainy season, when the earth became soft and muddy, we would find a colony of toads pressed in a corner of the wall. They resembled an ugly, dusty blob. It was an act of courage to touch them, interrupting their peace and making them jump in different directions out of their shelter. Meanwhile, we children ran shrieking into the house. It could happen that one of the toads escaped into the swimming pool where it hid in the drainpipe. I soon got used to their presence, and I felt like an expectant mother when the first strings of spawn were floating in the water; of course, my mother was never very enthusiastic about transforming the pool into a nursery for cute little toads and made sure that all of them were exterminated.

Another area was our fruit garden. There we had several tropical trees bearing exotic fruits like bananas, mangoes, goyabas, oranges, and papayas. It was a pleasure to observe the pretty blossoms turn into ripe, delicious fruit, and it was difficult for me to be patient and wait for the time when they could be picked and eaten. We had a little mango tree that was our pride. It was tiny and delicate, much smaller than its brothers and sisters, but the princess among them. It produced the largest and most beautiful mangoes, fruit so big and so numerous that it nearly collapsed under their weight, but it was always brave and never gave in to the valuable burden it had to carry year after year.   5

The lawn filled out the remaining area. It was our carpet, where we would run, jump, and sit with our dolls under the trees. There were some big trees; unfortunately, I was too small to climb them, but so were the boys. A tree that fascinated me was an old eucalyptus; it must have had hundreds of years of experience and wisdom, and it was as tall a tree as I had ever seen. Its bark was peculiar; it looked like peeling white skin. Its leaves were narrow and smooth. Since it stood near the pool, many of its leaves fell onto the water. There they glittered like polished silver, a magic I could never explain. All the other leaves looked plain and dull in the water.   6

When a storm was raging over the city, the eucalyptus swayed and groaned like an old man, threatening to crash onto our roof, but luckily it firmly resisted the heavy tempest. The morning after, the garden looked pitiful—leaves, branches, and dirt were spread all over the lawn and the pool looked like a dirty pond. It took us two days to restore its beauty. My mother deserves all the credit since she was the one who made the garden what it was; she worked in it daily, caring about every flower and tree, watering them, planting them in another place when she found that it was too sunny or too windy for them.   7

Maybe I should mention the animals that you could find in the garden. We literally established an orphanage for wild cats. We had a little kitten that was making its first steps through our garden when it came across a wild cat. Since then, every night the strange cat would appear on our terrace, drink the kitten's milk, and disappear into the night again. We were never able to touch it, but it was faithful to us. I wonder what it is doing now.   8

Besides cats, there were funny little lizards that lost their tails when we tried to catch them. There were hairy spiders, always treated with respect, grasshoppers (the boys loved to put them in the girls' shirts; since then I have an aversion to anything that is green and hops), and beautiful chameleons. Chameleons are peaceful creatures. We would walk around with them sitting on our arms, whether they liked it or not. Their tiny feet were very strong, and sometimes they clung to our arms so hard that it hurt.   9

I could go on forever talking about my garden. It was a wonderful time, and   10

I can say that there I learned what it meant to be a child. I miss that place a lot, and even if I had a chance to visit it now, twelve years later, I probably wouldn't do it. I'm afraid that it wouldn't look as it did when we left it and that strange people wouldn't have known how to take care of it. It would make me very sad to find out that my childhood dreams had disappeared and that none of them came true.

I feel better sitting here, remembering all the secrets of my garden, the laugh-   11
ter, the friends, and the fun I left behind. We can be expelled from paradise, but no one can take our memories away.

Personal Connections

1. How do you feel about going back to visit places that were important to you in the past? Would you like to return to your childhood home for a visit, or do you share Scherzer's feeling that it is better just to remember the happy times of the past without actually revisiting the places? Can you explain why you feel the way you do?

2. This essay contains many detailed descriptions of plants and animals. Take a few minutes to write a description of a plant or animal that you are familiar with. Make your description as detailed as possible.

Content and Writing Techniques

1. Reread paragraphs 2–6. Then draw a diagram or map of each section of the garden; label each part and what was in it. Underline the sentences or details in the essay that helped you as you drew the diagram. Compare diagrams with a partner. How are they similar or different? Look back at the essay to decide which one is more accurate.

2. Notice that Scherzer speaks to her readers directly in paragraph 8 when she says: "Maybe I should mention the animals that you could find in the garden." How would it be different if she had written: "Maybe I should mention the animals that could be found there"? Which way do you prefer? Why?

El Retorno
by Gloria Anzaldúa

In this passage from her book Borderlands/La Frontera (1987), *Gloria Anzaldúa writes of her return to the Lower Rio Grande Valley in south Texas, where she grew up. However, Anzaldúa's title,* Borderlands, *refers not only to the border, or dividing line, between Texas and Mexico, but also to the borders be-*

tween cultures, languages, social classes, and individuals. As you read, think about the "borderlands" in your own life. Do you feel that you spend all of your time on one side of the "border" or do you move back and forth across various "borders" depending on whom you are with and what you are doing?

> All movements are accomplished in six stages,
> and the seventh brings return.
> —*I Ching*[1]

> *Tanto tiempo sin verte casa mía,*
> *mi cuna, mi hondo nido de la huerta.*
> —*"Soledad"*[2]

I still feel the old despair when I look at the unpainted, dilapidated, scrap lumber houses consisting mostly of corrugated aluminum. Some of the poorest people in the U.S. live in the Lower Rio Grande Valley, an arid and semi-arid land of irrigated farming, intense sunlight and heat, citrus groves next to chaparral and cactus. I walk through the elementary school I attended so long ago, that remained segregated until recently. I remember how the white teachers used to punish us for being Mexican.

How I love this tragic valley of South Texas, as Ricardo Sánchez calls it; this borderland between the Nueces and the Rio Grande. This land has survived possession and ill-use by five countries: Spain, Mexico, the Republic of Texas, the U.S., the Confederacy, and the U.S. again. It has survived Anglo-Mexican blood feuds, lynchings, burnings, rapes, pillage.

Today I see the Valley still struggling to survive. Whether it does or not, it will never be as I remember it. The borderlands depression that was set off by the 1982 peso devaluation in Mexico resulted in the closure of hundreds of Valley businesses. Many people lost their homes, cars, land. Prior to 1982, U.S. store owners thrived on retail sales to Mexicans who came across the border for groceries and clothes and appliances. While goods on the U.S. side have become 10, 100, 1000 times more expensive for Mexican buyers, goods on the Mexican side have become 10, 100, 1000 times cheaper for Americans. Because the Valley is heavily dependent on agriculture and Mexican retail trade, it has the highest unemployment rates along the entire border region; it is the Valley that has been hardest hit.[3]

"It's been a bad year for corn," my brother, Nune, says. As he talks, I remember my father scanning the sky for a rain that would end the drought, looking up

[1] Richard Wilhelm, *The I Ching: or Book of Changes*, Cary F. Baynes, trans. (Princeton, N.J.: Princeton University Press, 1950), 98.

[2] *"Soledad"* is sung by the group Haciendo Punto en Otro Son.

[3] Out of the twenty-two border counties in the four border states, Hidalgo County (named for Father Hidalgo who was shot in 1810 after instigating Mexico's revolt against Spanish rule under the banner of *la Virgen de Guadalupe*) is the most poverty-stricken county in the nation as well as the largest home base (along with Imperial in California) for migrant farmworkers. It was here that I was born and raised. I am amazed that both it and I have survived.

into the sky, day after day, while the corn withered on its stalk. My father has been dead for 29 years, having worked himself to death. The life span of a Mexican farm laborer is 56—he lived to be 38. It shocks me that I am older than he. I, too, search the sky for rain. Like the ancients, I worship the rain god and the maize goddess, but unlike my father I have recovered their names. Now for rain (irrigation) one offers not a sacrifice of blood, but of money.

"Farming is in a bad way," my brother says. "Two to three thousand small and big farmers went bankrupt in this country last year. Six years ago the price of corn was $8.00 per hundred pounds," he goes on. "This year it is $3.90 per hundred pounds." And, I think to myself, after taking inflation into account, not planting anything puts you ahead.

I walk out to the back yard, stare at *los rosales de mamá*. She wants me to help her prune the rose bushes, dig out the carpet grass that is choking them. *Mamagrande Ramona también tenía rosales.* Here every Mexican grows flowers. If they don't have a piece of dirt, they use car tires, jars, cans, shoe boxes. Roses are the Mexican's favorite flower. I think, how symbolic—thorns and all.

Yes, the Chicano and Chicana have always taken care of growing things and the land. Again I see the four of us kids getting off the school bus, changing into our work clothes, walking into the field with Papí and Mamí, all six of us bending to the ground. Below our feet, under the earth lie the watermelon seeds. We cover them with paper plates, putting *terremotes* on top of the plates to keep them from being blown away by the wind. The paper plates keep the freeze away. Next day or the next, we remove the plates, bare the tiny green shoots to the elements. They survive and grow, give fruit hundreds of times the size of the seed. We water them and hoe them. We harvest them. The vines dry, rot, are plowed under. Growth, death, decay, birth. The soil prepared again and again, impregnated, worked on. A constant changing of forms, *renacimientos de la tierra madre*.

> This land was Mexican once
> was Indian always
> and is.
> And will be again.

Personal Connections

1. Anzaldúa begins this passage with a quotation from *The I Ching*, which is a book of Chinese philosophy often used to predict the future. In the quote used here, "All movements are accomplished in six stages, and the seventh brings return," the word *return* can have many meanings. For example, we can think of the six days of the week, with the seventh day being a return to where we started. *Return* can also mean the start of something new, as we start the new week just as we are ending it on the seventh day.

Look through the passage again. Try to find evidence of the meaning of return as in going back to a place from the past. Then find evidence of return as a new beginning.

2. Returning to the place where you spent your childhood is always an emotional experience. Try to imagine how Anzaldúa felt after this experience by writing a letter from *her* point of view (not your own). Address this letter to a close friend from her present life, and explain the feelings she had after visiting the place where she grew up. Try to write at least three or four paragraphs, and sign it "Sincerely, Gloria Anzaldúa." Begin the letter as follows:

Dear _____,

Today, after many years, I returned to the Lower Rio Grande Valley, the place where I spent my childhood.
As I looked at the land and the people, I felt . . .

Content and Writing Techniques

1. A distinctive feature of Anzaldúa's writing is the way she moves from one language to another without including translations. Try to guess the meaning of the Spanish expressions in this passage. If you get stuck, ask a Spanish-speaking classmate to help you figure out the meaning. Why, in your opinion, did Anzaldúa decide to include these Spanish expressions?

2. In paragraph 6, Anzaldúa mentions that the rose is Mexicans' favorite flower and goes on to add "how symbolic—thorns and all." A thorn is the sharp point on a rose stem, which can hurt your finger if you touch it. Which of the following things might the thorns symbolize? Discuss your answer with a partner or small group.

   a. The suffering of the Mexican people over centuries.
   b. The toughness or strength of the people.
   c. A kind of natural defense or protection from enemies.
   d. A religious symbol, such as the crown of thorns worn by Jesus before he died.

3. In paragraph 7, Anzaldúa describes how farmers in the Valley grow plants from tiny seeds and how these plants survive in a cycle of "growth, death, decay, birth." Anzaldúa seems to be saying that the people of the Valley also experience this cycle. For example, in paragraph 4, as her brother talks about the crops, she is reminded of earlier conversations with her father, who is now dead. Find two other examples that relate to the cycle of life, death, and rebirth.

The Coldest Winter of Beijing
by Jian Wei

In this essay, a Chinese student describes his visit to Tiananmen Square, a famous historical site in the capital of China. After leaving the tomb of Mao Tse-tung, the powerful chairman of the Chinese Communist Party, Wei begins to revise his thinking about this important political leader.

A shiver ran over my body. There was a nip in the air. I suddenly remembered it was already the end of the year, 1989.   1

The sun was nearly down. Shafts of light covered the empty Tiananmen Square, full silent, as if the Square were exhausted. There were only several teams of armed policemen, tiny and lonely in the empty vastness of the Square. From June 4, 1989, the bloody end of the greatest demonstration of the People's Republic of China, the Square had been closed for many months, and had just reopened. The bicycles drifted off, almost silent, and the buses ghosted past. Stopping to look in the Square was not permitted for the residents of Beijing. The Tiananmen (the Gate of Heavenly Peace) stood in the cold weather as a witness to the violent changes making up China's history and as a warning that the Communist Party still had absolute power in China. The red flags on the wall waved in the wind like hairs swaying on an old man's head.   2

I stood for a while looking for someone who could take a picture for me. But very few tourists stood in the Square. Before entering, the tourists had to pass through two sentry posts. They had to show the ID cards that they carried every day, and official proof that they were "good elements." Many people didn't come into the Square because they didn't have such proof.   3

For a while, no one passed me. I found some people waiting in line before the Chairman Mao Memorial Hall, so I decided to go there and ask someone to help.   4

When a young man was taking a picture of me, a plainclothes policeman called to us, "Hey, wait in line." "Why?" I asked. He came near and stared at me. His skin was black and rough, and his eyes were red. Obviously, the sharp wind of Beijing had caused it. In a harsh and imperious voice, he said: "Wait in line if you want to see Chairman Mao." Then he pointed at the bag I carried, "Deposit your bag." I noticed he was carrying a walkie-talkie, maybe also a gun under his clothes, and I did not ask the second "why." I suspected that his mission was to prevent a bomb scare. Later I found some policemen searching people's handbags and warning them not to take pictures or speak in the hall.   5

When I was walking into the hall, a big marble screen with Mao's writing caught my eye. Mao was a good poet in his early life. I appreciated one of his early poems. When he wrote it, he was a young man and China was an isolated country, struggling to stand up. The dreamy poem went like this: 6

Alone I stand in the autumn cold
And watch the river northward flowing
Past the Orange Island shore.

And myriad hills are all
Tier upon tier of crimsoned woods.
On the broad stream, intensely blue,
Hundreds of bustling barges float;
Eagles strike at the lofty air,
Fish hover among the shallows;
Millions of creatures under this freezing sky are
Striving for freedom.
In this immensity, deeply pondering,
I ask the great earth and boundless blue
Who are the masters?

Later Mao became the great dictator of China and remained in power until   7
his death. He became a famous idol, and his photographs and portraits were hung
in every corner of the country. He was the god of China.

An undercover policeman monitors Tiananmen Square on the sixth anniversary of the
student demonstrations.

Just then, some policemen hurried us. Through a dim passage we entered   8
the central room. Holding our breath, we looked carefully at Mao's dead body
through a glass screen. He lay in a crystal coffin far from us. Flowers circled him,
and a red party flag covered his whole body. Four armed soldiers stood at the corners. The bayonets cast some glittering reflections on their young faces.

At that moment, the remaining little motion of Mao's wit died in me. There   9
is a famous old proverb: "When the moon is fullest, it begins to wane; when it is
darkest, it begins to grow." Now the glories of Mao's wealth and power had turned
into passing smoke.

Light from unknown places shone on Mao's face, but it was too strong. It   10
was hard to recognize his familiar face from so far away. I felt that his face looked
wooden and not so real in the coffin. The air was blended with mystery and ten-
sion, which now seemed to grow and grow.

I heard a man murmuring when we got out, "Is he real?" I also had my   11
doubts. For the few seconds that I was in the room, what had I seen? I took a deep
breath. It felt good to walk in the fresh air again, although the air was much colder
than inside. I took out an old portrait of Mao from my pocket. But it was not
bright in the Square. The moon was just peeping over the horizon. I held the picture in the light. It was too old, somewhat crinkled, faded. Just when my eyes focused on Mao's face, a strange wind passed by, circling, and carried the picture
through my fingers, whistling, like someone's sigh. I extended my hand to try to
hold it. But it was too late. It had gone with the west wind. The picture was caught
in the light that spilled like fog from the Memorial Hall's windows, and waving,
rocking, it vanished in the dark.

Personal Connections

1. Have you ever visited a famous historical place? If so, did this visit
change your view of history in any way? Explain.

2. At one time Mao Tse-tung was a hero to millions of Chinese, yet since his
death in 1976, many people, like the writer of this essay, have become disillu-
sioned with their former hero. Who are some of your own heroes? Have any of
these heroes disappointed you? Freewrite about this question for a few minutes,
and then discuss your writing with a partner.

Content and Writing Techniques

1. Reread the first paragraph of this essay. Which of the following words
best describes the mood or atmosphere Wei creates in this paragraph: (a) happiness, (b) fear, (c) uneasiness, (d) excitement? Does this mood continue throughout the essay, or does the mood change at some point? Discuss your opinion with
your partner, group, or class.

2. Good writers often make their descriptions seem real by appealing to their
readers' senses—sight, hearing, taste, touch, and smell. For example, in paragraph 2,
Wei mentions "shafts of light" (sight) and describes the Square as "full silent" (hearing). Read through the entire essay, and underline every place where Wei appeals to

one of the five senses; each time, write in the margin which of the five senses is involved. What effect do these details have on you as a reader?

3. Look carefully at the last paragraph, in which Wei describes taking a photograph of Mao out of his pocket. What do you think this photo of Mao symbolizes? Wei creates an eerie mood when he says, "a strange wind passed by, circling, and carried the picture through my fingers, whistling, like someone's sigh." Do you think this really happened, or did Wei make this up to provide an effective ending for his essay? Give reasons to support your opinion.

The Dream Land
By Eun Soon Park

A student from Korea describes a place she now sees only in her dreams—her family's home, where she spent a happy childhood. Before you read, think about the home in which you grew up. What do you remember most about your childhood home?

I can't get rid of the memory of my old home even though I left there so long ago. When my family left our home, I told myself that I would get back there. But this was a dream and has not happened yet.   1

The house was surrounded by fruit trees such as apples, apricots, persimmons as well as tall and beautiful plants with flowers and fragrances. Every tree changed its color with the seasons, but the fence, which was made up of evergreen trees, remained green throughout the year. The house was inherited from my great-grandparents and actually included three separate houses as well as a playground, land for plants and gardening, and a well in the center that supplied the water for my family and the plants.   2

Fall was the time of year that my house looked best from the outside because many of the trees produced their fruits of yellow and red, and boasted about them competitively, especially the persimmon trees. During the autumn, pedestrians would stop by my house and take pictures of the trees and take persimmons too. But none of my family complained about these people. We enjoyed their coming and shared our happiness with them. When we picked the persimmons, we usually left one on the top of the tree, which we hoped would become food for a bird during the winter.   3

My parents always opened the door to the neighbors. The children who lived near my home came and played with us. There was a swing, a goal for soccer, a volleyball net, and a ping-pong table. I had a great time playing with the neighborhood children, and it became a part of my childhood memories.   4

My parents lived with their parents. During the summer, my grandparents' friends would come to my home and talk about their past experiences or other social things. Sometimes their stories were funny and interesting, and I could learn   5 about historical events from their conversations. But sometimes it was so boring to hear them that I would fall asleep in my grandparents' laps.

My old home was filled with love from my grandparents, parents, neighbors, and nature. I can't think about it without remembering their love.

Personal Connections

1. Complete the following sentence: "When I think about the house where I grew up, I remember _____." Use this sentence as the beginning of a piece of freewriting. Try to write for at least twenty minutes. Could you develop your freewriting into an essay?

2. In paragraph 5, Park talks about listening to the stories told by her grandparents and their friends. When you were a child, did you like to hear stories told by older people? What do children learn from listening to stories? Write down as many different answers to this question as you can, and then discuss your list with a partner.

Content and Writing Techniques

1. Write down one word that, for you, describes Park's childhood home. Compare your word with that of your partner, group, or class.

2. Analyze how Park has organized this essay. Read each paragraph, and write down a few words to describe the main idea. Why do you think Park arranged the paragraphs in this order?

Waiting Room
by Hypatia Foster

> *In this essay a student describes the place where she works—the reception area of an abortion clinic. Before you begin reading, think about how you feel as you sit in the waiting room of a doctor's office or hospital.*

My day starts at 6:00 A.M., when my two sisters and I wake up. By the time I get to the office it is already 9:00 A.M. After I sip on my coffee, regular, no sugar, and change into a light blue scrub suit with white lab coat and white shoes, I sit for a few minutes staring at the empty rooms. The quietness is interrupted by the noise of some surgical instruments and trays dropped at the far end of the hallway.

It is 9:30 A.M. The waiting room is empty, impersonal, businesslike. The people start arriving at 9:45 A.M. Some in blue jeans and worn sneakers, others sheathed in furs, some with children, others are children themselves. But whether they are junior-high or high-school students, models, actresses, middle-aged wives, or hold a Ph.D., all these women come to the office because they are pregnant and they do not want to be.

It is 10:00 A.M. I call the service to see if there are any more messages besides the ones I was given as soon as I came. "No messages" is the answer. I open the appointment book and see there are twenty patients scheduled for the day. The first patient should be processed soon; the doctor has called, saying he is on his way.   3

I call the first patient by her first name. A lady answers; she is in her fifties. I invite her to come in. As she sits, she tells me, "I am not the patient; my daughter is." I go out again and call the patient's name. This time a young kid answers. She seems a little scared. As I did with her mother, I invite her in. Taking the clinic history I learn that the girl is twelve years old. She is tall for her age, slim with two pig-tails and green ribbons. Her big black eyes have dark circles around them for having fasted from the previous midnight. Her slim body has started to take a different shape; her name, Natali.   4

While Natali's mother answers the questions for her, her eyes wander around the office, through every book, every sign, every picture around her. Suddenly her eyes stop for a moment, staring at a picture of a beautiful pregnant woman holding a carnation in her hands. There is silence for a moment. I stop asking questions. The three of us stare at the picture. Three women, Natali, her mother, and I. Three different persons, and while we stare at the same picture, we live and experience three different worlds. The phone rings, interrupting our thoughts and bringing us to reality. After I finish processing Natali, her mother says, "As you can see, she is a child; she cannot take care of herself." A few minutes later a doctor comes to the office to take the patient away.   5

After Natali, there are nineteen patients to process. At the end of the day the waiting room goes back to its quietness. I sit for a few minutes staring at the empty room; some newspapers and magazines were left behind. I open the appointment book and see that there are nineteen patients for the next day.   6

Personal Connections

1. Although abortion has been legal in the United States for many years, it remains a highly controversial issue. What is your opinion about abortion?

2. In paragraph 5, Foster describes a moment of stillness when she, the pregnant girl, and the girl's mother focus on the picture of a pregnant woman holding a flower. Write down what each of the three women might be thinking as they look at the picture on the wall. It is okay to guess.

Content and Writing Techniques

1. In paragraphs 1, 2, and 3:
   a. Underline any words that help create the mood of the story. How would you describe this mood?
   b. Circle all the verbs, and then change them to the past tense. How does this change the story?

c. Put an *X* over any words that have to do with time. What does time have to do with this story?

2. Which of the following ideas seems closest to Foster's feelings about abortion?

   a. She is opposed to it. She feels it is cruel and immoral.
   b. She doesn't like it, but she feels it is necessary in some cases.
   c. It is a personal decision that each woman must make for herself.
   d. She does not want to think about it too much. It is too complicated a subject.

Which of the above statements is closest to your own view?

3. **Writing Assignment**: Write a reaction to "Waiting Room." What is the mood of this piece? How does it make you feel? What does it remind you of in your reading or personal experience? What is your feeling about Foster's job? Would you be willing to do this work? Explain.

New Horizon of Beauty
by Sumiko Masaki

> *In this essay, a Japanese student tells of a visit to a small church in France — a visit that changed her outlook on life. Can you think of a place that has changed you in some way?*

It was early summer in the south of France. My husband and I were staying at a 1
small hotel near the beach in Nice. Opening the window of my room, I could look out over the sea, whose face changed according to the time of day or night. At this time of year, the darkness does not arrive until after eleven o'clock. People can enjoy the sensitive change of the color of the sky for more than four hours in the evening.

I love beauty — the color of the sky, the calm sea, the flowers in a Japanese 2
poem — but I always felt that it included something sad. I had been a kind of pessimist since my aunt's death ten years before. She was a beautiful lady, like a white rose. When she was in the hospital called the Cancer Center, one day she asked me to bring her white roses, which she loved very much but nobody gave her because white flowers are not considered appropriate. One week after that, she passed away with those roses. I could not understand why a wonderful person like her had to die young. But after that, I lost still more — two grandmothers. When I recovered from my great sorrow, I had to face new sadness. These happenings made me a person who thinks that a sunshine day must change to a rainy day. I came to believe that there is no happiness which never ends and there is no beauty which has no limit.

The day was sunny. The morning sky and sea were truly blue. The bright 3
sunlight of southern France made everything vivid. I strolled along the beach with

my husband. It was a beautiful and happy time, but I could not enjoy it completely because of my thought that sadness always comes after joy.

We had planned a trip to Vence to see a chapel decorated by Matisse, an artist whom my husband admired very much. Vence was about a thirty-minute drive from Nice. As we drove into the town of Vence, we could see the small brick houses with their brown roofs. We went up along the road through the peaceful village, looking for the church. Our guidebook said that Matisse had designed the stained glass, the tile work on the walls, and even the priest's vestments. He worked for a sister in that church, because she had taken care of him and comforted him when he was very ill. It was one of the greatest works of Matisse's last years.   4

Although the church was on top of a hill, we nearly missed it because it was small. There was a small wooden sign on a fence which only said, "Chapelle décorée par Matisse." I was just a little disappointed. While we were standing at the entrance, two sisters invited us to come in. The door was opened.   5

At first, I could see stained glass in front of me. It was at the corner of the white stairs leading to the chapel. It was the simplest glass I have ever seen. The color was only white and blue, and the motif was a dolphin and a star, which a child might draw. It was so lovely that it made me smile. We went down the stairs and came into the chapel.   6

Chapel? I was surprised by the warm atmosphere and the light coming through two big stained-glass windows. I have never seen such a bright chapel. There was no confession room, authoritarianism, or heavy atmosphere. It was small, like one room of a kindergarten. We could be children in this room. Sunshine through the stained glass dyed the white floor yellow, green, and blue. The design of the glass was some kind of plant or seaweed. But I felt that they were flowers of joy.   7

There were three walls covered with white ceramic tiles on which Matisse had drawn three scenes using only black lines. One was a big priest wearing a cape. Another was flowers and the Virgin Mary embracing a baby. The third one was the scene of the Resurrection. What simple and genuine pictures! I was struck by a strong emotion. Although I am not a Christian, the pictures spoke to the deepest place in my heart. They showed me that I must be a child in front of God and I must enjoy my happiness. I cried in my mind sitting in the small chair in the beautiful church. At that time a candle of my heart was lighted.   8

My husband and I strolled along the beach that evening. The sky was sensitive orange, like a picture by an impressionist painter. The sea was like a piece of golden cloth. I felt the warmth through the arm of my husband. I was pleased that I had found a new horizon. For years I had been a person lacking in moral courage. I had been afraid of making my heart uncovered. I had forgotten the smile of children. But now I could truly enjoy the air of southern France, because I could return to the genuine child in front of great beauty. I closed my eyes and breathed deeply. At that time I saw the flowers of joy drawn by Matisse shimmering on the golden waves of my mind.   9

Personal Connections

1. Have you ever visited a place that made a very strong impression on you, as the chapel did on this student?

2. In paragraph 2, Masaki says, "I had been a kind of pessimist since my aunt's death ten years before." Do you consider yourself an optimist or a pessimist? Can you explain why?

Content and Writing Techniques

1. In this essay, which describes the work of a well-known artist, Masaki uses words to create visual images, almost like painting with words. Underline three visual images that you find in this essay. How do they relate to the ideas being expressed? Do they add to your enjoyment of the essay?

2. Sometimes writers describe a turning point, which marks a major change of some kind. What, in your opinion, is the turning point of this essay?

3. In paragraphs 6–9, find as many references to children as you can. How do these references relate to Masaki's main idea? Why do you think she repeated this idea so often?

4. Reread the last paragraph of the essay. What part of this paragraph do you like the most? Can you explain why?

ACTIVITIES

Before you decide on a particular place to write about, it is helpful to do some activities in which you focus on description.

THE CAREFUL OBSERVER

In this activity you will go to a place with your class or with a partner and write while you are there. Select a nearby place such as the college cafeteria or a local park. Plan to spend about thirty minutes on this activity.

1. Choose a partner from your class to work with, and take along a notebook and pen.

2. Once you have arrived at the place, find a comfortable spot to sit or stand near your partner. Observe carefully for five minutes; think about what makes this place different from other places.

3. Now freewrite for ten minutes. Say as much as you can about this particular place. You will probably notice what the place looks like, but do not ignore the other senses: smell, hearing, touch, and taste.

4. After you have finished writing, rest for a minute. Then exchange notebooks and read what your partner has written. Discuss how your observations were similar and different.

Reactions

At the next class meeting, compare notes with other students. Work in small groups of three or four students. It is not necessary to be in the same group with your partner. Have each student read his or her freewriting out loud. After everyone has had a chance to read, discuss these questions:

- Which description was the most interesting to you? Why?
- If you had never visited this place, which description would have given you the clearest picture of what it was like?
- Working as a group, can you find examples of specific details that appeal to each of the five senses?

Examples

To practice responding, read the freewriting done by two students who were partners for this activity:

Central Park

by Elsa McAdams, Haiti

Here I am, sitting on the thick green grass in the middle of the "East Green" part of Central Park, enjoying the warm caress of the afternoon sun. I look around, observing people, their gestures, the way they talk, laugh, express themselves. This is one of my favorite hobbies that I practice everywhere and at any time: on the subway, the bus, on the streets, in restaurants, in class, and in the park. 1

Right now I am looking at two ladies sunning themselves and conversing with each other. They both have very blond and probably dyed hair. It makes me wonder what kind of people hang around the park at this time of day. Obviously people who can allow themselves breaks of this kind, maybe wealthy people. 2

And my thoughts drift back to the fact that this is a beautiful afternoon and the weather is so agreeable. The sounds are cottony soft. I guess it is because of the nature surrounding me. 3

On my right, there is a group of boys playing a game of baseball, but it seems disorganized. Their supervisor tries to settle them down. The boys look excited and full of energy like children usually are: impulsive and very natural. 4

Now, one of the blond ladies gets up to talk with a little Asian girl. They try to talk to each other in French, my native language. I try to understand what they are saying. They introduce each other with the habitual salutations. I get bored and my eyes wander around and finally fix on the yellow flow of cars passing by. People living near this neighborhood don't use the subway. They take cabs. That's why there are a lot of those bright colored cars. 5

I love those hours spent in the park. 6

Central Park

by Sissi Cavadini, Switzerland

The park! Wow, the park! It's the very first time I have come to the 1
park this summer. And on top of it, it is summer, at least I feel it's summer. I
hope that no mosquitoes bite me. I hate mosquitoes. They always bite me.
It's the worst thing about summer. But the rest is great. I notice a fat woman
wearing a jumpsuit. A white jumpsuit for a fat woman is the worst. This
woman is trying to speak French. I don't know why, when I'm in New York,
it annoys me so much when I hear somebody speaking some European language. I always think they must be stupid. I don't give them any chance. I'm
sure I'm wrong. But this woman really looks stupid. She's doing exercise, but
she should eat less. . . .   While I was writing this, a little bug was crossing
my paper, and she was orange like the orange juice I wish I had here now. All
the others are looking at the boys playing baseball. I don't understand the
rules of baseball, but the boys are cute. They must be from some private or
special school.

Questions for Discussion

1. Which of these two descriptions do you like better? Can you explain
why?
2. Locate the following details in both descriptions:
   a. discussion of weather and season
   b. the French-speaking lady
   c. the boys playing baseball
3. How are these details handled differently in the two descriptions? What
do these differences tell you about the writers?

USING THE SENSES

When asked to write a description, student writers often rely almost entirely on
the sense of sight and ignore the other senses. Yet to describe a place vividly, you may
want to use information from the others as well. This activity requires you to use the
senses of touch, hearing, smell, or taste.

1. Think of a convenient place you would like to observe.
2. Go to the place. Be sure to take along a notebook and pen.
3. Find a comfortable spot to sit or stand.
4. Write down all the information that can be gathered using only the senses of
hearing, smell, touch, and taste. Do not use any information that you get from the
sense of sight. It might help you to close your eyes for a few minutes and then write
what you learned from the other senses.
5. Read over what you have written and add any new details that you think
of.

Reactions

At the next class meeting, share the results of this experiment with a group of three or four students by reading your notes aloud and discussing what you learned. Did you use your other senses more when you were not allowed to use the sense of sight? When you closed your eyes, did you notice things you might not have noticed with your eyes open?

Example

Read the following selection and notice how the other senses became more active when the student decided to close his eyes.

Subway

by Marco Beria, Colombia

I close my eyes trying to imagine that I am not here. I have no idea how many times I have been in the same awful train, reading the same ads, watching the most horrendous people and their routine attitudes. Today I believe that I have been doing it for centuries.   1

I open my eyes, noticing that I hate their smells. I hate the shocking perfume of an old woman because it is cheap and too strong. I hate the smell of the fresh-printed newspapers and the wet second-hand coats that people wear on rainy days.   2

I close my eyes and pretend that I'm sleeping because I don't know where to direct my eyes anymore. I'm tired of seeing what surrounds me inevitably on this daily trip to the city. Now everything is dark. I start experiencing a different sensation, the sound of the train. Its repetitious noise to which I have become addicted is methodical; I could say that it almost hypnotizes me. The time passes by and I feel that people are looking at me. I feel uncomfortable and finally I'm dying to see what's going on in the car.   3

When I open my eyes again, I realize that I have missed my stop.   4

Questions for Discussion

1. This selection creates a mood or attitude that some people have described as hostile or angry. Others say it is humorous. Which adjective do you think reflects the writer's mood: hostile or humorous? Explain your answer.

2. Beria uses many descriptive adjectives to convey his feelings about the people and things around him. Underline six adjectives that reveal his feelings.

A PLACE FROM THE PAST

The first two prewriting activities asked you to go to a place, observe, and then write about it. This activity asks you to describe a place clearly using only your memory of what that place was like.

1. Think of a place from your past that was important to you for some reason, such as a special place from your childhood, a work place, a place where you went with friends.

2. Make a brief list of details to describe the place, using these categories:

      sight   sound   smell   feelings

3. Show your list to a partner and talk about what this place was like.

4. Begin writing a description of the place. Try to express your feelings about the place by showing rather than telling what it was like. In other words, don't *tell* the readers that the place was "mysterious." Instead, *show* them by the details you include: "When I climbed down to the cool, moist ditch behind our house, it was like entering another world."

GRAMMAR IN CONTEXT

MAKING SUBJECTS AND VERBS AGREE

In English, as in many other languages, certain verbs have to "agree" with their subjects. To see how this works, fill in the blanks in the following chart with a common verb such as *play* or *sing*. Keep all the verbs in the present tense. For example, "I sing in the shower."

	Singular		*Plural*	
	Subject	*Verb*	*Subject*	*Verb*
First person	I	_____	we	_____
Second person	you	_____	you	_____
Third person	he, she, it	_____	they	_____

Which of the blanks had a different form of the verb? Now, try the same thing using the past tense of the same verb. Were any of the forms different?

If all went well, you should have discovered that only in the *third-person singular* and only in the *present tense* does the verb change by adding *-s*. (As an experiment, try filling in this same chart using subjects and verbs from your native language. Does this explain some of the problems you have in English?)

If you tend to have trouble with subject-verb agreement, remember that it is almost never correct to have an *-s* ending on both the subject and the verb. For example, it is correct to say "The girl plays" or "The girls play." But it is not correct to say, "The girl play" or "The girls plays."

Remember this basic rule: A verb should end in *-s* if, and only if (1) it is in the present tense, and (2) it has a singular subject that is not "I" or "you."

Activity

The following student description of the difference between snacks and meals uses the plural forms of these two words. To see what changes occur when the subject is singular, change the form to "a snack" or "a meal" wherever possible. Also change the pronouns that refer to snacks and meals to singular form. For example, in paragraph 2, you would write: "A snack is light food we eat between meals." And in paragraph 5, you would write: "A meal, on the other hand, is the more elaborate and serious way of eating." The goal of this activity is not to correct errors but rather to examine how English grammar works.

Snack/Meal

by Abu Tyeb Salleh

Food is essential to our lives. We spend an average of three hours each day eating; one-eighth of our lives is spent consuming food. Therefore, we "invented" two ways of enjoying it—snacks and meals. 1

Snacks are light food we eat between meals. They satisfy our craving for food and let us eat without having to sit at the table. They help us to exercise our jaws and yet let us enjoy the taste. Snacks need little or no preparation, and we can snack almost anywhere, any time, and in any mood. 2

You munch when you are on the bus. You munch when you are in the classroom; you munch when you are hungry; you munch when you are not; you munch when you are depressed; you munch when you are glad; you munch with your bunch of friends, but often you munch solitarily. 3

Snacks bring life to parties. They help to make the atmosphere happy and informal. Snacks are fast to eat, and you don't have to worry too much about manners. But in terms of nutritious value, your doctor and parents would advise you to minimize your consumption of snacks because they kill your appetite when you have to eat a meal. 4

Meals, on the other hand, are the more elaborate and serious way of eating. We are accustomed to eat two or three meals a day, and meals are the most impor- 5 tant source of energy we need for activities during the day. Their importance and nutritional value are therefore high.

You can skip snacks, but you can't skip meals. Because of their importance,   6 we tend to spend more time on meals, preparing and enjoying them. Meals can be romantic—candlelight dinners and breakfasts in bed are favorites among lovers. Meals also bring family members and friends around the table and create a warm, loving, cozy atmosphere. Meals are the more formal type of eating, and table manners are considered important. Meals, on the whole, should be taken seriously.

As we can see from the above, snacks and meals differ in the way of eating,   7 time consumed, emotional involvement, and nutritious value. But they both make the intake of food enjoyable. Although meals are considered more important, snacks are sometimes more fun.

(See Answer Key, pages 318–19.)

KNOWING WHEN TO ADD -ED TO THE VERB

Many students have trouble getting the proper endings on their verbs. One reason for this is that it is very difficult to hear these endings when we speak. Try repeating these two sentences to some friends and see if they can tell the difference:

The game will be play at eight o'clock.
The game will be play*ed* at eight o'clock.

While the difference between these two verb forms may seem small in speaking, it is viewed as a large difference in writing. Only the second sentence is considered correct in written English.

Understanding a few fairly simple rules can help to greatly reduce errors related to verb endings.

1. The most obvious reason for adding *-ed* to a verb is that the verb is in the past tense.[1]

Past tense: Yesterday I ask*ed* him to go.

---

[1]Remember that irregular verbs (such as *to write*) never add *-ed*. In situation 1 use the past tense form (*wrote*), and in situations 2, 3, and 4 use the past participle form (*written*). See pages 305–308 for a list of irregular verbs.

2. An *-ed* ending is also called for if the verb is in the present perfect or past perfect tense.

Present perfect: I have ask*ed* him to dinner many times, but he always refuses.

Past perfect: She married Carlos in 1995, but three years earlier I had ask*ed* her to marry me.

3. Sometimes *-ed* is added to a regular verb not because of its tense but because it is in the passive voice.

Passive voice: I was interview*ed* for that job.

4. Sometimes *-ed* endings are needed to change a verb into an adjective.[2]

Adjective form: Physics 350 is a very advanc*ed* course.

5. Some common expressions always end in *-ed*: accustom*ed* to, bas*ed* on, so-call*ed*, suppos*ed* to, and us*ed* to.

Activity

Read the following paragraphs taken from a student essay and underline all the *-ed* endings.

Goodbye to the High Tatras

by Jan Kalousek, Czechoslovakia

It was in January 1982 when I visited the High Tatras for the last time. The   1
High Tatras are mountains in Czechoslovakia. This region is one of the last pieces
of wild, unspoiled nature in Europe. From the age of fourteen I was a member of
the mountaineering club, and I used to visit these mountains every month. This
visit was my last farewell to the place I loved so deeply, because I knew that the
next month I would leave Czechoslovakia forever.

High in the mountains there is a place called "White Fall," where there is a   2

---

[2]It is often difficult to tell the difference between an adjective form and passive voice. Here is a trick that some teachers use to tell the difference: add *very* before the word in question. If it makes sense, the word is being used as an adjective. If it sounds strange, the verb is in the passive voice.

> *Example:* The student was [very] bor*ed*. (This makes sense, so *bored* is an adjective form.)
> She was [very] marri*ed* in 1989. (This sounds strange, so *married* is in the passive voice.)

hut used by mountain climbers. I had to walk eight hours to reach this place. The snow was deep, my rucksack was heavy, and I was alone and tired.

The weather was cold and windy, but I had expected it. I examined the hut closely. A couple of years ago there had been a fire and the hut had partly burned up. The roof had a lot of holes, and burned beams hung dangerously in the air. I searched inside for the best place to sleep and prepared my "bed" in one corner which was better protected than the others. It was gloomy inside the hut and I had to strain my eyes, especially when I cooked the soup.

Meanwhile, outside the visibility was getting poorer because of the clouds which appeared in the sky. It was getting colder and the first snowflakes started to fall. Soon the wind changed to a gale and the snowstorm began.

I went back to the hut. Snowflakes were whirling even there; rotten beams were creaking and squeaking. I went to sleep afraid, and I dreamed heavy, ugly dreams about avalanches and other disasters.

Activity

1. After you have finished underlining the *-ed* verb endings in the preceding story, choose a partner to work with.

2. Working with your partner, indicate *why* each *-ed* ending was used: (1) past tense, (2) present perfect or past perfect tense, (3) passive voice, (4) adjective form, or (5) common expressions that always end in *-ed*.

(See Answer Key, pages 319–20.)

USING ADJECTIVES FOR DESCRIPTIVE WRITING

Adjectives are words that are used to describe people, places, things, actions, or ideas. For example, in "My Garden" (pages 98–100) Suzanne Scherzer writes, "It was an immense garden." The word *immense* is an adjective describing the garden, telling us how big it was. The writer did not have to use the word *immense*. She could simply have said the garden was *big* or *large*. But the word *immense* tells her readers that they are seeing the garden through the eyes of an eight-year-old girl for whom this garden was her whole world. Scherzer needed a special word like *immense* to give her readers that sense of a child's-eye view.

Activity

Look at the following sentences or phrases taken from some of the essays in this chapter. Try to think of two or three other adjectives that might be used instead of the ones the writers have chosen. Then, with a partner or group, compare your adjectives with the ones chosen by the writers. Which ones do you like better? Can you explain why?

Example: It was an <u>immense</u> garden
                huge
                gigantic
                tremendous

1. From "My Garden" (paragraph 4): " . . . a colony of toads pressed in a corner of the wall. They resembled an <u>ugly</u>, dusty blob."

2. From "My Garden" (paragraph 5): "It was a pleasure to observe the <u>pretty</u> blossoms turn into ripe, delicious fruit."

3. From "*El Retorno*" (paragraph 2): "How I love this <u>tragic</u> valley of South Texas. . . . "

4. From "The Coldest Winter of Beijing" (paragraph 7): "Later Mao became the <u>great</u> dictator of China and remained in power until his death."

5. From "The Dream Land" (paragraph 5): "Sometimes their stories were <u>funny</u> and interesting. . . . "

COPING WITH ARTICLES

There are only three articles in the English language (*a*, *an*, and *the*). But students whose native language does not contain articles are often amazed by how much trouble these three little words can cause.

It may help you to remember some general rules. Choose *the* when you are referring to a particular thing—for example, "That is *the* best movie I have seen all year" (referring to a particular movie). Choose *a* or *an* when you are referring to a general thing—for example, "Tomorrow I may go to *a* movie" (meaning any movie; the speaker has not yet decided on a particular movie).

Deciding whether to use *a* or *an* is easy. Use *a* when the word that comes next begins with a consonant or consonant sound—for example, "a *peach*" or "a *union*." Use *an* when the next word starts with a vowel or vowel sound—for example, "an *apple*" or "an *hour*"; the reason for adding the *n* is simply to make the phrase easier to pronounce.

The best way to improve your use of articles is to do what American children do as they are learning the language: listen carefully to native speakers and notice where they use articles. Also pay attention to the use of articles as you read. It is a good idea to keep your own list of special expressions you want to remember; one student kept these on tiny cards that she flipped through while riding the bus to school.

Activity

Underline all the articles in this excerpt from student writing.

In contrast to my home in Japan, the place where I am staying now is a   1
house. Actually, I don't live in a house; I live in a building of the Salvation Army.
Although I don't have a kitchen, the place I rent has enough facilities to live in. I
have a closet, a desk, drawers, a bathroom, and a bed. They serve us meals and I
eat them with the other residents as if we were a family, but we are not. The bed
I sleep in every night is not my own. In my rented room I have never thought that
I am home. This feeling is like that of a homeless person who lives in a shelter but
does not think of it as a home.

Home is where I was born and where I grew up. Home is where I laughed   2
and cried. Home is warm, as if it were a living creature. On the other hand, a
house is cold and only a building.

Reactions

With a partner or small group, discuss the use of articles in the excerpt. Why
do you think an article was needed in each case? How did the writer know which of
the three articles to use?

Activity

Fill in each blank with the missing article—*a, an,* or *the*. Then discuss your
choices with a partner or small group. In some cases, both *a* and *the* may be correct.

_____ dictionary definition of "house" is _____ building to live   1
in, and _____ definition of "home" is _____ place where one lives. To
me, _____ house is _____ building made of pieces of wood and
_____ couple of bricks, but home has _____ lot of meanings to me.

When I am home, I feel so comfortable and relaxed. It is   2
_____ place where I spend most of my time, and also it is _____ place
where I learn things which build me up as _____ human being.

It is _____ important thing to have _____ building in which we   3
can build _____ home, because I think that without my home, I wouldn't

exist now. Also without _____ home, people would be like animals without _____ master. They would wander.

(See Answer Key, pages 320–21.)

Activity

Now write your own description of the difference between a house and a home. After you have finished, underline every article you used. Share your description with a partner, and discuss any problems you had with article use.

ASSIGNMENT

In this chapter you have been asked to observe, write, and talk about places, and you have read descriptions written by others. You may already know what place you want to describe in your essay. If you are still not sure, take some time now to think about the possibilities. Look back through this chapter and reread the writing you have done so far. The most important thing is to choose a place that is meaningful to you—a place that you care about.

The purpose of this essay is to describe the place so clearly that it seems real to the reader; you should also reveal your feelings about it. Imagine your readers to be interested classmates who have never visited the place you are describing.

SUGGESTED TECHNIQUES

Certain techniques that you observed in the readings and practiced in the activities in this chapter will help you to make your place seem real:

1. *Be a careful observer and recorder of details.* The secret to describing a place vividly is to include significant details that will help the readers to re-create the place in their own minds. For example, in the first paragraph of "Waiting Room," Hypatia Foster tells us how she begins her morning at work: she drinks her coffee "regular, no sugar," and then puts on "a light blue scrub suit with white lab coat and white shoes." Foster's careful choice of details helps us to feel present at the scene.

If possible, plan to revisit the place you will be describing. Take a notebook and pen and write down your observations. If an actual visit is out of the question, revisit the place for a few minutes in your imagination. Close your eyes and pretend you are there. Then write down all the ideas that came into your mind. Refer to this list as you are writing the first draft.

2. *Use information from the five senses.* Think about how the writers featured in this chapter made the places they were describing seem real. One important technique was the effective use of sensory details. For example, Jian Wei appeals to the reader's sense of feeling when he writes, "A shiver ran over my body. There was a nip in the air." Eun Soon Park appeals to the sense of sight when she states, "Every tree changed its color with the seasons, but the fence, which was made up of evergreen trees, remained green throughout the year."

Before you begin your essay, take a few minutes to list the possible sensory details you could include. Write down as many things as you can think of, and keep this list nearby while you are working on the first draft.

3. *Try to convey the mood or atmosphere of the place.* By the words they use and the details they include, writers can evoke a particular atmosphere. The place may be cold and impersonal like the abortion clinic described by Hypatia Foster or warm and peaceful like the chapel described by Sumiko Masaki.

Is the place you are describing happy or sad, peaceful or tense? Think about how you will create this impression in the reader's mind.

4. *Try to express why this place is important to you.* This does not mean that you should tell the reader directly by saying, "I chose to write about this place because . . . " But it does mean that after reading the essay, the reader should understand why it was important for you to write about this place.

For example, Eun Soon Park links her childhood home in Korea with memories of her warm and loving family. Sumiko Masaki wrote about the chapel decorated by Matisse because her visit marked an important change in her outlook on life.

After you have completed your first draft, choose a partner to work with, exchange papers, and fill out the Peer Response Sheet located at the end of this chapter. If you choose to continue working on your essay, refer to Part III: Rethinking/Rewriting for suggestions about revising and editing.

PEER RESPONSE SHEET:
WRITING ABOUT PLACES

Writer's Name: _____

Reader's Name: _____

Date: _____

(*Note to the reader:* As you respond to the writer's draft, try to focus on the ideas rather than the grammar and spelling. Discuss only those mistakes that interfere with understanding.)

1. What did you like best about this paper? _____

_____

_____

_____

2. Did the writer describe the place clearly? List any parts that were not clear to

you. _____

_____

_____

_____

3. Did the writer appeal to the different senses? List two sensory details that you

especially liked. _____

_____

_____

_____

4. How would you describe the mood or the atmosphere of this place? _____

_____

_____

_____

5. Why do you think the writer chose to write about this place? _____

_____

_____

_____

_____

6. How could the writer improve this paper when he or she rewrites it? Make only *one* suggestion. _____

_____

_____

_____

_____

INTERIM PROGRESS REPORT:
A MIDTERM SURVEY

Instructions: As you finish your work in the chapters on personal writing, it is an appropriate time to think about the progress you have made so far and your goals for the rest of the course. Before answering the questions, please review your responses on the Beginning Survey. Save both surveys so that you can refer to them at the end of the course.

1. How satisfied are you with the course as it has been presented so far?

Very   Somewhat   Not
Satisfied   Satisfied   Satisfied

Explain: _____

_____

_____

_____

_____

2. What activity has been the most helpful for you? (Some possible answers might be small group discussions, freewriting, reading, peer conferences, rewriting essays.) Identify the activity and explain *why you think it has helped you.*

_____

_____

_____

_____

_____

3. What activity has been the least helpful? Can you explain why it did not help you?

_____

_____

_____

_____

_____

4. Go through your writing folder and check to see if you have done all the writing assignments so far. If you are missing any, write down the date(s) when you expect to hand them in.

_____

_____

_____

_____

5. Which of the essays that you have written so far do you feel is your best one? How did you get the idea for this paper? Did you write more than one draft? If so, how many?

   What do you think the strong points of your paper are? What parts could use more work? Did you enjoy writing this paper? Why or why not?

_____

_____

_____

_____

6. Have you noticed any changes in your attitude toward writing since the beginning of this course? If so, explain.

_____

_____

_____

_____

More Formal Writing

When deciding what to wear to a party, most people try to choose an outfit that is appropriate for the occasion. For example, you would not wear shorts and a T-shirt to a formal wedding or a dress suit to a picnic.

With writing, it is also important to consider the occasion. The writing you do for a love letter is different in style and content from a paper for an economics class. Even within academic settings, there can be a wide range of opinion on what is appropriate and acceptable. Some professors like and encourage students to write about their own experiences and feelings. Others prefer facts and analyses of texts; they may not even want to see the word *I* in an essay.

While we value and enjoy personal writing, such as the essays presented in the previous three chapters, we also understand that the style and form of these essays may not be appropriate for all writing contexts. That is why in the following chapters we present essays and activities that will help you take advantage of the skills and knowledge you already have and apply these to more formal types of writing. Such writing might include a science report in which you explain the results of an experiment you conducted, an essay for a literature class in which you analyze the theme of a novel, or a research paper for a history course in which you compare the causes of U.S. involvement in the Korean and Vietnam wars.

The readings in these chapters include both personal and more formal essays. We include the personal essays to show how people often become concerned about a cultural or social issue because they have had some personal experience with it. For instance, the experience of meeting a homeless person on the street can be the beginning of an essay analyzing the causes of homelessness. The story about the changes in a student's family after moving to the United States can form the basis of an essay about cultural differences. Your essays are likely to be more interesting to your reader, and to *you*, if you feel personally involved with your subject.

What changes as you move from personal to more formal writing is not so much the skills needed or the subject matter, but your approach to the subject matter. You may write about some of the same experiences, people, and places you wrote about in earlier chapters, but now you will be concerned not only with your own personal reactions, but with how these reactions can be linked to broader subjects. You may need to gather information beyond your own experience by reading, interviewing others, or doing library research.

We have found that most students feel more "at home" when writing in personal contexts. This makes sense because personal writing such as letters, journal entries, and autobiographical essays, in many ways, resembles conversations. When you ask your mother to make spaghetti for dinner, you do not need to give her three reasons why you want it. You may not have to give any reasons at all. That is because you and your mother already share much common knowledge that does not need to be explained—that you like spaghetti, that you always eat spaghetti on Thursdays, and so on. But if you are writing an essay explaining the nutritional value of pasta, you will have to present your information in a different way. You cannot assume that the reader knows everything that you have learned about the subject. Your role shifts from that of a storyteller to that of a teacher; you have to demonstrate what you know rather than how you feel.

As you work in these chapters, we hope that you will discover new ways of exploring your ideas and exchanging them with others in the academic community.

7
Learning From Others:
Interviewing

In a sense, all of us have been interviewing other people ever since we learned to talk. In every conversation with a friend, there is the natural give-and-take of questions being asked and answered. When we interview someone as part of a writing assignment, it may feel more formal, but the process is essentially the same.

However, the purpose of an interview is quite different from that of an ordinary conversation. Its goal is to gather material to reflect on and possibly write about later. For instance, you may not have realized that your grandmother has fascinating stories to tell about life in old China or that your uncle remembers the assassination of the dictator of the Dominican Republic in 1961.

The assignment for this chapter asks you to conduct an interview and later to write an essay in which you make generalizations about what you have learned. As in most formal writing situations, you are expected to support your generalizations with specific evidence — in this case, material from the interview.

As you read the essays that follow and begin to do some interviews of your own, we hope that you will discover how much you can learn by listening to the people around you.

READINGS: LIFE-HISTORY INTERVIEWS

What does the word *history* mean to you? One response might be "the famous events of the past that we study in history class." But another answer, and an equally valid one, is "the stories that surround us." In order to become a permanent part of history, of course, these stories must be preserved in some way. Usually this means writing them down.

In the following selections you will learn about a woman who lived in a poor, rural area of Puerto Rico, a man who left China during World War II, and a migrant worker in the United States. By reading about ordinary people such as these, we also learn about the history of their time and place.

Interview with My Grandmother
by Eleonor Maldonado

Eleonor Maldonado, a student from Puerto Rico, decided to interview her grandmother, Mercedes Rojas. Later she translated the interview from Spanish into English. What follows is a transcript of the highlights of this interview. As you will soon discover, the grandmother is a gifted storyteller. Do you know someone who loves to tell stories? If so, would it be possible for you to interview this person?

Question: Grandma, can you describe your childhood in the village?

Answer: Look, Granddaughter, those were dog days. We were living in a small shack built of straw and bamboo sticks. During the day the rain and the sun rays filtered throughout the many holes in the walls and ceiling and at night we fell asleep counting the stars and praying to God for a pleasant night without rain. Also we didn't have beds. My mother slept in a hammock and my sister and I every night made a bed out of burlap sacks filled with straw. There was also no running water or toilet. The water was carried in a tin can from a nearby well, and the biological necessities were done under some bushes near the house.

Q: Who helped your mother to support the family?

A: My mother was the only breadwinner of the family so she worked on a farm picking sweet potatoes all day and at night spent many hours weaving "Panama hats." Each Saturday morning Don Thomas, our neighbor, would take the hats to sell them at the nearby town, and with the money received he would bring us some groceries and once in a while, especially for Christmas or during the town's feasts, a piece of cloth for making dresses, a box of Pompeii face powder, or a small bottle of Evening in Paris perfume. Our diet consisted of sweet potatoes, corn meal, and dried cod fish. A half pound of coffee was blended with other toasted grains so there was enough coffee for the whole week. Meat we ate only at Christmas time, when the owner of the farm for whom my mother was working killed a pig and gave us a piece.

Q: Grandma, at what age did you get married?

A: I think I was fourteen years old when I met your grandfather. He was a very handsome Spaniard who was well known for being a good dancer. He was also very poor and at an early age started to work in the field to help his mother raise three brothers and two sisters after his father's death. He also didn't have the opportunity to go to school so his life was a continuous struggle. A year later we got married, and while he was working in the field cutting sugar cane, I was home taking care of a few domestic animals.

Q: How many children did you have?

A: Oh, please, I don't know how to count as I didn't have the opportunity to go to school, but my oldest son said that I have eighteen alive and a couple of what people called miscarriages.

Q: When a woman was giving birth to a child at that time, what was the preparation for the event?

A: Oh, girl, I don't even want to talk about that, but I will try to please you. When the woman was pregnant, she would ask the neighbors to bring her some pieces of old clothes to use as diapers. During pregnancy the woman worked in the field or in the house but never went to a doctor for a checkup. When it was the time for delivery, a midwife was called, and the woman was asked to be seated on a round piece of wood. That wood was a mold used to give the hat its shape, and whenever the woman had a contraction she would pull from a piece of rope which was attached to the ceiling. The woman was in that position sometimes for two days or up to delivery time. Then when the baby was born, the umbilical cord was cut with a pair of regular scissors and the baby was bathed with aromatic oil. Chicken broth was given to the mother and she was asked to stay in bed for forty days. I never had the chance to stay in bed all that time because your grandfather was too demanding. I had to take care of the animals, the children, and also do the house chores.

Q: Grandma, I would like to ask you something else. How do you compare the life you have today with the one you had years ago?

A: Oh my God, today I feel like a rich person. I have a house with electricity and running water. Also I have a toilet in the house. Quite a few dresses and shoes and a Social Security check. I don't have to worry about anything but still I would like to know how to sign my name instead of making a cross symbol every time I have to sign my name.

Personal Connections

1. From this interview it is clear that Maldonado's grandmother lived much of her life in poverty but that she was a very strong person. How do you think poverty affects people? Does it make them give up or cause them to fight for a better way of life?

2. The grandmother is obviously an extremely intelligent woman. Yet at the end of the interview, she mentions that she still does not know how to sign her name. Do you know an older person who has not had much education but is very intelligent? Write your own definitions of the words *education* and *wisdom*. Is it possible to have one without the other?

Content and Writing Techniques

1. Look at the beginning of the interview. List the details you find that show that Mercedes came from a poor family.

2. Find parts of the interview that show the following aspects of Mercedes' character:
   a. pride
   b. strength
   c. wisdom
   d. happiness

A Reward from Buddha
by Zhong Chen

> *The life-history assignment gave Zhong Chen, a student from China, an opportunity to have a long conversation with a respected member of his family, his ninety-two-year-old great-uncle. Before you read, think about the elders in your own family. Is there an older relative you would like to interview?*

Entering this traditional living room furnished with old-fashioned Chinese furniture, such as a redwood sofa and chairs decorated with colorful shells, I seemed to come back to my hometown and couldn't help feeling comfortable. I looked at the bleached wall on which some Chinese calligraphy and old photographs were hung. This apartment, located in Manhattan, is the home of my great-uncle, who emigrated to the United States forty-eight years ago during World War II. Now he is ninety-two years old. 1

In order not to disturb my uncle's afternoon nap, I walked to the window over the plush carpet in silence. As I looked out through the soft white curtains, I noticed the contrast between this peaceful Chinese room and the noisy American street eleven floors below. It made me curious about my uncle's extraordinary experience—about his life in China, his immigration to America, and how he dealt with the contrast between the two countries. 2

"Oh, Zhong Zhong (my nickname), I am really glad to see you," my uncle said with strong dialect as he walked briskly out of his bedroom. "Have you been here long?" 3

"I didn't want to bother you. Did you have a nice nap?" 4

"Just like every day. Now my life has become nonsense without working and challenge. Have a seat!" 5

We sat down. With a distinctive movement, he took an old wood frame from the center of the shelf and began to wipe off imaginary dust. In the frame there was a precious certificate praising his service in the American Navy during World War II. 6

"Why do you emphasize this certificate so much?" I asked. 7

"Actually, I never got any certificate in my life except this one. You know, I didn't receive any formal education. Even though I can't understand each word in this certificate, I know its real meaning," he said, and then looked around the room. Compared with the small house of his childhood, the room was like a paradise. 8

He began to remember. My great-uncle was born in a small village in 1902. At that time, China was still ruled by the Qing Dynasty. Most of the people suffered from poverty caused by constant civil war, especially in the underdeveloped remote countryside, where my great-uncle lived. As a result, he had to struggle for food and clothes in order to survive. 9

During his childhood, he lived with his parents, two brothers, and three sisters in a small wood house with no windows, which was on the verge of collapse. They all depended on their father's low salary and frequently had to endure hunger. 10

My great-uncle never owned any toys. Instead, he had to play with mud. When he was seven years old, he should have started school, but there was no 11 school in his village, and his parents couldn't afford to send him away to a nearby village to study.

He remembered it sadly: "At that time I was very anxious to go to school, but I couldn't. When I saw my friends carrying their book bags, I envied them and said, 'Ah, so you must study hard now, really study hard since you have the opportunity.' " 12

At age nine, my great-uncle was already regarded as a man because his father had died of disease, and his mother couldn't manage alone. As the eldest son, my great-uncle had to find a job to support the family. Finally he found work as an apprentice in a tobacco store. His job was to polish approximately two hundred pipes every day. It was such hard work for a nine-year-old boy that his fingers were swollen day and night. Still, he didn't give up. On the contrary, he was delighted that he could earn nearly ten yuan a month to support his poor family. 13

"Hard work can create a better life," he often says. "The more you work, the more you gain." 14

When my great-uncle became a teenager, he began to worry about his future. Poverty and painful experience had made him decide to be a successful man who depended only on himself. Having worked at a boring job for three years, he realized he could learn nothing more in the tobacco store. He didn't want to spend his whole life there. He hoped to leave the small village and explore the outside world. Finally he decided to go to the modern city to learn a skill. However, he didn't have enough money. At his mother's urging, he swallowed his pride and asked for his uncle's help. His uncle, a wealthy merchant in their village, had scorned his father many years ago. Afterward, they didn't communicate any more. 15

"When I went to his house to ask for help, he showed his scowling face and refused me without mercy," my great-uncle said. "At that time, I realized that the only one who could help me was myself." His words impressed me. Even though he was an old man, what he said was full of energy and vitality. 16

Before long, he found a job in a shipping company. Although it was hard work, he was excited to be a sailor and learned a lot working on domestic cruise ships. But soon World War II broke out, and he was hired by an American shipping company that transported weapons all over the world. His family advised him not to accept this dangerous job. Nevertheless, he refused to give up the opportunity. 17

On the ship, he began to learn English from Americans. "I just tried my best and memorized every word they told me. For example, when they pointed to a chair, I would keep repeating *chair, chair.*" Gradually, he was able to talk with Americans freely. 18

I was interested in his experience in the war: "Were you ever afraid?" 19

"Generally not. But one night in Denmark, more than ten bombers attacked the port. Flames brightened the whole sky. We just sat in the dark cabin and kept silent. I prayed for Buddha to bless me. Eventually we were lucky to escape. I think my life was a reward from Buddha." 20

After World War II, my great-uncle arrived in the United States and made up his mind to stay. "I began to love this country the first time I saw her." 21

Because he had served in the American Navy, he was naturalized as a U.S. citizen. In New York City, he began his new American life working as a chef in a Chinese restaurant. In contrast to his previous job, this one seemed easier. Ten 22 years later, he opened his own restaurant and began to earn a lot of money. He was completely satisfied with his life in America.

"Do you think of yourself as an American or a Chinese?" I asked. "Me? I think   23
I'm a Chinese," he answered with hesitation. "Although I have lived in America for a long time, there are all Chinese thoughts in my deep mind after all. To this day, I still keep the Chinese lifestyle and customs. As soon as you see this room, you can feel it, right? And, I was honest and loyal when I communicated with other people here. I made a great effort to show how a Chinese immigrant should be."

We had talked for more than two hours. It was already dusk outside. I   24
looked out the window. The sun was starting to set, though the sunshine was still dazzling and splendid.

Personal Connections

1. Do you know anyone who, like Chen's great-uncle, has lived for long periods of time in two different cultures? Would you describe this person as monocultural (mainly influenced by one culture) or bicultural (strongly influenced by both cultures)?

2. Who is the oldest living member of your family? Think of a story you know about this person and write it down quickly. Could you expand this story into a longer essay?

3. In paragraph 6, the great-uncle proudly displays the certificate he received for serving in the U.S. Navy during World War II. What object in your own life are you most proud of? Can you explain why?

Content and Writing Techniques

1. Write down one word that you think best describes the great-uncle's character. Then reread the essay, and underline every part that reminds you of your word. Compare your word and supporting evidence with a partner or small group.

2. What does the title "Reward from Buddha" mean to you? Do you think the great-uncle really believes that his success was a reward from some powerful force outside himself? Or do you think he believes that he earned his success through his own hard work? Underline parts of the essay that support your opinion.

3. Although Chen has included quite a few direct quotations in this essay, they represent only a small part of the entire two-hour conversation. Underline one direct quotation that you feel is especially effective. Discuss your quotation with a small group. Based on your group's selections, what are some of the characteristics of good quotations?

4. Reread the last paragraph of the essay. Circle any words you don't know and look them up in the dictionary. Do you think the meaning of this conclusion is strictly literal (based on the explicit meaning of the words). Or does the meaning exist on a symbolic level also (representing something else as well as the literal meaning)? If you think there is a symbolic meaning, what could it be?

From *Uprooted Children*
by Robert Coles

In this excerpt from his book Uprooted Children, *the well-known child psychiatrist Robert Coles talks with migrant farm workers about their children's lives. As the selection begins, Coles is listing the "facts of life" as one mother explains them to her children. What do you know about the lives of migrant workers in the United States or in your native country?*

She tells them that no, there aren't any second helpings; no, we don't dress the way those people do, walking on that sidewalk; no, we can't live in a house like that; no, we can't live in any one house, period; no, we can't stay, however nice it is here, however much you want to stay, however much it would help everyone if we did; and no, there isn't much we can do, to stop the pain, or make things more comfortable or give life a little softness, a little excitement, a little humor and richness. 1

Still, the children find that excitement or humor, if not the softness and richness; to the surprise of their parents they make do, they improvise, they make the best of a bad lot and do things—with sticks and stones, with cattails, with leaves, with a few of the vegetables their parents pick, with mud and sand and wild flowers. They build the only world they can, not with blocks and wagons and cars and balloons and railroad tracks, but with the earth, the earth whose products their parents harvest, the earth whose products become, for those particular children, toys, weapons, things of a moment's joy. "They have their good times, I know that," says a mother, "and sometimes I say to myself that if only it could last forever; but it can't, I know. Soon they'll be on their knees like me, and it won't be fun no more, no it won't." 2

The "soon" that she mentioned is not figured out in years, months or weeks. In fact, migrant children learn to live by the sun and the moon, by day and by night, by a rhythm that has little connection with hours and minutes and seconds. There are no clocks around, nor calendars. Today is not this day of this month, nor do the years get mentioned. The child does not hear that it is so-and-so time—time to do one or another thing. Even Sundays seem to come naturally, as if from Heaven; and during the height of the harvest season they, too, go unobserved. As a matter of fact, the arrival of Sunday, its recognition and its observance, can be a striking thing to see and hear: "I never know what day it is—what difference does it make?—but it gets in my bones that it's Sunday. Well, to be honest, we let each other know, and there's the minister, he's the one who keeps his eye on the days, and waits until the day before Sunday, and then he'll go and let one of us know that tomorrow we should try to stop, even if it's just for a few hours, and pray and ask God to smile down on us and make it better for us, later on up there, if not down here. . . ." 3

Does she actually forget the days, or not know them, by name or number or whatever? No, she "kind of keeps track" and "yes, I know if it's around Monday or Tuesday, or if it's getting to be Saturday." She went to school, on and off, for three or 4 four years, and she is proud that she knows how to sign her name, though she hasn't done it often, and she is ashamed to do it when anyone is watching. Yet, for her children she wants a different kind of education, even as she doubts that her desires will be fulfilled: "I'd like them all, my five kids, to learn everything there is to be learned in the world. I'd like for them to read books and to write as much as they can, and to count way up to the big numbers. I'd like for them to finish with their schooling. I tell them that the only way they'll ever do better than us, their daddy and me, is to get all the learning they can. But it's hard, you know, it's very hard, because we have to keep going along. There's always a farm up the road that needs some picking, and right away; and if we stay still, we'll soon have none of us, because there won't be a thing to eat, and we'll just go down and down until we're all bones and no flesh—that's what my daddy used to tell me might happen to us one day, and that's what I have to tell my kids, too. Then, they'll ask you why is it that the other kids, they just stay and stay and never move, and why is it that we have to move, and I don't hardly know what to say, then, so I tells them that they mustn't ask those questions, because there's no answer to them. And then the kids, they'll soon be laughing, and they'll come over and tell me that they're real glad that we keep going up the road, and to the next place, because they get to see everything in the world, and those other kids—well, they're just stuck there in the same old place."

Personal Connections

1. In paragraph 4, Coles quotes the migrant woman as saying that she hopes her children will get a good education even though she herself was not able to go far in school. Many parents share this hope that their children will get a better education and have a better job than they did. Freewrite about your own reaction to this desire. Do you think the mother's wishes will come true? Why or why not?

2. The migrant workers interviewed by Robert Coles have a very low status in American society. Yet they perform an essential service by harvesting the food that the rest of us eat. Why, in your opinion, are some types of work less respected than others? Think of a worker you have known who held a low-status job. Why do you think this particular job was low in status?

Content and Writing Techniques

1. Why do you think that Coles does not identify the people he is interviewing by name?

2. In paragraph 2, Coles tells how the children of migrant workers often manage to have fun in spite of their poverty. Divide a piece of paper into two columns and list the advantages and disadvantages of a migrant's life from a child's point of view.

3. Paragraph 4 contains a very long quotation from one of the migrant workers. Carefully reread this quotation. What things do you notice about the woman's speech that are different from standard English? Why do you think Coles decided not to correct the grammar of her speech?

READINGS: TOPICAL INTERVIEWS

Sometimes students prefer to focus their interviews on a topic rather than a person. If you are interested in what it's like to live through a war or revolution, you may want to interview someone who has had this experience. Or perhaps you're interested in a particular career and would like to find out more about it by interviewing a person who works in that field. Interviews provide a natural way of getting more information on topics of interest.

As you read the next three essays, think of topics you would like to know more about. How could you use interviewing to gather information?

Unfinished Interview
by Tatyana Dyachenko

Tatyana Dyachenko, a student from the former Soviet Union, had always wanted to know more about her mother's experiences as a child during World War II. An interview provided the chance for Dyachenko to ask about her mother's painful childhood, a conversation that led to a deeper understanding of her mother's character and values.

All my conscious life I remember my mother as working: knitting, embroidering, or sewing. She could do several jobs at the same time. Her hands—always busy. Her eyes—always slipping around for "what else to do." 1

At the time I visited her for an interview, she was busy as always. First of all, she asked me her usual question: "Have you already had your breakfast?" (or dinner, or lunch, depending on the time of day). This question always has opened each of our meetings. And it doesn't matter whether the answer is yes or no, she'll serve me a meal. The most important thing for my mother is to keep her children satisfied. 2

When she put everything on the table, I asked her to sit down and said, "I'm going to interview you." She laughed. "Me? I'm not a movie star." Then I said, "Mom, I need your help. I'm going to write an essay." She asked, "What's it about?" I answered that I was going to write an essay about her life. My mother said, "I'm not a famous person. There is nothing to write about me." "I'll try to find something," I said. "You just sit down, please, for twenty minutes." 3

The first question I asked was about her childhood. My mother was born in 1930, in the city of Kiev. Her childhood was very short because of World War II. When the war started, she was ten years old. Her father was killed at the beginning of the war; her mother died from starvation in Bukhara, Uzbekistan, where the family was evacuated. And my mother was left with her four-year-old sister. In her ten years, life had turned her into an adult person; she became the mother for her sister. 4

Then they were evacuated to Irkutsk, Siberia. When I asked her how two lit- 5 tle girls could survive in the severe conditions of that land, my mother refused to answer this question. She said, "My children don't have to know anything like this." She stood up and began to clean the table. "Twenty minutes haven't passed yet," I said. "Could you sit down, please, and tell me more about the war in your life." But the answer she shouted was sharp: "That's all about it."

I knew she wouldn't say anything more, but I tried again. "OK, answer me, please, the last question. What was most terrifying for you during the war? You were only ten years old. I mean, were you afraid of bombs exploding, or were you afraid of death around you?" I was surprised by her answer. She said that she wasn't afraid of explosions or death, fires or cries. When my mother saw my astonished eyes, she explained, "It wasn't because I was a brave girl, but because when you see tragedy, horror, and ruin, death and tears all around you every day, every hour, you get accustomed to these awful things. It is terrible, but it is true. But, of course, there was one thing that I was afraid of most of all." "What was that?" My mother read this question in my eyes. She looked at me (I was finished eating her homemade cookies and drinking some tea) and said, "Starvation." I froze with an open mouth, unable to swallow the bite of cookie. My mother continued, "I experienced the terrible feeling of starvation. There was nothing to eat. I wanted to eat all the time. I wanted to eat when I went to sleep and when I got up. I woke up at night because I wanted to eat. I got crazy from it. When I'd found something to eat, I gave it to my little sister." Here, my mother saw my expression (still with a piece of cookie that stuck in my throat) and cried to me, "How many times have I told you, don't ask me questions about it! My children do not have to know these things!" And she went to the living room. 6

I understood that she wouldn't say anything more. My interview wasn't finished, but I knew that was the end. My mother was already knitting in the living room. She always knits when she gets nervous because it calms her down. I stayed in the kitchen. Suddenly I recollected one thing from my childhood. Like most children, I very often whined about meals: "I don't want to eat. I'm not hungry." But my mother would say, "You'll eat everything that I give you. There is no question about it!" Sometimes I sat at the table for one hour or more to eat my meal, which became cold and not tasty. But my mother wouldn't let me go until I finished. I cried and ate my meal with my tears. And now, in the kitchen, I learned in less than twenty minutes, that it was because somewhere, in the past, my dear mother cried and ate just her tears without any meal. I understood why every time we meet or call each other, her first question is "Have you already eaten something today?" 7

It is impossible to write about a person's life in a few pages. Just one episode of my mother's life took several pages. Of course, she has a lot to tell, but she doesn't like to talk about herself. I just want to add that my mother tried to build all her castles in the air for her children, my brother and me. When I look at her rough, overworked hands, I understand why my hands are soft and smooth. When I look at her wrinkled face, I understand why I look young. She found her happiness in her children's lives, and I will try not to let her down. I'll try to be happy for her and for me. 8

When I was about to leave that day, I asked my mother the last question, "What do you want most of all?" She said, "To see my children smiling, happy, and never knowing what war is." We kissed goodbye and I went home.

Personal Connections

1. Do you know anyone who has lived in a country that was at war? If so, ask if he or she would be willing to talk about what it was like. Freewrite about what you learned.

2. In this essay, Dyachenko explains how she grew to understand her mother's behavior better as a result of this interview. Think about your own parents. Is there anything about their behavior that you didn't understand when you were a child but have come to understand now that you are older?

Content and Writing Techniques

1. Dyachenko includes many details related to eating or food. Go through the essay and underline all the parts that refer to food. Why do you think she included so many of these references?

2. In essays for U.S. schools and colleges, writers are expected to introduce direct quotations with their own words, as Dyachenko does in paragraph 2: "First of all, [my mother] asked me her usual question: 'Have you already had your breakfast?'" Reread paragraphs 3 through 6 and underline three places where Dyachenko introduces a quotation with her own words. Working with a partner or small group, write down several other ways that Dyachenko could have introduced the same quotations. Discuss which ways you like the best.

3. Write one sentence that describes the overall meaning of this essay. Then write one word that sums up the meaning of your sentence. Discuss your sentence and word with your partner, group, or class.

My First Interview
by Larisa Zubataya

In this essay a student from the former Soviet Union investigates a subject of great interest to her personally — prejudice against people of other racial or ethnic groups. As a Jew, Zubataya had experienced discrimination in her native country, and she was eager to learn more about the position of Jews in the United States. This conversation with an American-born Jew gave her the chance to discover the answers to some of her questions.

I first met Irving in a happy, but at the same time, difficult period of my life. My family came to America from Russia, escaping from national prejudice against us as second-rate persons because we are Jews. We immigrated to a community where we could be accepted as equals. On the other hand, I experienced what Americans call "culture shock." I lost my ease of communication and my professional experience because we arrived in a society with a different language. I met

1

Irving and continued to see him every Sunday in the Jewish Center, where he works as a volunteer helping newcomers adapt to a new environment and understand their new country, its culture, and its citizens.

Fate presented me with another chance to meet Irving the next year. Accidentally, I met him in the computer laboratory at my college. This old man is enrolled in a special college program to learn about the computer.

I chose Irving for my interview because he is an American-born wise man. Thus, I could get sensible answers to my questions. I had experienced discrimination as a Jew in Russia, and I wanted to know an American's point of view on this problem.

I began my interview with a question that worries me: "What do you think about prejudice?" He replied, "I think that pre-judging people is an ignorant and horrible thing. One is not born with prejudice. It has to be learned. If children were taught from their early years to accept people of different colors, customs, and religions, the world would be a better place." I was listening to him, and I agreed with his position.

Prejudice is always dangerous if it is against people of a different color of skin, a different religion, or a different social status. I remember my dismay when I heard in a job interview in my former country: "This is not Israel! We cannot take a Jew to work in our research center!"

Irving's mother's family came from Riga in Russia in 1888 to find a better life in America. His father's family also came here in 1888; they came originally from Spain to England and then to South Carolina. Thus, Irving grew up, was educated, and worked in the United States. He grew up during the Great Depression and attended Brooklyn College at night for seven years while he worked during the day. He was a chemist for most of his life. He is the father of three children and has one granddaughter. Irving is an observant Jew and a supporter of Israel.

I asked Irving whether he had ever experienced discrimination or prejudice as an American Jew. He sighed, then answered me, "I experienced prejudice several times in my life, especially when applying for a job when someone of another religion told me of her misconceptions about Judaism. Fortunately, it was possible for me to change her negative viewpoint to a positive one."

Irving continued: "I feel fortunate to have been living as a Jew in America all my life. I have never been seriously discriminated against in college or in my profession." He added that he has always been very proud of his Jewish heritage, proud also of the great strides Jews have made in science, art, literature, and music. Although Jews in America are a very small part of the population, their achievements greatly outweigh their numbers.

I noticed a similar pattern in Russian society, where fewer than 1 percent are Jews, but a high proportion of Jews are scientists, engineers, and technicians. However, they are forced to hide their Jewishness. Jews cannot observe traditions in Russia. A circumcision was done for my fifteen-year-old son only here, in America. I expect that those prohibitions have influenced the Russian Jews' mentality. Thus, I asked, "Do you see a difference between American and Russian Jews?" He answered, "I see many differences between American and Russian Jews, and I believe that I know the reasons for these differences. I agree with you that in Russia

Jews are made to feel ashamed of the label 'zhid.'[1] Russian Jews know nothing about Jewish history. It was against the law to circumcise a male child or have a Jewish marriage ceremony. Here in America a Jew has the privilege of choosing whether he wants to observe his traditions or not."

I was full of questions: "Why the Jews? Why were these people who never   10 constituted more than a small minority singled out as scapegoats in Russia?" His answer was full of wisdom and understanding, "It is always necessary to have a scapegoat; it relieves people of the responsibility of taking the blame for their own problems and mistakes. The Jews in Russia have always been disliked and treated badly. Perhaps it is because they excelled in all fields. They worked hard to become educated and performed well in whatever positions they held."

During the interview, Irving, his wife, and I were sitting at a table in their   11 comfortable, small apartment. I asked questions about what worries me about Jewish emigration from the former Soviet Union and his attitude toward the new immigrants, about the advantages and disadvantages he sees for America. Because I am an emigrant, I've received assistance to come to America. I thank Americans for this help and feel sorry because it takes money from American taxpayers. Irving smiled, then answered, "America is a country of immigrants. The only native-born Americans are the American Indians. This country has welcomed the oppressed and the persecuted since its inception. If you study American history, the arts and sciences and social institutions of this country, you will find that people who settled here from every country in the world added to the greatness of America. I am sure that some Russian emigrants will contribute in a positive way to this country."

I enjoyed meeting with Irving and his wife. I received full and truly interest-   12 ing answers to my questions. And I had a comfortable and relaxed feeling, as if I were in my grandmother's house.

As we parted, Irving said, "Larisa, you made the right choice to come to   13 America. You are making many efforts to achieve your goal and to improve your English. My wife and I will be happy to help you. We invite you, when you have time, to come visit us. Take care! Be happy!"

Personal Connections

1. In paragraph 4, Irving states, "One is not born with prejudice. It has to be learned." Do you agree with this statement? With a partner or small group, discuss some of the different ways in which children learn to be prejudiced against people who are different from them in some way.

2. Think of a topic that interests you in the same way that prejudice interested the writer of this essay. Write your topic at the top of a sheet of paper, and then write five questions about this topic. Who could you interview to find out the answers to these questions?

---

[1]*zhid*: an insulting name for a Jewish person.

Content and Writing Techniques

1. In paragraph 10, Irving says, "It is always necessary to have a scapegoat; it relieves people of the responsibility of taking the blame for their own problems and mistakes." Look up the word *scapegoat* in the dictionary. Freewrite for ten minutes about your understanding of this word. In your own experience, do you know of any people or groups who have served as scapegoats?

2. Questions provide the foundation for every successful interview. Reread the essay and underline every question that Zubataya asked. Put a *D* next to questions that are expressed in direct speech using quotation marks: for example, *"Where were you born?"* Put an *I* next to questions that are expressed in indirect speech without quotation marks: for example, I *asked Irving where he was born.*

Interview with Andrei
by Young Ja Lee

Young Ja Lee, a student from Korea, interviewed a Russian man she had met in one of her previous English courses. She decided to focus her interview on a common problem experienced by older immigrants—the difficult adjustments involved when people are forced to give up the prestigious jobs they held in their native countries and to work in low-level jobs in the United States. As you read this essay, think about whether you know anyone who reminds you of Andrei.

I often see many immigrants in the United States who used to hold highly 1 professional jobs in their native countries but now make their living by working in low-skilled fields. These jobs are far from their once prestigious professions.

Andrei (not his real name) is a Russian native who was born and raised in 2 Siberia. He went to college and became a metallurgical engineer. He worked for the Siberia Railroad Company for many years. Then he immigrated to the United States. At that time he was in his early fifties. Since his immigration to this country, he has been working as a cleaning man.

I asked him how he liked his present job. He sighed, then answered with a 3 strong Russian accent, "I don't like the job. Doesn't have any interest. I can't talk to people about art, literature, or anything. *"No discussion about intellectual things!"* He shook his head with a slight motion of resignation.

He tried to find a job as an engineer in the railroad construction and mainte- 4 nance fields only to learn that the railroad business in the United States was history for bygone days. He said, "Nobody construct railroad in this country. I had a very interesting job in Russia. I loved it. So much activity in my job. I was in-charge metallurgical engineer of the railroad company covering from the Pacific Ocean to Lake Baikal." He added that Lake Baikal was the coldest area in Siberia. And he lived near this lake.

When he graduated from high school, he didn't want to go to engineering   5
school at all. "I wanted to study languages. But I was forced to go to engineering
school by my parents." He added, "Because in Soviet Union, you make more
money and have more opportunities in society. When I first got a job as an engineer, my salary was three times more than my sister's. Do you know she was a professor in the university at that time?" He was content with his job and enjoyed his
high salary. He was happy that he had listened to his parents' advice.

I asked him why he gave in to his parents. He smiled, saying, "In my coun-   6
try, children were and are raised to respect their elders. That's why, even though I
wanted to study languages, I listened to my parents and their advice. In the United
States young people don't have much respect toward their elders like parents, old
people, or teachers. It's sad. I think this is a serious problem. Old people are much
wiser and know what is the best for the young ones."

I pointed out that a cleaning job wasn't highly regarded socially. I asked, "Do   7
you feel uncomfortable to tell your friends, especially Russians, what you do for a
living now?" He replied quickly with a slight tinge of impatience, "I never make any
secret. Doesn't matter who they are. All my friends, actors and scientists, when they
ask me, I tell them without hesitation. For the time being, I have to do something.
The real shame is being lazy and don't do nothing. I believe in hard labor."

"Hard labor!" he repeated. Then, in my imagination, I drew a picture of An-   8
drei wearing a fur coat, a fur hat, and a pair of fur boots working in snow-covered
Siberia filled with arctic wind, constructing the endless railroad over the bare horizon. It must have been hard labor physically. But for this very intelligent man
working as a cleaning man, it must be hard labor emotionally. "Do you miss your
old job?" I asked. "Yes, I do. Sometimes, a lot," he quietly answered.

Since there wasn't any hope of working as an engineer for the railroad as long as   9
he lived in the United States, I asked him whether he was going to keep his present job as a lifelong occupation. He leaned his chest toward the table. His voice became sharp. He stared at me for a couple of seconds. Then he declared, "No! No! No!
Never!! Young, if someone tells me today that I would be a cleaning man the rest of
my life, I'll draw all my money from the bank, spend them all, then I'll commit sui-
cide!" His voice and his eyes revealed his misery, which he had never spoken of before,
and at the same time displayed his determination to get out of his present situation.

He speaks four languages very fluently besides his mother tongue, Russian: 10
German, Slovak, Polish, and English. He is studying at Hunter College, majoring
in Russian and Slavic languages. He had always wanted to study languages, even
when he was a young boy. Now as a middle-aged man, he is pursuing his lifelong
wish. I remember the two beautiful short essays which he wrote in our English
class. They were so well written they became the professor's collection items. He
said, "I want to become a translator in United Nations in international committee.
Also I look forward to be a teacher of Russian literature."

Now it was time for him to go to work, the night shift. He studies during the   11
day and works at night. He headed for the subway. The air was cold. But still the
crisp October sunlight was falling on his back. Suddenly I felt that he was lonely
and homesick right at that moment. I called out, "Andrei!" He looked back. I put
my thumbs up. "You will make it!" I shouted. He grinned and waved. Then he disappeared into the crowd.

Personal Connections

1. Do you know anyone who, like Andrei, once held a prestigious job but was forced to work in a low-level job after immigrating? How do you feel about this problem?

2. In paragraph 6, Andrei states that it is a shame young people in the United States do not listen to the advice of their elders. Do you agree with Andrei about this?

3. In paragraph 8, Lee focuses on Andrei's phrase "hard labor" and talks about two kinds of hard labor, physical and emotional. Write a definition for each of these two kinds of labor. Then try to give examples from your own life or the experiences of people you know to illustrate both types of hard labor.

Content and Writing Techniques

1. Look back at the essay and find one direct quotation from Andrei that tells something important about his attitude toward his present job. What do we learn from Andrei's own words that we might not have understood if Lee had expressed these things in her own words?

2. In this essay Lee reports on Andrei's nonverbal reactions to her questions. In paragraph 3, for example, she tells us that after saying what he did not like about his job as a cleaning man, "He shook his head with a slight motion of resignation." Find two other examples of places in the essay where Lee describes Andrei's nonverbal communication — tone of voice, facial expression, body language, and so on. What do these things tell us about Andrei?

3. Look at the concluding paragraph of the essay. Why do you think Lee decided to end her essay this way? Do you like this ending? Why or why not?

ASSIGNMENTS
Option 1: Life-History Interview

For this assignment, you will be asked to interview a person about his or her life, and use the information from the interview to analyze the person's life: Is there a common theme that runs through all the experiences? Is it a story of fulfillment or lost opportunities? How was the person's life shaped by economic or political forces beyond his or her control? These questions, and many more, arise when you begin to reflect on someone's personal history. The purpose of this assignment is for you to learn something about the person's life by asking questions such as these and then to teach the readers of your essay what you have learned.

One good source of material for a life-history essay is your own family. And many times the older members will have more interesting stories to tell simply because they have "lived more history." If you have a grandparent or a great-aunt or great-uncle who lives nearby and likes to talk, you may have an easy time choosing a person to interview. But consider all your options before you select a participant. One outstanding life-history essay was based on an interview with the writer's mother conducted by long-distance telephone. Other essays have been written about the parent of a friend, the night watchman at a dormitory, even a deaf teenager whom the writer tutored after school (the interview was conducted in sign language).

In planning for this assignment, you should consider whether you will conduct your interview in English or some other language. If you do the interview in another language, you will need to translate parts of the interview into English to share the results with your class and, later, to include some direct quotations in the essay.

Option 2: Topical Interview

This assignment asks you to focus your interview and writing on a topic of your own choice. Possible topics include a political event such as a war or depression, a social issue such as the criminal justice system or the changing role of women in society, or a career or job you would like to learn more about.

The choices of topics and people to interview for this assignment are practically unlimited. For example, in one class a student interviewed his uncle about the recent civil war in his native country of Moldova; another student interviewed a classmate to learn more about the position of women in Russia; a third student, who was researching the medical practice of cesarean section, interviewed his sister, who had had two babies delivered by this method; a fourth student interviewed a professor at her college about a career in foreign-language teaching. As you can see from these examples, you can choose to interview someone you know well or a total stranger. You might want to do several short preliminary interviews with different people before you decide to focus on one person. Or you might decide to interview two or three people to get different perspectives on your topic.

The purpose of this assignment is to draw a conclusion based on the results of your interview. You may decide to limit your analysis to just the one person you interviewed. Or you may choose to explain how this person's experience fits into some larger pattern.

INTERVIEWING TECHNIQUES

Whether you decide to concentrate on a person's life history or a more narrowly focused topic, you should start to think about what makes an interview successful. Make a point of listening to interviews on television or the radio, paying special attention to the different interviewing styles.

The following pre-interview activities will help you to become a more sensitive and skillful interviewer.

Out-of-Class Activity

This activity gives you a chance to practice interviewing in an informal situation. This is just a practice session and not designed to provide material for your interview essay.

1. Think of a friend or family member you could interview informally. Pick a person you feel comfortable with who is enthusiastic about being interviewed.

2. Prepare a short list of questions ahead of time. The questions may be on any subject but will, of course, be influenced by the person you have chosen to interview. Examples of questions you might ask include:

- What is your earliest memory?
- When did you first come to this country?
- What were your expectations?

3. During the interview be sure to take notes or tape record the conversation.

4. Afterward, freewrite for ten or fifteen minutes about what you learned about interviewing. What question got the longest answer? Why? What question got the shortest answer? Why? What question led to the most interesting response?

Out-of-Class Activity

This activity is designed to help you understand the interviewing process from the point of view of the person being interviewed. Allow fifteen to twenty minutes for this activity.

1. Ask another person to interview you. It could be the person you interviewed in the previous activity or someone else. It is a good idea to have the other person write down four or five questions ahead of time.

2. After the interview take five minutes to write down your own reactions to the other person's questions and to the way in which the person asked these questions. What did you learn about interviewing methods from this experience?

Reactions

In the first class meeting after you have completed these out-of-class activities, discuss your results. What things will you try to do when you interview someone more formally? What will you try to avoid doing?

CHOOSING A SUBJECT

Now that you are familiar with basic interviewing techniques, you should begin to think about what person you will interview and what questions you will ask. The following activity will help you to make these decisions.

In-Class Activity

You may or may not decide to interview the person you had in mind when you did this activity. The important thing is to think carefully about whom you would like to interview and to decide what kinds of questions you will need to ask.

1. Write down five people you might choose to interview—for example, a teacher, a friend, your grandmother, a waitress at your favorite restaurant, a neighbor.

2. Show your list to a partner and discuss the choices.

3. Choose one of the people from your list.

4. Write down five questions you might want to ask this person in an interview.

5. Discuss the list of questions with your partner.

6. Next to each question write down what general area it is related to—for example, family relationships, education, economic situation, work, religion, goals for the future. With your partner, discuss why you decided on these general areas.

7. Practice asking your partner these questions in a mock interview. Note which questions got the longest responses. Why do you think this was so? How could you improve the questions that did not get very long responses?

NOTE TAKING

There are several ways to keep a record of your interview: taking notes during the interview, tape recording the conversation and taking notes later, or combining these two methods. You might want to ask the person you are interviewing which method he or she prefers. In any case, you should have several questions in mind ahead of time. But also be sure to ask spontaneous questions that occur to you as the interview progresses.

If you are taking written notes, use abbreviations to make your note taking faster. If the person says something that seems especially important or interesting, try to copy it exactly and put it in quotation marks. Remember that you can ask the person to pause for a minute while you finish writing something down. Also remember to take notes on nonverbal aspects of the interview such as the person's physical appearance, facial expressions, or body language. If you conduct the interview in a language other than English, you can translate your notes into English later on.

As soon as possible after the interview, do the following post-interview activity.

Out-of-Class Activity

1. Read over the notes you took during the interview or listen to the audiotape.

2. Spend twenty to thirty minutes writing an informal report on your interview. Here are some questions you might want to consider:

- What was the most important thing you learned from the interview?
- Did anything surprise you?
- Were there any questions that the person was not able to answer?
- What were some of the nonverbal aspects of the interview—tone of voice, gestures, and so on—that caught your attention?
- Which two or three direct quotations of the person's exact words seemed especially important?
- What one word would you choose to sum up your interview? Can you explain why?

3. Bring your notes from the interview and your informal report to the next class meeting.

REPORTING

After completing the interview, share your findings with others in your class by giving a short oral report. Follow the directions below.

In-Class Activity

1. Work in a small group with two or three other students.

2. First give some background information about the interview. (For example, for a life history interview you might tell when and where the person was born, where the person lives now, and why you decided to interview this person; for an interview about work, you might describe the person's job and his or her feelings about it.) Then read part of your informal report on the interview. Finally, read one direct quotation from the person you interviewed and explain why you think this quote is important.

3. The listeners should ask questions and offer comments.

4. Continue until every group member has had a chance to report.

5. Each group should select one report to be presented to the entire class at the end of the period.

WRITING STRATEGIES

The two strategies explained in this chapter are helpful when writers are faced with a large amount of material—in this case the results of an interview—and must decide how to focus this information and shape it into a coherent essay.

CLUSTERING

This strategy is useful for getting some ideas down on paper quickly and for seeing how they relate to each other. Before you begin, reread your interview notes or listen to the tape again. Then spend ten to fifteen minutes on this activity.

1. Write the topic for your essay in the center of a blank piece of paper and circle it.

2. Think of several subtopics and write them around the main topic. Circle them and draw lines connecting them to the main topic.

3. List examples, facts, and specific details that relate to the different subtopics. List as many things as you can think of, even though you may not use all of them in your essay. Circle them and draw a line connecting them to the subtopic they relate to most closely.

4. Look at these clusters and think about which ones you might want to discuss in your essay. Which are the most interesting to you? Which do you have the most information about?

Figure 7–1 shows a cluster based on Eleonor Maldonado's interview with her grandmother, which appears on pages 132–134.

LOOPING

Looping is a strategy that involves short periods of freewriting, with the goal of finding a central focus, or main idea, for your essay. This section explains how looping works.

Loop 1:

1. At the top of a sheet of paper, write your topic, for example, "My friend's work as a cleaning man."

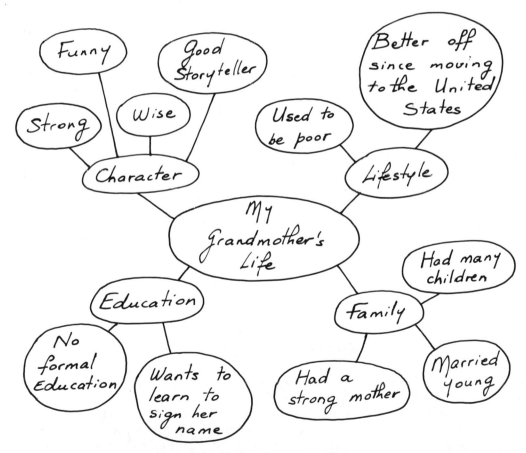

Figure 7–1   Cluster Diagram

2. Now freewrite on this topic for six minutes. If possible, use a timer that rings or beeps, so you will not have to keep watching the clock. Force yourself to keep writing. If your mind goes blank, just write, "I can't think of anything to say, I can't think of anything to say," until your thoughts start to flow again.

3. When the six minutes are up, stop writing. You have completed the first "loop." Read over what you have written, and underline the part or parts that seem most important. You may underline one complete sentence or words and phrases scattered throughout the loop. At the end, write the words "Summary Statement" and a sentence that expresses the most important idea from the first loop. Take a break and do something else for five or ten minutes to rest your brain.

Additional Loops:

1. Begin the second loop; remember to time yourself for six minutes. Start by copying the summary statement from the previous loop.

2. When the time is up, go through the same process described in step 3 above. Write a summary statement for the second loop at the end.

3. Continue with these six-minute loops (most writers do at least three or four) until you think you know what you want to focus on in your essay.

General Statement:

1. When you have written as many loops as you think you need, try to write a general statement that could serve as the main idea of your essay. Sometimes it helps to think of this general statement as the answer to a question. For example, if you have done a life-history interview, you might want to ask, "What is there about this person's life that is unique or different?" or "How did outside forces such as economic conditions or historical events affect the person's life?" If your interview was focused on a person's work, you might ask, "What accounts for the person's success (or failure) in his or her work?" or "What main conclusion can you draw about the nature of the work itself?" or "What is the person's attitude toward his or her work, and how do you account for this?"

2. Write several possible main ideas, and put an asterisk (*) beside the one you like best.

Examples

The examples were taken from a looping exercise by Rebecca Mlynarczyk.

Topic:
My mother's work as a high school teacher

Loop 1:   My mother has always been a worker. Whether at home or at school, she is rarely idle. For her, work is play, and she is either going full tilt or totally at rest—taking a nap. She really loves working; maybe it's part of her German heritage. Her own mother worked all the time also but didn't seem to get the same type of enjoyment from it. <u>My grandmother seemed to dwell on the imperfections of her work rather than to delight in the rewards.</u>

Summary Statement:

Work is a pleasure for my mother because she delights in its rewards rather than dwelling on its imperfections.

Loop 4:   My mother's positive attitude as a teacher is illustrated by how she handled a class labeled as "slow learners." That class was a difficult assignment and it reminds me of <u>another difficult assignment she is handling well—old age.</u> My mother retired from teaching when she was 62. Now she is 78—an age when many people are sitting at home worrying about their health and waiting to take the next pill. But not my mother. She is always on the go. Three times a week she attends an exercise class made up of other retired people. She remains open to new ideas and is always reading the latest books. She also tries to help take care of "the old people" by going around to nursing homes. Ironically, quite a few of these people are younger than she is, but you'd never guess it.

Summary Statement:

My mother's positive attitude has helped her not only in her work as a teacher but also in her retirement.

Possible Main Ideas:

My mother delights in the rewards of work rather than dwelling on its imperfections.

My mother's energy and positive attitude help to explain her success as a high school history teacher.

*Energy and a positive attitude have helped my mother to succeed in her work as a teacher—and in life.

Rebecca Mlynarczyk's Comments on Looping:

I was surprised by the way that looping enabled my thoughts to move in a different direction from what I had originally intended. At the beginning I thought I wanted to write about my mother's work as a high school teacher, but by the end my interest had shifted to a much broader subject—how my mother's positive attitude has helped her in every aspect of her life and is now helping her to deal with old age. I don't think I would ever have ended up with this idea if, instead of looping, I had started by writing an outline.

GRAMMAR IN CONTEXT
USING DIRECT AND INDIRECT QUOTATIONS

Understanding how to use direct and indirect quotations is important for many college writing assignments. Every time you quote from a published source, you are using a direct quotation; every time you paraphrase, or explain in your own words what an author said, you are using an indirect quotation.

Basically, a direct quotation consists of a person's exact words—either spoken or written; it is set off from the rest of the text with quotation marks. (Examples are adapted from Tatyana Dyachenko's essay, "Unfinished Interview.")

> **Example:** When my mother saw my astonished eyes, she explained, "It wasn't because I was a brave girl, but because when you see tragedy, horror, and ruin, death and tears all around you every day, every hour, you get accustomed to these awful things."

An indirect quotation (sometimes called a paraphrase) contains the same information but not the speaker's exact words; it does not use quotation marks.

> **Example:** When my mother saw my astonished eyes, she explained that when people see tragedy all around them, they become accustomed to it.

Activity

The following opening paragraphs from a student essay contain some direct quotations, but the quotation marks have been omitted. See if you can punctuate this passage correctly, restoring the quotation marks and adding commas and capital letters where they are needed.

Crisantina Orellana is a very old woman who was born in the quiet village of Chalatenango in the northern countryside of El Salvador. During my interview, I asked her about her age. She replied I really don't know it. The only thing I'm sure of is that I was born at some day in the past and I'm still alive. 1

One thing is notorious in Crisantina Orellana's personality. She always looks happy and full of joy. When I asked her what was the secret that has kept her full of life, she said life is life. The only thing we have to worry about is how to live it. Once you learn the way of doing so, you'll see the difference. 2

(See Answer Key, page 321.)

USING THE PRESENT PERFECT TENSE

The present perfect tense is formed by using *has* or *have* plus the past participle of the verb. It usually indicates activities that started in the past but extend into the present or changes that have occurred over a period of time.

Examples: The world <u>has gotten</u> smaller.
The population <u>has increased</u>.
Scientists <u>have found</u> a cure for cancer.

Activity

Imagine that the year is now 2007, and you are looking back over the last ten years. Write a short description telling how the world has changed over the past decade. Refer to the following categories, and use the present perfect tense where appropriate. Underline all the examples of the present perfect tense in your description.

Categories: Population
Ecology
The economy
Your own personal life

Sample Paragraph: The world <u>has changed</u> a lot since 1997. The population <u>has increased</u> by more than 50 percent. There is so much pollution that people need to wear gas masks just to go outside. Inflation <u>has gone</u> up so that you need $95 just to buy a slice of pizza. I <u>have gotten married</u> and <u>divorced</u> five times and <u>have had</u> fifteen children.

REVIEW OF SUBJECT-VERB AGREEMENT

The exercise that follows, based on an interview essay by Marina Petlakh, will give you practice in choosing verbs that agree with their subjects. If you need to review this grammar area see the section on Making Subjects and Verbs Agree on pages 115–17.

Activity

Supply the correct present tense form of each verb in parentheses. Use either the simple present tense or the present progressive, whichever seems more appropriate. Compare your answers with those of a partner, and then check yourself by using the Answer Key.

Example: Julia (be) _____*is*_____ one of my best friends in this college.
She (major) *is majoring* in art.

Julia (be) _____ an eighteen-year-old girl, who (seem)   1
_____ to be a very ordinary person. She (like) _____ art, and she
(take) _____ an art course this semester in college. But I did not suspect
that she (be) _____ so advanced, not only in drawing but also in ceramics.

I realized how talented she (be) _____ when I came to interview   2
her _____ and saw her room decorated with interesting abstract pictures on the walls and some ceramic works on the shelves. Although I
(be) _____ not a professional artist and I (do) _____ not like abstract painting, Julia's strange pictures, her perception of colors, and her free flow
of imagination delighted me. Since I (do) _____ not have any talent at all,
I always (admire) _____ people who (be) _____ gifted in something. Julia (be) _____ one of those people. Therefore, I made up my
mind to interview her without any doubts.

(See Answer Key, pages 321–22.)

SUGGESTED TECHNIQUES

When writing about an interview, there are no set rules that every student must
follow. Each essay will be unique just as each of the people interviewed is. However,
it is a good idea to follow these five general suggestions.

1. *Try to identify the major theme of the interview.* Think about the main impression you want your readers to receive from reading your essay. What point do you
want to make? What is your purpose for writing? For example, Tatyana Dyachenko
was focusing on her mother's experiences during World War II, particularly, the
theme of starvation, and she selected details that related to this theme. Young Ja Lee
was interested in the contrast between Andrei's job in his native country and his cur-
rent work in the United States; thus, she chose material from the interview that was
connected with this theme.

2. *Include specific details to get your readers actively involved.* The most successful
interview essays include carefully selected specific details. You may want to describe
the physical appearance of the person you interviewed or to describe the physical setting in which the interview took place. Or you might include specific details that reveal something important, as Robert Coles does when he says that migrant children
do not have traditional toys such as blocks and wagons but instead play "with sticks
and stones, with cattails, with leaves, with a few of the vegetables their parents pick,
with mud and sand and wild flowers."

Before you begin to write your own first draft, carefully read through the notes from your interview and underline all the specific details that you think are interesting. After you have written your first draft, go back and see how many of these details you have actually included.

3. *Use some direct quotations from the interview.* One of the most obvious and effective ways to make the person you interviewed seem real to the reader is to include his or her voice in the essay by means of direct quotations. In choosing which quotations to use in your essay, try to capture the flavor of the person's speech, even if it means including a few awkward expressions or grammatical errors.

Before beginning the first draft, reread the notes from your interview or listen to the tape again. Write down the quotations that you feel are most interesting or important. Which comments reveal the personality of your participant? Which ones tell us how this person talks or thinks? Are there any quotations that emphasize a point you want to make?

Remember to introduce the quotations you select with your own words. The most common way to do this is with simple phrases like "she said" or "he replied." But for variety think of other ways. If you have trouble introducing quotations, look back at the readings in this chapter to see how other writers have done it.

4. *Use indirect quotations when the exact words are not important.* Although direct quotations from the interview are often the highlight of the essay, be careful not to overuse them. If you include too many direct quotations, the essay will seem more like the transcript of an interview rather than your own analysis of it.

As you try to decide which quotations to include, ask yourself what was more important: what the person said, or how he or she said it. In the first case, you may be able to paraphrase the quotation, that is, to express the same idea in your own words as an indirect quotation. Use direct quotations only where the person's exact words are particularly effective.

5. *Try to include some information about the nonverbal communication of the interview.* Nonverbal communication—revealed by such things as facial expression, tone of voice, body language—is sometimes as important as the exact words we use. For instance, when Young Ja Lee tells us that Andrei "leaned his chest toward the table" and that "his voice became sharp," we know that he is about to say something very important.

As you prepare to write your first draft, think about the nonverbal communication that occurred during the interview. When did the person speak loudly or softly, look straight into your eyes, or avoid looking at you? When did the person seem eager to tell you more, and when did he or she want to move on to a new topic? Nonverbal clues such as these can be important in assessing the overall meaning of the interview.

Shaping the material from your interview into a meaningful and well-written essay is difficult, and at times you may feel like giving up. But remember that you are working on a first draft; the important thing is to get some ideas down on paper.

After completing your first draft, exchange papers with a classmate and fill out the Peer Response Sheet located at the end of this chapter. Also refer to Part III: Rethinking/Rewriting for suggestions on how to improve your first draft.

FINAL THOUGHTS

By talking to and writing about the people around us, we often come to understand them and ourselves better. This is one way "to celebrate life the way it is," in the words of a student writer. "Not only great historical events, but also ordinary experience can make life interesting, if we are sensitive enough. Not only Napoleons are interesting people, but also all the people around us, because everybody can say something to us. Something new."

Now that you have completed an essay based on an interview, take a few minutes to freewrite about two or three of these questions:

1. Have you ever interviewed anyone before? Explain.
2. What were your feelings about the interview itself? Was it easy or difficult? If you had a chance to do the interview over, what would you do differently?
3. Do you think that doing this assignment helped to improve your writing skills? If so, what specific skills improved?
4. Do you feel that doing this assignment will help you in other college writing assignments? If so, what type of assignments? Explain.
5. What was the most difficult part of this assignment for you?
6. What was the most rewarding part?

PEER RESPONSE SHEET:
WRITING ABOUT INTERVIEWS

Writer's Name: _____

Reader's Name: _____

Date: _____

(*Note to the reader:* As you respond to the writer's draft, try to focus on the ideas rather than the grammar and spelling. Discuss only those mistakes that interfere with understanding.)

1. What did you like about this essay? _____

_____

_____

_____

2. Were there any places where the writer's meaning was not clear? If so, what were they? _____

_____

_____

_____

3. What is the main conclusion you would make about the results of the interview? (Try to express your idea in one sentence.) _____

_____

_____

_____

4. Write down one direct quotation from the interview that you thought was effective. _____

_____

_____

_____

5. Do you feel that there are too many quotations from the interview, too few quotations, or about the right number? Explain. _____

_____

_____

_____

6. What *one* thing would you advise the writer to do when he or she rewrites this essay? _____

_____

_____

_____

8

Looking at Difference: Cultural Contrasts

Girls playing basketball in Guatemala

Culture is not an easy term to define because it includes so much. According to *The Random House Dictionary of the English Language*, culture is "the sum total of ways of living built up by a group of human beings and transmitted from one generation to another." To further complicate matters, most of the time we are not aware of the ways in which culture governs our lives. Edward T. Hall explained this idea in his influential book about culture, *The Silent Language*: "Culture is not an exotic notion studied by a select group of anthropologists in the South Seas. It is a mold in which we are all cast, and it controls our daily lives in many unsuspected ways. . . . Culture hides much more than it reveals, and strangely enough what it hides, it hides most effectively from its own participants" (New York: Doubleday, 1973, pp. 38–39).

In other words, as long as you are living in a culture, you are largely unaware of how your life is shaped by cultural forces. But as soon as you enter another culture, you are immediately aware of enormous differences. *Culture shock* is not too strong a term to describe this new awareness. Once you have recovered from the initial shock, however, you can begin to analyze and understand the new culture and, through this comparison, understand your native culture better as well.

The readings in this chapter deal with several topics related to culture: changing family structures, concepts of polite behavior, and the pace of life. We have included some readings that emphasize personal reactions and some that employ a more analytical approach. These different approaches demonstrate our belief that the type of essay you write will depend largely on your purpose and intended audience.

READINGS: CHANGING FAMILY STRUCTURES

Today cultures all over the world are changing rapidly as a result of political and economic forces and technological developments such as air travel, television, and computers. Dramatic changes are occurring in family structures, marriage patterns, and religious practices. Think of some of the ways in which cultural changes are affecting your own life. For example, perhaps your family life changed when your mother took a job outside the home. Or maybe your ideas about dating and marriage are different from those of your parents. Or the younger members of your family may have discarded some of the religious practices of the older ones.

Traditional vs. Modern Family
By Wan L. Lam

In this personal essay, a student from Hong Kong describes the dramatic transition that took place as her family was transformed from a traditional to a modern family structure. What does "traditional family" mean to you? How does this type of family differ from a "modern family"?

The traditional family structure no longer exists in the modern world. It's not surprising that the modern family structure has replaced it. My family, for example, has made a great leap from traditional to modern in which I can feel the existence of freedom.

It seems like a characteristic of traditional families that men are dominant. When I was born, my grandfather urged my mother to give me up, for I was only a girl. He suggested that my mother throw me into the sea or give me to my aunt and uncle, who didn't have any children. Under the pressure of my grandparents and relatives, my mother did give me to my aunt. But she brought me back a few hours later because of her regret in doing so.

In my childhood, all my family members and relatives lived in a big old building in Hong Kong. They had the same kind of job—the sculpture of ivory— and they worked together in that big building. In my family, my grandpa had the power of making all significant decisions, such as stopping my father, who was an outstanding student, from going to high school, and forcing him to work as a skilled worker in ivory sculpture.

There was no exception for my mother. She had to obey the men absolutely with no argument. From what my mother said, I don't think she was the daughter-in-law of my grandparents. Maidservant is a better word to describe my mother's role in the family. She had to do all the housework by herself without any help or any machines, and had to take care of the children and the elderly parents as well.

By the same token, children had to obey what the older people, especially my father, said, such as going to bed by nine o'clock exactly, going home right after school, and not walking alone or with other children in the streets. We, my brother, sisters, and I, had to do whatever my father said without question.

The ripple of change began when we moved out of the old building. Every individual family moved to a different place. I think the reason for not living together was that my grandpa had died, and another building was very expensive. My mother began to work outside to support the family (to pay the rent on the small apartment and other expenses). We had to share the housework when my mother was out. However, my father was still stubborn and strict with us as long as we lived in Hong Kong.

But things really started to change when we came to the United States two years ago. My father began to be concerned about his children and tried to communicate with us. To a large extent, we now have the right to make individual choices and have a certain freedom, like coming home later at night, which we were never permitted to do before. Perhaps my parents are getting old or maybe we have grown up.

Undoubtedly, to a large extent, the modern family is better than the traditional one. At least there is a great improvement in the relationship between family members, and everybody plays an important role in the family.

Personal Connections

1. Unfair treatment of women is something that Lam associates with the traditional family structure. How do you feel about the points concerning the treat-

ment of women in paragraphs 2 and 4? Do you know of any cases where this type of treatment still occurs?

2. Lam feels that the modern family is better than the traditional one. However, many people today are concerned about the breakdown of traditional family values. How do you feel about this issue? What are some of the good things about traditional families?

Content and Writing Techniques

1. Look at the following list of categories related to family structure. In the space provided, briefly describe these categories as they relate to traditional and modern families.

Category	Traditional	Modern
a. Where family members live	All together	In nuclear families
b. The role of men		
c. The role of women		
d. Attitude toward the elderly		
e. Relationship between parents and children		

2. This essay follows a chronological sequence beginning with Lam's birth and continuing up until the present. On a piece of paper, draw a vertical line, and list the major events that occurred in Lam's family. Circle any of the events that reflect traditional or modern aspects of her family, and label them with a *T* (for traditional) or an *M* (for modern). For example:

T ↓ Lam is born.
    (Mother pressured to give up baby girl.)

3. Draw a time line that shows the major events in the history of your own family. Circle the events that illustrate either traditional or modern family structure, and label them with a *T* or an *M*. After you have completed this time line, discuss it with a partner or small group.

The Family in Society
by Isabella Kong

In this essay, a student from Hong Kong responds to the previous essay and discusses the underlying reasons for traditional family structure. She explains why this system is not as suitable in modern society. Before you read, think about some of the reasons why families all over the world are changing.

Nothing is perfect. The modern family and the traditional family both have   1
their merits and demerits. What makes one more desirable than the other depends
on the context of the society, the values and attitudes of the people, and the economic system. In short, we have to look beyond the culture of the society. The
family patterns are the products of the culture, but they also shape the culture.

The traditional family, which Wan Lam described, had survival values in the   2
primitive Chinese society for which farming was the principal economic activity.
The family owned the land and depended on it for its living. If the traditional family structure had broken down, every family unit would then claim its share of
land for itself. This would be disastrous as the land would be divided into such
small portions that none of the family unit could survive because there would not
be enough to feed them. Thus, all of the land was passed down to the eldest son.

Moreover, the traditional family also provides a stronger union and closer re-   3
lationship among family members, which is vital if they are to defend themselves
against outside threats. However, the more people living together, the more complicated their relations will be. Disputes and conflicts may often arise and thus
threaten the existence of the family. As a means to counteract the disintegrating
force within the family, an authoritarian leadership is needed to decide on important issues and settle disputes. This is often the job of the eldest son in the family.
In turn, everyone has to obey and submit to the authorized figure; that is, they
have to pay the price of giving up freedom for family union, which Wan Lam
found unreasonable and disagreeable.

Nowadays, when individualism and equality are the most prevailing ideas in   4
the world, people may find it very hard to adjust themselves to a traditional family.
The means of production has changed so that the adaptive value of the traditional
family is no longer obvious. The modern family has its advantages, as it will be
more open and free, but it will also devastate the respect for the older generation
that once was the dominant force in the traditional family.

It is clear that family structure changes in accordance with the changes in so-   5
ciety. Yet, no matter what their differences are, all share one universal and everlast-
ing theme of affection, companionship, and warmth, which underlies any family
in any place and any time.

Personal Connections

1. Kong begins her essay with the statement, "Nothing is perfect." What
does this statement mean to you? Do you agree or disagree?

2. Do you agree with Kong that "the more people living together, the more
complicated their relations will be"? What experiences from your own life support
your conclusion?

Content and Writing Techniques

1. This essay analyzes why the traditional family was useful in Chinese society in the past, and why it is changing in today's world. List three reasons why the
traditional family was so prevalent in the past. Then list three reasons why it is not
as useful in modern society.

2. This essay is more formal than the personal essay by Wan Lam. Kong was asked to analyze why different family structures have evolved in different societies. Compare her essay carefully with the one by Wan Lam. Then indicate which of the following statements apply to each essay. Be prepared to point to specific evidence to support your answers.

> **Example:**
> Uses first-person narrative   Lam ✔   Kong _____
> (*I, my, we*).

a. Uses personal experience as   Lam _____   Kong _____
    examples.

b. Makes generalizations about   Lam _____   Kong _____
    sex roles.

c. States a preference for one   Lam _____   Kong _____
    type of family over another.

d. Attempts to explain behavior   Lam _____   Kong _____
    rather than judge it.

Traditional Family and Modern Society in Africa
by Papa Aly Ndaw

> *In Africa the family used to be of supreme importance— "one and indivisible, powerful and sacred," as this student from Senegal puts it. However, African families, like the Chinese families described earlier, are being changed drastically by the demands of modern life. In this essay, Ndaw, a student from Senegal, comments on some of the problems that can arise when families change. In your opinion, what are some of the problems that modern families face?*

The culture of a group can be defined as all the social, economic, and metaphysical aspects contributing to make a group specific and its members recognized as entities belonging to that group. In fact, every group, large or small, having a common past or heredity, has its own culture, even though some common cultural aspects can be found in all cultures. Another common denominator is that almost all traditional societies are going through some cultural changes caused by the introduction of new concepts or aspects of modern life. In Africa one structure that couldn't be unaffected is the family.

In traditional Africa the family used to be one and indivisible, powerful and sacred. Every member had rights and responsibilities he could assume as long as they didn't conflict with those of the group. The family was like the body and soul

1

2

of a person, the members like the different parts of the body, separate but vital in keeping the body and soul alive.

Today the economic and political conditions have changed, changing at the same time people's mentality and behavior. The result is a tendency to individualism, to self-concern, to division, which is not the goal of the traditional family.   3

The transition from the traditional family to the nuclear family was so quick and unpredictable that I wonder if its members were prepared for such a change in their way of living. One of the first things to change was the size of the family. It used to be a big family with Grandpa, Grandma, Mom, Dad, their brothers and sisters, and their children. Now it's a nuclear family that only includes Dad, Mom, and their own children. Many reasons are given: the house is not big enough, or it is better to have a small family so the children can have a better education, or the couple thinks their life can't be like the one their father and mother were having a few years ago. And for all these reasons and many others, the family needs to change to be able to cope with the rhythm of the twentieth century.   4

When the size of the family had decreased, the next step was to increase the rights of the nuclear family members, either by giving them more freedom or by giving them more power. The result was an establishment of new relations among the family members, who started seeing their differences and particularities.   5

The wife, whose role used to be giving a good education to the children and taking care of her husband, says she needs to be independent, and refuses to be confined to just household work. Her next thought will put her out of the house, looking for a job, leaving behind her a big hole and irresponsible and unprepared children.   6

The children, left to themselves and without supervision, think they are free. For them now, everybody except for Mom and Dad is an intruder in their education. And like the adage says, "When the cat is away, the mice will play." In fact, it was their mother's job to teach them their responsibilities, to correct them when they made mistakes, and to punish them when they violated the family's rules. Now, with Mom working outside the home, they will spend much of their time deciding for themselves, a right they didn't have before. In fact, it's a beginning of freedom!   7

The father, once the support of the family, feels less powerful, because his wife can now assume that function: to bring money home. To compensate for what may be called an inferiority complex, he tries to have more control over the children, who don't look at him any more as the symbol he used to be, but rather Mom's equal. At this stage, the notion of groups has lost its old power; the family has lost its traditional roots and function; every member thinks about himself first before thinking about the family.   8

But as we know, when society progresses, human beings gain more power over nature, bringing at the same time some changes in many aspects of life, culture included. These cultural changes, as long as they are not negative, contribute in a sense to the development of the group, because what they bring into the society are new attitudes that are needed for us to cope with the new environment in which we are living. At this time it may be too soon to understand and accept these developments, and to perceive them as achievements. The increase of   9 women's rights, their contribution to the economic power of their countries as a working force, couldn't be accomplished if women were just household workers.

A lot of things can be said about the cultural changes in human societies, 10 since we know that Man's life is an evolution, and evolution means improvement; and we know there is no improvement by simply repeating the old ways, but instead it comes with innovation and variety, which always lead to changes. The only thing to remember is that as long as these cultural changes bring improvement, they shouldn't be refused even though we know that every group tends to be conservative of its traditional values.

Personal Connections

1. In paragraph 7, Ndaw seems to be saying that it is not good for children to have too much freedom. How do you feel about children being left on their own without adult supervision?

2. In your own words, explain the idea stated in the conclusion to this essay: ". . . Man's life is an evolution, and evolution means improvement; and we know there is no improvement by simply repeating the old ways, but instead it comes with innovation and variety. . . ." Do you agree with this idea? Why or why not?

Content and Writing Techniques

1. In paragraph 1, Ndaw gives a definition of the word *culture*. What does this word mean to you? Write your own personal definition of culture and then look the word up in the dictionary. How does your definition compare with the dictionary definition?

2. In paragraph 3, Ndaw states that families are changing as a result of changing economic and political conditions. List some examples of economic and political changes that are affecting family life.

3. In paragraphs 6–8, Ndaw explains some of the serious problems that modern families face. Then, in paragraphs 9 and 10, he states that cultural changes usually lead to improvement. Do you feel that this conclusion is supported by the rest of the essay? If Ndaw were to write another draft, what advice would you give him about the essay's conclusion?

READINGS: CONCEPTS OF POLITE BEHAVIOR

You may have thought that politeness was the same the world over—based on common human decency rather than cultural learning. But as you will see in the readings that follow, what is seen as polite behavior by a person from one culture may seem rude to a person from another. As you read these essays, think about how we learn what it means to behave in a polite manner.

Everyday Life: Israel in Comparison to New York
by Sigalit Dallal

> *In this personal essay, a student contrasts the everyday behavior of people in New York City with the behavior of people in her native Israel. Not surprisingly, she finds strengths and weaknesses in both cultures. Before you read, think about a time when a stranger was very polite—or very rude—to you.*

I walked into the supermarket to buy some things. I stood in line to pay. Then while I was paying, I saw, from the corner of my eye, someone "jumping" on my stuff and collecting it into a big brown bag. I didn't understand what was going on. Then I realized there was one person at each counter who was packing the customers' stuff. I was very surprised when the cashier thanked me. "Would you believe that?" I asked myself. "She *thanked me* for buying here!" 1

This situation, which happened not long after I arrived in New York, caused me to think about how such little things influence one's day. Maybe other people don't pay so much attention to the difference between saying "thank you" or not saying it, but I see it as a very important issue. It really affects my day if people treat me nicely. 2

In Israel I never saw such a thing as saying "thank you" in a supermarket. People have to pack their own purchases and nobody thanks them for buying. It would sound ridiculous if a seller would thank a buyer. 3

Here in New York everybody is much more polite. "Thank you," "please," "excuse me" are part of everyday life. In Israel, you don't hear these words so much. People are more rude. If they don't like what you do, they will tell you right up front. It doesn't matter where you are and who is around you; they will just say what they think. 4

For example, when I sit here, on a bus, the driver sometimes looks like a statue to me. He doesn't get involved with the passengers. In Israel, many times there are arguments between the driver and one or more passengers, or between the passengers themselves. If someone doesn't like the way the driver drives, he will tell him. 5

Another thing is that in Israel people hate to stand in line. Usually it causes trouble, because whoever has the force to push himself to the front gets to be the first, even though he might have been the last one to arrive. 6

The above examples don't show a very nice picture of Israel. However, there are some things that are much more positive in Israel than they are here. Israelis know much better how to take care of problematic situations. Even the clerks in public offices usually are not so strict as the ones here. From what I have seen here, everybody just goes by the rules of the "book," and if something a little bit different happens, they can't handle it. In contrast people in Israel show much more initiative and are much more able to solve problems. 7

Another good thing in Israel is that when someone is in trouble, he will get more than one hand to help him. Even strangers on the street will jump to help. 8

In comparison, here everybody only takes care of their own business. In one way, it's good. Everybody has the freedom to do whatever he likes without anyone sticking his nose in other people's business, but on the other hand when someone needs other people to stick their noses in and help him, it won't happen.

Some time ago a murder took place in New York City. A young woman was stabbed in front of her apartment building in the early hours of the morning. She yelled for help, but people just stood at their windows and watched. No one did anything. Even after the murderer left, nobody came out to help. The woman was lying there, not able to move, and people stayed in their safe homes. Then the murderer came back and finished what he began. Now the young woman was dead. Suddenly, someone had the "courage" to call the police. This was after he had called a friend from another town and asked him what he should do. He didn't even telephone from his own apartment. He went to an old woman's apartment and called from there.[1]   9

I know it's an extreme example, but in Israel such a thing could never, ever happen. People are more likely to help.   10

In the United States people do help, but only in safe situations. They will be delighted to show you where a certain street is, but they won't help if they see any shadow of risk to themselves.   11

When I went back to Israel, after my trip here last year, I had an argument with my sister. I told her how impressed I was with the people in New York, how nice and polite they were. She had visited the United States before me and told me she didn't like it. She said it is all fake and hypocritical. Nobody is real here. It's like one big show. She asked me if I prefer people to lie and be polite rather than to be honest. She said that the smiles that the sellers give you in the shops are not real smiles, but special smiles for buyers, and they will smile even if they don't like you. I wasn't sure if she was right. She also said that people here are cold, in contrast to Israel, where people are warm and act according to their feelings.   12

She was right in some of the things she mentioned, but I came to the conclusion that it's better to be nice and polite, even though you sometimes have to keep bitter feelings to yourself. It's better than getting involved in ugly situations.   13

In conclusion, I can say that nothing is black and white. Life is mostly gray. Nobody is perfect, and no country is perfect. Everyone and every country has its own advantages and disadvantages.   14

Personal Connections

1. Compared with people in your native culture, do you find Americans to be polite, rude, or somewhere in between? Think of two specific examples from your own experience to support your opinion.

---

[1]The case being referred to occurred in 1964 in Kew Gardens, Queens, NY. A twenty-eight-year-old woman named Kitty Genovese was stabbed to death while more than thirty neighbors watched from nearby homes.

2. In paragraph 9, Dallal includes the shocking example of the young woman who was murdered while her neighbors watched. If you had been one of the neighbors who saw the woman being attacked, what would you have done?

    a. Called the police immediately.

    b. Yelled out the window for the man to stop.

    c. Rushed outside to help the woman.

    d. Watched but done nothing.

    e. Gone back to bed.

Discuss the reasons for your choice with others in your class.

Content and Writing Techniques

1. What, in your opinion, is the main idea of this essay? Underline the one sentence that you feel comes closest to expressing the main idea. In which paragraph is this sentence located?

2. In this essay Dallal compares the behavior of people in New York City with that of people in Israel. Look through the essay, and write *NY* in the margin whenever she is discussing people in New York City. Write *I* whenever she talks about people in Israel. Were you confused by this shifting back and forth between New York City and Israel? Why or why not?

3. Reread the last paragraph of this essay. Do you think this is an effective conclusion? Discuss your opinion with a small group of classmates.

Behavior in Public: Japan and the United States
by Masami Kazama

In contrast with the previous writer, who found Americans to be polite, this student from Japan feels that they sometimes assert themselves in a rude way. Yet Kazama, like the previous writer, comes to the conclusion that there are advantages and disadvantages to both cultures. Before you read, think about a time when you and a friend reacted to the same event in a very different way.

A Japanese friend who was living in New York once said, "I feel comfortable here because I don't have to care about other people. Unlike in Japan, nobody criticizes me, whatever I wear or however I behave." Her comment can be explained by the difference of characteristic features between Americans and Japanese. Generally speaking, Americans are individualistic, and Japanese are not. The standard which regulates people's behavior is different; that is, compared to Americans, who think the important thing is whether they themselves feel comfortable, for Japanese, other people's eyes become the standard of our behavior. We Japanese

    1

tend to dislike being different from others, and others, too, expect us to be the same as them. This tendency can be observed in every aspect of our life.

For example, Americans choose their clothes freely without caring about other people. As a result, we can see people in torn jeans and T-shirts and people dressed formally at the same place. Also, even older Americans wear vivid colors. Some elderly ladies wear elaborate make-up and take care of their hair and nails. I was surprised to see an old lady who couldn't walk without someone's help wearing red lipstick. We hardly ever see such a scene in Japan, where others expect us to be like so-and-so. If a seventy-year-old woman wore red in Japan, she would be criticized for not acting her age, and she would stop wearing it immediately. Uniforms in Japanese high schools reflect our inclination to conformity as well.   2

Another example can be seen in our feelings about age. Since I came here, I have scarcely thought of my age. In America no one puts pressure upon me because of age. In Japan, however, our surroundings make us constantly conscious of our age. For instance, we have a marriageable age. When someone, especially a woman, remains single beyond that age, people refer to her as an "old maid." One of my friends got married unwillingly only because she didn't want people to regard her as an old maid. Though, of course, this is an extreme example, our behavior is influenced by our concern for what others will think of us.   3

The Japanese way of thinking of others sometimes meets with good results. In contrast to Americans, who express their opinions in a self-assertive way, Japanese tend to speak and act with consideration of others' feelings and point of view. One day recently I observed an interesting incident. During a movie a baby burst into tears. In spite of the complaints of others, the mother stayed there, insisting on her right. According to her, she had a right to see the movie because she had paid for it. As the baby kept crying, some people shouted to her to leave. They emphasized their right to see the movie quietly. Because of this dispute, many viewers were not able to enjoy the movie. I was so surprised at their self-centered conduct. People who cursed each other never thought of other viewers. What was important for them was to protect their own right. At that time I thought that too much emphasis on individualism creates egocentrism.   4

It is said that our environment forms our character. The different ways that Americans and Japanese relate to others probably have something to do with each country's circumstances. For example, America is a big country called a melting pot, and Japan is a small, single-ethnic country. Anyway, since our features are acquired, we have a chance to modify them. Taking advantage of living in a different culture, I want to accept the good aspects of both. Without going to extreme "me-ism," I want to be an autonomous person who isn't excessively concerned about what others think of me.   5

Personal Connections

1. Do you agree with Kazama that Americans tend to be individualistic and behave according to their own desires rather than the standards of the group? Give an example from your own experience to support your opinion.

2. In paragraph 4, the writer describes a dispute that broke out in an American movie theater when a baby started to cry. If you had been with the baby, what would you have done?

  a. Left as soon as the baby started to cry to keep from disturbing the rest of the people.
  b. Left as soon as other people started to complain.
  c. Insisted on your right to stay and see the movie since you had paid for your ticket like everyone else.

Content and Writing Techniques

1. Underline the sentence (or sentences) that serves as the main idea of this essay. In which paragraph does it appear? Discuss your answer with a small group of classmates.

2. Although this is a more formal essay than the one by the Israeli student, Kazama uses several examples from her own experience to illustrate her ideas. List three of these personal examples. Do you think these examples strengthen or weaken the essay?

Mixed Metamessages across Cultures
by Deborah Tannen

> *In this passage from her book* That's Not What I Meant, *Deborah Tannen helps to explain why the Israeli student and the Japanese student interpreted the behavior of Americans so differently. According to Tannen, different cultures have different ways of showing politeness, and what is considered polite behavior in one culture may be considered rude in another.*

The danger of misinterpretation is greatest, of course, among speakers who actually speak different native tongues, or come from different cultural backgrounds, because cultural difference necessarily implies different assumptions about natural and obvious ways to be polite.   1

Anthropologist Thomas Kochman gives the example of a white office worker who appeared with a bandaged arm and felt rejected because her black fellow worker didn't mention it. The (doubly) wounded worker assumed that her silent colleague didn't notice or didn't care. But the co-worker was purposely not calling attention to something her colleague might not want to talk about. She let her decide whether or not to mention it: being considerate by not imposing. Kochman says, based on his research, that these differences reflect recognizable black and white styles.   2

An American woman visiting England was repeatedly offended—even, on bad days, enraged—when Britishers ignored her in settings in which she thought   3 they should pay attention. For example, she was sitting at a booth in a railroad-station cafeteria. A couple began to settle into the opposite seat in the same booth. They unloaded their luggage; they laid their coats on the seat; he asked what she would like to eat and went off to get it; she slid into the booth facing the American. And throughout all this, they showed no sign of having noticed that someone was already sitting in the booth.

When the British woman lit up a cigarette, the American had a concrete object for her anger. She began ostentatiously looking around for another table to move to. Of course there was none; that's why the British couple had sat in her booth in the first place. The smoker immediately crushed out her cigarette and apologized. This showed that she had noticed that someone else was sitting in the booth, and that she was not inclined to disturb her. But then she went back to pretending the American wasn't there, a ruse in which her husband collaborated when he returned with their food and they ate it. 4

To the American, politeness requires talk between strangers forced to share a booth in a cafeteria, if only a fleeting "Do you mind if I sit down?" or a conventional "Is anyone sitting here?" even if it's obvious no one is. The omission of such talk seemed to her like dreadful rudeness. The American couldn't see that another system of politeness was at work. (She could see nothing but red.) By not acknowledging her presence, the British couple freed her from the obligation to acknowledge theirs. The American expected a show of involvement; they were being polite by not imposing. 5

An American man who had lived for years in Japan explained a similar politeness ethic. He lived, as many Japanese do, in frightfully close quarters—a tiny room separated from neighboring rooms by paper-thin walls. In this case the walls were literally made of paper. In order to preserve privacy in this most unprivate situation, his Japanese neighbors simply acted as if no one else lived there. They never showed signs of having overheard conversations and if while walking down the hall, they caught a neighbor with the door open, they steadfastly glued their gaze ahead as if they were alone in a desert. The American confessed to feeling what I believe most Americans would feel if a next-door neighbor passed within a few feet without acknowledging their presence—snubbed. But he realized that the intention was not rudeness by omitting to show involvement, but politeness by not imposing. 6

The fate of the earth depends on cross-cultural communication. Nations must reach agreements, and agreements are made by individual representatives of nations sitting down and talking to each other—public analogues of private conversations. The processes are the same, and so are the pitfalls. Only the possible consequences are more extreme. 7

Personal Connections

1. Has there ever been a time when you had trouble communicating with someone because of cultural differences? If so, tell about it in writing.

2. Paragraphs 3–5 present the example of an American woman visiting England who was offended by the behavior of a British couple who shared her booth in a restaurant. If you were in this situation, how would you react?

a. Feel uncomfortable, finish your food as quickly as possible, and leave the booth without saying anything.

b. Not care about the couple one way or the other and finish your meal without paying any attention to them.

c. Be pleased by a chance for some company, introduce yourself to them, and try to start a conversation.

d. Be annoyed and tell them that they are rude to sit down without asking your permission first.

Freewrite about why you made the choice you did. Do you think your choice was personal or cultural?

Content and Writing Techniques

1. What is the main idea of this passage—the one statement that everything else relates to? Underline the sentence that comes closest to stating the main idea. In which paragraph does this sentence appear?

2. To support the main idea, Tannen gives three specific examples from real life. What are they?

3. For each of the three examples, Tannen explains how it relates to the main idea of the passage. Underline the sentence or sentences in which she explains how each example is connected to the main idea.

READINGS: THE PACE OF LIFE

"Pace of life" is not easy to define. It has to do with so many things—the speed of traffic, how quickly one gets served in a restaurant, how long it takes to complete a business deal. Even the speed of walking and speaking are influenced by this pace.

Of course, the pace varies from culture to culture, from city to countryside, and even from family to family. A midday meal that might take half an hour in the United States could take three times as long in Italy or Spain. The signing of a contract that might require a three-hour meeting in New York might take three weeks of meetings in Tokyo.

In the following essays, you will read about how people react to the pace of life in a culture not their own. What the writers choose to observe can tell us a great deal about their own personal and cultural values.

Social Time: The Heartbeat of Culture
by Robert Levine with Ellen Wolff

> *In this article, which was originally published in* Psychology Today *magazine, an American professor describes the very different pace of life he encountered when he accepted a teaching assignment in Brazil. In fact, he became so interested in the different sense of "social time" that he decided to make it the subject of his research. Before you read, think about your own adjustment to life in the United States. What one cultural difference would you most like to study and write about?*

"If a man does not keep pace with his companions, perhaps it is because he hears a different drummer." This thought by Thoreau[1] strikes a chord in so many people that it has become part of our language. We use the phrase "the beat of a different drummer" to explain any pace of life unlike our own. Such colorful vagueness reveals how informal our rules of time really are. The world over, children simply "pick up" their society's time concepts as they mature. No dictionary clearly defines the meaning of "early" or "late" for them or for strangers who stumble over the maddening incongruities between the time sense they bring with them and the one they face in a new land.

I learned this firsthand, a few years ago, and the resulting culture shock led me halfway around the world to find answers. It seemed that time "talks." But what is it telling us?

My journey started shortly after I accepted an appointment as visiting professor of psychology at the federal university in Niteroi, Brazil, a midsized city across the bay from Rio de Janeiro. As I left home for my first day of class, I asked someone the time. It was 9:05 A.M., which allowed me time to relax and look around the campus before my 10 o'clock lecture. After what I judged to be half an hour, I glanced at a clock I was passing. It said 10:20! In panic, I broke for the classroom, followed by gentle calls of *"Hola, professor"* and *"Tudo bem, professor?"* from unhurried students, many of whom, I later realized, were my own. I arrived breathless to find an empty room.

Frantically, I asked a passerby the time. "Nine forty-five" was the answer. No, that couldn't be. I asked someone else. "Nine fifty-five." Another said: "Exactly 9:43." The clock in a nearby office read 3:15. I had learned my first lesson about Brazilians: Their timepieces are consistently inaccurate. And nobody minds.

My class was scheduled from 10:00 until noon. Many students came late, some very late. Several arrived after 10:30. A few showed up closer to 11:00. Two came after that. All of the latecomers wore the relaxed smiles that I came, later, to enjoy. Each one said hello, and although a few apologized briefly, none seemed terribly concerned about lateness. They assumed that I understood.

[1]Henry David Thoreau (1817–1862) is a well-known American writer. In his essay "Civil Disobedience," he stated that individuals should act according to their own concepts of right and wrong even when these conflict with government policies.

The idea of Brazilians arriving late was not a great shock. I had heard about   6
manhã, the Portuguese equivalent of *mañana* in Spanish. This term, meaning "tomorrow" or "the morning," stereotypes the Brazilian who puts off the business of
today until tomorrow. The real surprise came at noon that first day, when the end
of class arrived.

Back home in California, I never need to look at a clock to know when the   7
class hour is ending. The shuffling of books is accompanied by strained expressions that say plaintively, "I'm starving. . . . I've got to go to the bathroom. . . .
I'm going to suffocate if you keep us one more second." (The pain usually becomes unbearable at two minutes to the hour in undergraduate classes and five
minutes before the close of graduate classes.)

When noon arrived in my first Brazilian class, only a few students left imme-   8
diately. Others slowly drifted out during the next fifteen minutes, and some continued asking me questions long after that. When several remaining students
kicked off their shoes at 12:30, I went into my own "starving/bathroom/suffoca-
tion" routine.

I could not, in all honesty, attribute their lingering to my superb teaching   9
style. I had just spent two hours lecturing on statistics in halting Portuguese. Ap-
parently, for many of my students, staying late was simply of no more importance
than arriving late in the first place. As I observed this casual approach in infinite
variations during the year, I learned that the *manhã* stereotype oversimplified the
real Anglo/Brazilian differences in conceptions of time. Research revealed a more
complex picture.

With the assistance of colleagues Laurie West and Harry Reis, I compared   10
the time sense of 91 male and female students in Niteroi with that of 107 similar
students at California State University in Fresno. The universities are similar in
academic quality and size, and the cities are both secondary metropolitan centers
with populations of about 350,000.

We asked students about their perceptions of time in several situations, such   11
as what they would consider late or early for a hypothetical lunch appointment
with a friend. The average Brazilian student defined lateness for lunch as thirty-
three-and-one-half minutes after the scheduled time, compared to nineteen minutes for the Fresno students. But Brazilians also allowed an average of about fifty-
four minutes before they'd consider someone early, while the Fresno students
drew the line at twenty-four.

Are Brazilians simply more flexible in their concepts of time and punctual-   12
ity? And how does this relate to the stereotype of the apathetic, fatalistic and irresponsible Latin temperament? When we asked students to give typical reasons for
lateness, the Brazilians were less likely to attribute it to a lack of caring than the
North Americans were. Instead, they pointed to unforeseen circumstances that the
person couldn't control. Because they seemed less inclined to feel personally responsible for being late, they also expressed less regret for their own lateness and
blamed others less when they were late.

We found similar differences in how students from the two countries charac-   13
terized people who were late for appointments. Unlike their North American
counterparts, the Brazilian students believed that a person who is consistently late

is probably more successful than one who is consistently on time. They seemed to accept the idea that someone of status is expected to arrive late. Lack of punctuality is a badge of success.

Even within our own country, of course, ideas of time and punctuality vary considerably from place to place. Different regions and even cities have their own distinct rhythms and rules. Seemingly simple words like *now*, snapped out by an impatient New Yorker, and *later*, said by a relaxed Californian, suggest a world of difference. Despite our familiarity with these homegrown differences in tempo, problems with time present a major stumbling block to Americans abroad. Peace Corps volunteers told researchers James Spradley of Macalester College and Mark Phillips of the University of Washington that their greatest difficulties with other people, after language problems, were the general pace of life and the punctuality of others. Formal "clock time" may be a standard on which the world agrees, but "social time," the heartbeat of society, is something else again. 14

How a country paces its social life is a mystery to most outsiders, one that we're just beginning to unravel. Twenty-six years ago, anthropologist Edward Hall noted in *The Silent Language* that informal patterns of time "are seldom, if ever, made explicit. They exist in the air around us. They are either familiar and comfortable, or unfamiliar and wrong." When we realize we are out of step, we often blame the people around us to make ourselves feel better. 15

Appreciating cultural differences in time sense becomes increasingly important as modern communications put more and more people in daily contact. If we are to avoid misreading issues that involve time perceptions, we need to understand better our own cultural biases and those of others. 16

When people of different cultures interact, the potential for misunderstanding exists on many levels. For example, members of Arab and Latin cultures usually stand much closer when they are speaking to people than we usually do in the United States, a fact we frequently misinterpret as aggression or disrespect. Similarly, we assign personality traits to groups with a pace of life that is markedly faster or slower than our own. We build ideas of national character, for example, around the traditional Swiss and German ability to "make the trains run on time." Westerners like ourselves define punctuality using precise measures of time: five minutes, fifteen minutes, an hour. But according to Hall, in many Mediterranean Arab cultures there are only three sets of time: no time at all, now (which is of varying duration) and forever (too long). Because of this, Americans often find difficulty in getting Arabs to distinguish between waiting a long time and a very long time. 17

*   *   *

As you envision tomorrow's international society, do you wonder who will set the pace? Americans eye Japan carefully, because the Japanese are obviously "ahead of us" in measurable ways. In both countries, speed is frequently confused with progress. Perhaps looking carefully at the different paces of life around the world will help us distinguish more accurately between the two qualities. Clues 18 are everywhere but sometimes hard to distinguish. You have to listen carefully to hear the beat of even your own drummer.

Personal Connections

1. Robert Levine captures his readers' attention with a story—a detailed description of the first class he taught in a Brazilian university. Write one of your own stories that reveals something about cultural differences. Force yourself to be specific by beginning with the phrase, "I remember the time when. . . ."

2. In paragraphs 3 through 9, Levine describes the differences he observed in how students and teachers in Brazil and in the United States behave in class. Freewrite for a few minutes, describing a typical class in your native country. How is classroom behavior in your country different from what you have observed in the United States? In your opinion, what are the reasons for these differences?

3. Paragraph 14 refers to the experiences of Americans who volunteered for the Peace Corps—a U.S. organization in which Americans try to help improve the quality of life in developing countries. According to the research cited here, the most frustrating cultural difference for the American volunteers, except for language, was the difference in the pace of life. Based on your own experiences living in the United States, make a list of the three cultural differences that have affected you the most. Discuss these lists with a small group of classmates.

Content and Writing Techniques

1. Research in the social sciences is often based on questionnaires in which each participant answers questions posed by the researcher. For example, paragraphs 10–13 describe a research project to compare the time sense of American and Brazilian college students. Working with your whole class, write a short questionnaire to discover and compare the different concepts of time among class members. Have every student write one question, and pick the most appropriate questions to make up a short questionnaire that everyone will complete. Then summarize the results. Can you draw any conclusions from the questionnaire responses? You may decide to continue this research by administering the questionnaire to a group of people outside the class.

2. The last paragraph states that "speed is frequently confused with progress." Think about the relationship between these two concepts by writing down three good things about doing things quickly. Then list three bad things that sometimes result from doing things quickly. Write your own definition of progress. What role, if any, does speed play in progress?

3. See "Vocabulary Practice: Idioms" on page 188 for vocabulary practice related to this essay.

What's the Rush?
by *Paulo Vieira-Moreno*

In this essay, the writer responds to the previous essay, explaining some of the problems a Brazilian student faces in trying to adjust to the faster pace of life in the United States. Before you read, think about the meaning of the title of this essay. Based on this title, what do you think the writer will say in the essay?

It is hard to be a foreigner in a country where the language and the culture are totally different from yours. The process of adjustment is long and gradual. How do I know that? I came from Rio de Janeiro, Brazil, to New York, U.S.A., in December 1989. I was already twenty-one years old. I had my own principles and ideas formed. My culture was already in my thoughts and attitudes. So, when I read the article written by Robert Levine, who had lived and taught psychology at a university in Brazil, I realized that we Brazilians are always late. The article, "Social Time: The Heartbeat of Culture," talks about how people behave toward time. What does it mean for us Brazilians to be late? 1

I agree with what Professor Levine has written about how we act when the issue is time. Like him, I have some experience living in another culture which is obviously different from my own. I would like to share this experience with you. 2

I have been in the United States for approximately three years, and I still do not understand why people have to rush all the time. For example, when I walk around at lunch time, I see people walking and eating at the same time, eating and reading on the subway, and when the shuttle train arrives at 42nd Street-Times Square, they run to get on the train that will leave a few minutes earlier. It does not make sense to me. 3

I have a friend, Dagoberto, who is Cuban and has been living in this country since 1963. He goes to Rio de Janeiro every year for Christmas and Carnival. He always says, "*Yo amo Brasil y los brasilenos pero esa tal 'calma' e que no suporto,*" which means "I love Brazil and the Brazilians; however, this '*calma*' kills me." *Calma* has several meanings in English such as "wait," "hold on," "be patient." It is true we Brazilians do not rush to do anything and still we do everything we are supposed to by the end of the day. 4

The behavior of a Brazilian student is not very different from what Professor Levine describes in the article. As a matter of fact, when I read it, I thought it was an article written by my American professors about me. I felt pretty bad, though! I am always late for my classes; however, I never meant to be rude to my teachers. It is something that I do normally, and now, when I look back, I am much better than I used to be. 5

Anyway, to be late is part of my life, and because of that I got myself in trouble with my friends so many times. Now, when we go out, they always tell me to arrive at least thirty minutes early so then I will be on time. However, I think I am better than I used to be because I am only ten or twenty minutes late, instead of forty to fifty minutes. I guess I am learning the new culture. 6

In conclusion, I just want to say that in Rio we have a different kind of life   7
than we have in New York, and being late does not mean to be lazy or irresponsible. The concept of time is part of a culture, and we cannot judge it by saying that
it is right or wrong. We have to try to understand the way it is, to accept it, and to
try to adjust to other people's culture. By the way, that is what I am trying to do.

Personal Connections

1. Think about the prediction you made before reading this essay. In what
ways was your prediction correct? In what ways was it incorrect?

2. During your first few weeks in the United States, did you find the pace of
life here slower or faster than in your native country? Write about a specific experience that made you realize what some of the differences were. Discuss your writing with a partner.

Content and Writing Techniques

1. In paragraph 7, Vieira-Moreno writes, "The concept of time is part of a
culture, and we cannot judge it by saying that it is right or wrong. We have to
try to understand the way it is, to accept it, and to try to adjust to other people's culture." Do you agree or disagree with this statement? Can you think of a
time when you tried to adjust to another person's culture? What were the results?

2. Imagine that Vieira-Moreno is one of your classmates, and you have been
asked to help him revise his essay. If he were to write another draft, what would
you like to know more about? What specific parts of this essay, in your opinion,
need to be expanded?

WRITING STRATEGIES
FORMULATING A THESIS STATEMENT

One thing that American professors consider important in more formal writing
is a clear thesis statement. Basically, a thesis statement is the main idea of an essay. In
personal writing the thesis is often implied rather than stated directly, but in more
formal writing it is desirable to state the main idea explicitly, usually toward the beginning of the essay.

In most college writing a simple explanation of the topic—for example, "In
this essay I plan to discuss the changes that have taken place in American family
life as a result of women working outside the home"—is not considered an acceptable thesis. You must take it one step further and state an opinion (what you believe) about how these changes have affected American family life—perhaps the
assertion that "American family life has benefited because of women working outside the home."

In-Class Activity

This activity will give you a chance to practice developing a thesis.

1. Working with a small group of classmates, read and discuss the following sample thesis statements.

> **Topic:** Old people in American society
> **Possible thesis statements:**
> a. Old people are not respected in American society.
> b. American television commercials are responsible for the lack of respect toward the elderly.
> c. Because the United States is a youth-oriented culture, old people are not respected.
> d. As a larger proportion of the population becomes elderly, old people will gain more respect in American society.

Although some of these statements are obviously more complex than others, they all fulfill the basic requirements for a thesis statement.

2. With your group, choose *one* of the following topics and try to formulate an acceptable thesis statement for it. Discuss your ideas as much as you need to, and come up with two or three possible thesis statements. When the group has settled on a thesis, have one group member write it down.

> **Topic A:** The American university system
> **Topic B:** The difference between high school and college
> **Topic C:** Dating customs in the United States
> **Topic D:** The role of women (or men) in your native culture

3. Share the groups' results with the class by having a member of each group write the thesis statement on the board. What do the various thesis statements have in common? How are they different? What have you learned from this activity?

OUTLINING

We have defined the thesis as a statement of what you believe about a particular topic. It may help to think of an outline as a shortened way of explaining why you believe this. In other words, an outline lists the major reasons or evidence used to support the opinion stated in the thesis.

Outlining is a tool to help in organizing ideas. Some writers like to get their ideas down in outline form before they write the first draft. Others prefer to write a rough draft and then go back and improve the organization.

In-Class Activity

This activity will give you a chance to practice outlining and to observe how other students approach this process. You can then decide whether outlining would be a useful strategy in your own writing.

1. Work with the same group of students as for the activity on thesis statements (see pages 183–84). Practice making an outline for an essay using your group's thesis. (Your teacher will let you know whether or not you will eventually write an essay based on the outline you develop.)

2. Working as a group, develop an outline to support your thesis statement, using this basic outline format:

> **BASIC OUTLINE FORMAT**
> I.   Tentative thesis statement for essay
> II.   First major supporting idea and evidence
> III.   Second major supporting idea and evidence
> IV.–? Continue with additional ideas
>   Conclusion

3. Once your group has written its outline, discuss what else you might need to do before writing the first draft. For example, you might need to look up some facts and figures to support the points you are making.

4. Have one student from each group write the outline on the board. How are the outlines alike? In what ways are they different? How would you use an outline such as this in writing an essay?

GRAMMAR IN CONTEXT
USING THE MODALS

The modals are necessary to add important shades of meaning to verbs. Among the most common modals are these nine:

can, could, may, might, will, would, must, ought to, should

These words indicate different degrees of ability, possibility, or permission. Because it is difficult to explain the exact meanings of these words, it is best to experiment with using them, and then discuss their meaning with your teacher or classmates.

Activity: A Grammar Mystery Puzzle

The following activity is a kind of guessing game in which you are asked to figure out the professor's mistake. In addition, you are asked to choose the correct verb forms to use with certain modals such as *may*, *must*, and *would*. Note that the modals in this passage are underlined and that all the verb forms are influenced by the fact that the event being described took place in the past.

Fill in the blanks with the correct form of the verbs in brackets to solve the mystery of the missing students.

Example: The professor <u>might</u> [have] _____*have*_____ _____*had*_____ jet lag.

An American professor was rushing to the classroom where he was   1
scheduled to give his first lecture at a Brazilian university. When he arrived, he was surprised to find Room 101 was empty. He didn't know what <u>had</u> [happen] _____. However, being a professor, his mind went to work, and he came up with some interesting theories.

The professor's watch <u>might</u> [stop] _____ _____. Or   2
the students <u>might</u> [forget] _____ _____ that a class was scheduled for that day. Or possibly, they all <u>might</u> [decide] _____ _____ to drop the class.

There were other possibilities as well. The university <u>might</u>   3
[close] _____ _____ early that day for a strike or protest. But surely if there had been a strike, the professor <u>would</u> [hear] _____ _____ about it from someone.

Maybe there was a cultural explanation. Perhaps in Brazil, it <u>might</u>   4
[be] _____ acceptable for students to come late to class, or not to come to class at all.

As it turned out, the answer was quite simple. As a professor,   5
he <u>should</u> [know] _____ _____ better, but he obviously <u>had</u> not [check] _____ the schedule of classes carefully enough. Although he had copied down the day and time correctly, he <u>must</u> [make] _____ _____ a mistake about the room. He <u>had</u> [go] _____ to room 101 when, in fact, he <u>should</u> [go] _____ _____ to Room 110, which is where all his students were waiting.

(See Answer Key, pages 322–23.)

PROOFREADING FOR VERB ENDINGS

If you feel unsure of your answers for the following activity, review the section entitled "Knowing When to Add *-ed* to the Verb" on pages 118–20. For general advice about proofreading, see page 309.

Activity

The following short essay contains many errors in verb endings. Correct the errors, and above each correction write a number indicating the reason for the change: (1) past tense, (2) present perfect or past perfect tense, (3) passive voice, (4) adjective form, or (5) common expressions that always end in *-ed*.

I have never live in a so-call traditional family in which people live with   1
their grandparents, uncles, aunts, and other relatives. Even though I have never
live in a traditional family, I still prefer to live in a modern family.

Our family is consider average in size, my parents, my two sisters, and me.   2
Since there are only three children, we are given a lot of attention and freedom. I
remember when we were still in Hong Kong, we always have new clothes, school
supplies, etc. Everything we need was provide for us.

On the other hand, my parents were very strict about our homework, and   3
how we do in school. I remember every night they spended time to sit down with
us while we were doing our homework, and they have to sign all our test papers.

In our family, most of the housework was done by my parents. I use to wash   4
a few dishes at night and sweep the floors. During the weekend we were allow to
stay out late. Sometimes, my friends and I decide to go up to the mountains and
spend a few days there. My parents usually like to go with us. I will never forget
those times.

Things haven't change much since we came to this country, except we don't   5
have family trips any more because our parents are busy working every day, and
we kids are busy studying and going to school.

(See Answer Key, page 323.)

VOCABULARY PRACTICE: IDIOMS

Idioms are expressions that convey special meanings which may not have anything to do with the usual meanings of the words used. For example, the expression "It was raining cats and dogs" has nothing to do with household pets. It's just a way of saying it was raining very hard.

Activity

Look at the examples of idioms taken from "Social Time: The Heartbeat of Culture" on pages 178–81. Write out your own definition for the underlined words. If you are not sure of the meaning, discuss it with a partner, small group, or your teacher.

1. From paragraph 1: "This thought . . . strikes a chord in so many people that it has become part of our language."
2. From paragraph 1: "The world over, children simply 'pick up' their society's time concepts as they mature."
3. From paragraph 13: "Lack of punctuality is a badge of success."
4. From paragraph 14: "Seemingly simple words like *now*, snapped out by an impatient New Yorker, and *later*, said by a relaxed Californian, suggest a world of difference."
5. From paragraph 14: ". . . [P]roblems with time present a major stumbling block to Americans abroad."

(See Answer Key, page 324.)

ASSIGNMENTS

Option 1: Cultural Change

Think of an aspect of your culture that is changing. Write an essay in which you discuss this change and state whether you prefer the traditional way or the modern way. (See the essay by Papa Aly Ndaw, pages 168–70, for an example of how one student approached this assignment.)

The purpose of this assignment is to demonstrate how a change in your own or your family's experience can reflect some of the larger patterns of change taking place in a culture or society. For example, in the past it was unusual for women to work outside the home. Today it is common, maybe even expected. Yet this change did not come about overnight. It happened gradually, one family after another. It is only now, looking back, that we can see that a fundamental change in the roles of women and men was taking place. Imagine your readers to be students who are interested in what you have to say but are not familiar with your family or your culture.

Generating Ideas

1. Write down three or four aspects of your culture that are changing—for example, dating or marriage customs, religious practices, the role of women, the role of men, attitudes toward the elderly. Look at your list and decide which of these changes is affecting your own life the most. Freewrite about this change for a few minutes. If you have trouble writing, pick another topic from your list and try again.

(Let's assume that you have chosen to discuss changing family structures. If you have chosen another topic such as marriage patterns or religious practices, remember to write in your own topic as you complete the following steps.)

2. Write a description of what you consider to be the traditional <u>family struc-ture</u> in your culture.

3. Write a description of what you consider to be the modern <u>family structure</u> in your culture.

4. Discuss your descriptions in groups. Be prepared to discuss how <u>family structure</u> is changing and what you, personally, think about these changes.

Organizing Ideas

Using the following organizational pattern, write down some advantages and disadvantages of the aspect of culture you have chosen. For example, students comparing traditional and modern families would use this pattern:

Traditional Family

I. Advantages	*II. Disadvantages*
_____	_____
_____	_____
_____	_____

Modern Family

I. Advantages	*II. Disadvantages*
_____	_____
_____	_____
_____	_____

Working toward a Thesis Statement

1. What overall statement can you make based on the advantages and disadvantages you have noted? What do you believe this change reveals about your culture? For example, Isabella Kong stated that what makes a particular type of family structure "more desirable than the other depends on the context of the society, the values and attitudes of the people, and the economic system."

2. Working in a small group or by yourself, write two or three possible thesis statements. (Review pages 183–84 if you are not sure how to do this.) For which of these thesis statements do you have the most supporting ideas? Which do you think would result in the best essay?

Option 2: Cultural Comparison

Compare some aspect of your native culture with the same aspect of American culture. Be sure to state what conclusion you draw from these cultural differences. (See Masami Kazama's essay on pages 173–74 and Paulo Vieira-Moreno's essay on pages 182–83 for examples.) If you have not lived in two cultures, choose Option 1, which asks you to discuss a change within your own culture.

The purpose of this assignment is to make a generalization about two cultures based on a comparison of their differences. Consider possible readers of your essay to be people from your own culture, interested people outside your culture, and students of anthropology or sociology.

Generating Ideas

1. First you need to find an interesting topic to write about. Start by freewriting for ten to fifteen minutes about this question: What cultural differences surprised you most during your first few months in the United States?

2. Read what you have written and underline parts that seem interesting to you. In the margin write down what different aspects of culture you seem to be talking about. Some examples might be behavior in public places, behavior on dates, hospitality toward guests, child-rearing practices, treatment of old people.

3. Working with a small group of classmates, read some of your freewriting aloud and discuss possible ways to use this material in an essay. Each student should explain what aspects of the two cultures he or she plans to write about.

Organizing Ideas

Next, try to list your ideas in a more structured way. At the top of a piece of paper, write down what aspect of the two cultures you plan to discuss. For example, Masami Kazama wrote: "Behavior in Public: Japan and the United States." Then list the similarities and differences you have observed, using the following format. Remember that for each point of similarity or difference, both cultures should be discussed.

Aspect of cultures being discussed:

	Culture A	*Culture B*
Similarities 1.	_____	1. _____
2.	_____	2. _____
3.	_____	3. _____

Differences 1. _____   1. _____

            2. _____   2. _____

            3. _____   3. _____

Working toward a Thesis Statement

What do these differences and similarities mean? What is the main conclusion you would make based on the information you have listed?

1. Freewrite about these questions for twenty to thirty minutes. Read over your freewriting and underline ideas that seem important.

2. Following the general procedures described on pages 183–84, write three or four possible thesis statements for your essay and pick the one that best expresses your meaning.

3. Discuss your proposed thesis statement with a partner.

SUGGESTED TECHNIQUES

Whether you have chosen Option 1 or Option 2, try to follow these suggestions, which generally apply to more formal types of writing.

1. *Give your essay a title.* Simply forcing yourself to think of a title can serve to focus your essay on one main idea. Once you have written the essay, try writing two or three titles and choose the one that seems best. The title should inform the readers of your topic and also make them curious as to what you have to say. Titles such as *Gone with the Wind*, *Profiles in Courage*, or *The Power of Positive Thinking* have the effect of arousing readers' curiosity.

2. *Include a thesis statement.* After you have written the first draft, check to make sure that you have included a thesis statement that clearly states the main idea of the essay. For example, in the selection entitled "Mixed Metamessages across Cultures," Deborah Tannen states the thesis at the end of paragraph 1: "cultural difference necessarily implies different assumptions about natural and obvious ways to be polite."

Remember that thesis statements have a way of evolving during the writing process. Do not limit yourself by sticking with a thesis that no longer expresses what you believe about your topic.

3. *Check to make sure that your essay is clearly organized.* After you have found your thesis statement, check your supporting evidence. What are the major points you give to support your thesis? Is each major point explained in a separate paragraph?

4. *Write an effective conclusion.* Most of the time the conclusion serves to sum up an essay and let the reader know it is coming to an end. In addition, the conclusion can emphasize your opinion, suggest a way to solve a problem, or explain what you have learned.

Read over the last paragraph of your essay. Does it sound like an ending? Does it function in one or more of the ways mentioned above? As with titles, it is often a good idea to write several possible endings and choose the one you like best.

Before handing in the first draft to your teacher for comment, exchange essays with a partner and fill out the Peer Response Sheet located at the end of the chapter. Be sure to discuss your reactions after you have answered the questions in writing. If your teacher asks you to revise the essay, refer to Part III: Rethinking/Rewriting.

PEER RESPONSE SHEET:
WRITING ABOUT CULTURE

Writer's Name: _____

Reader's Name: _____

Date: _____

(*Note to the reader:* As you respond to the writer's draft, try to focus on the ideas rather than the grammar and spelling. Discuss only those mistakes that interfere with understanding.)

1. What was one thing you learned about culture from reading this essay? _____

_____

_____

_____

_____

2. Did the writer include a thesis statement explaining the main idea of the essay? If so, copy it in the space below. _____

_____

_____

_____

_____

In which paragraph did this thesis statement appear? _____

3. Were there any places where you got confused? If so, what were they? _____

_____

_____

_____

_____

4. Reread the last paragraph of the essay. Do you think it is an effective conclusion? Why or why not? _____

_____

_____

_____

_____

5. What could the writer do to improve the next draft? Make only *one* suggestion.

_____

_____

_____

_____

_____

9

The American Dream: Immigrant Perspectives

There is an old joke about an immigrant who came to the United States. He said, "When I was in the Old Country, I thought the streets in America were all paved with gold. But when I finally got here, not only did I discover that the streets were *not* paved with gold, but that *I* was expected to pave them."

When we think of the expression "The American Dream," many thoughts come to mind such as freedom, equal rights, a good education, a home of one's own. Though America seems to hold out the promise of all these things to everyone, many people, particularly recent immigrants, are aware of the difficulties they face in obtaining this Dream. Discrimination, the language barrier, and poverty can make the Dream seem far from reality.

In this chapter, we will examine the American Dream from the differing perspectives of several different immigrants: a successful lawyer, a working student, a political refugee, and an illegal alien. We will also look at one of the greatest difficulties faced by new immigrants: overcoming the language barrier.

As you read these essays, consider your own ideas about the American Dream. Are the promises America offers readily available to everyone? Are the sacrifices necessary to attain the Dream worthwhile?

READINGS: EQUAL OPPORTUNITY?

The American Dream means different things to different people. For some it means freedom and democracy. For some it means a house with a yard and two cars in the garage. For others it means opportunity, but not without hard work and struggle. And for still others it is just a dream and not reality at all.

An American Success Story
by Samuel Nakasian

> *Samuel Nakasian, a successful lawyer who immigrated to this country from Armenia as a child, gave this speech at the naturalization ceremony for a group of new American citizens on December 12, 1983. As you read this personal statement, think about Nakasian's description of America. Is it realistic? Does it match your own experience?*

Some forty years ago, in a U.S. District Court in New York—a court in the neighborhood of the Statue of Liberty and Ellis Island, where I entered America—I applied for American citizenship and received it, just as you did today in the same time-honored ceremony. I was given my naturalization certificate, as you were given yours today. May I share with you what this certificate has meant to me?

This is my American birthright. I have cherished it above all other posses-

1

2

196

sions for forty years. It means something very special, for no other country in the
world offers as much as this certificate guarantees.

If you came here to escape discrimination because you are a member of a mi-   3
nority in your religious beliefs, ethnic origins, or political preference, *here* you are
guaranteed your religious rights and personal freedom. This court and other
courts are here to serve you by protecting your rights and to hear your petitions
with impartial justice. If you came here to make a better life for yourself and your
family, to have the opportunity of formal education to the highest level of your ca-
pacity, ours is one of the few countries where you can climb the economic, intellectual, and cultural ladder to the top.

I must now, unavoidably, become personal—to emphasize this point. I was   4
brought here very young, very poor, by one surviving parent of a massacre, and
shortly after arriving in the United States I was orphaned. After a few years in an
orphanage, my first job was as a farm hand. I had a dream to be a lawyer; there-
after, I made steady progress: educationally, professionally, and economically. Taking advantage of America's opportunities, I was able to support a family of four
children, each of whom now has a college education at my expense and has employment of his or her choice. And how nice it is that my wife and I are not financially dependent on our children as we approach the later years.

Do you know what I hate to hear? "You are a self-made man." I am *not* a self-   5
made man. I am the product of this great country and its generous people. *America* made me!

The opportunity to work is here. The schools are here and available, whether   6
or not you can afford the tuition for college or graduate school. If you have
dreams and make the effort, *you* can make it or—more accurately—America can
make *you.*

The major difference in America is the 200-year-old system. I know the dif-   7
ference firsthand, because since World War II, I have traveled to almost every
country in the world as a representative of our government and as an overseas ne-
gotiator for American companies. Whatever the country of origin, people who
come to America are remade by our free society system. They become dedicated
Americans regardless of their ethnic origins. . . .

Before World War II, immigrants were regarded one or two notches below   8
the social level of old American families. The greatest social prestige came from
having an ancestor on the Mayflower or in the War of Independence. . . . Today,
all is changed. You are respected for your diligence and honor. It doesn't matter
that your skin is darker, eyes more slanted, or speech heavily accented. You are respected for what you can contribute to your family, community, and country.

Read the awards of the Nobel Prize; read the list of distinguished scientists;   9
read the election sheets; read *Forbes* magazine listing the richest Americans today.
You will find immigrants in all those records of achievement. . . .

In recent years immigrants fly in, so perhaps many of you have not had the   10
opportunity to see the Statue of Liberty. Would you, the first chance you get, visit
there and read what is inscribed? The statue is the symbol of America's outreach to
the world's people. America is great because it is composed of almost every race
and religion in the world. It is a community which has been enriched by what im-

migrants brought here and planted here to flourish in a free society—a society based on government as the *servant* of the people and not government as the *master* of the people. What you do with your lives is your decision, not the government's. . . .

Finally, let me say this. A popular song goes, "If I can make it here [in New York], I can make it anywhere." I believe that. I also believe that if you can't make it in *America*, you were not likely to make it anywhere else.   11

You will make it here, no doubt, because you came here to work. You will find, as I did, that America's rewards are generous.   12

Personal Connections

1. Nakasian's view of America is idealistic; that is, he only talks about the positive things and ignores the darker side. Which of the following statements might explain Nakasian's positive outlook?

  a. He is not aware of such things as discrimination, language problems, or poverty because he never experienced them himself.
  b. He knows that problems exist in the United States, but he wants to offer encouragement to new citizens.
  c. He is proud of his adopted country and wants people to see the positive things as opposed to the negative things usually reported in the press.
  d. He truly believes that the United States allows anyone who really wants to succeed to overcome any obstacles or barriers.

Discuss your answer with your partner, small group, or class.

2. In paragraph 8, Nakasian says that before World War II, recent immigrants were regarded as socially inferior to people whose ancestors came to this country much earlier. But he continues, "Today, all is changed. You are respected for your diligence and honor. It doesn't matter that your skin is darker, eyes more slanted, or speech heavily accented." Do you agree with this statement? Explain why or why not.

3. Think of a successful immigrant whom you know personally or have read about. Try to estimate what percentage of his or her success was related to personal characteristics such as intelligence, motivation, or skill. What percentage was related to opportunities provided by the United States? What percentage was related purely to luck? Write a brief explanation of why you assigned these particular percentages.

Example: Samuel Nakasian

Personal Characteristics: 90%. Nakasian must have been an intelligent and talented student in order to complete law school. He also must have been highly motivated to work so hard to achieve his goal.

Opportunities in the United States: 5%. The United States offered the educational opportunities he needed to fulfill his goals. It also provided a strong economy and a high standard of living. There are many talented lawyers who cannot make a lot of money because they are living in poor countries.

Luck: 5%. Nakasian was lucky to be rescued from war and to survive. Many children from Armenia died at that time. He was also fortunate enough to arrive in this country during one of America's greatest periods of economic growth.

Exchange papers with a classmate, and read and discuss them with each other.

Content and Writing Techniques

1. What, in your opinion, is the main topic of this speech? Where does Nakasian state it?

2. According to Nakasian, what advantages does the United States offer? List all the advantages that he mentions, and next to each advantage, write down the paragraph or paragraphs in which it is discussed.

3. List the different forms of evidence that Nakasian offers to support his opinion that the United States offers more opportunities to immigrants than does any other country. Do you find this evidence convincing? Can you think of any other evidence to support his opinion?

4. In what ways was Nakasian's speech influenced by his audience — a group of new American citizens? How might his speech have been different if he had been speaking to a different audience — for example, prison inmates or people on welfare?

A Reaction to "An American Success Story"
by Aneta Siwik

> *Aneta Siwik was born in Poland and emigrated to the United States with her family in the early 1990s. In responding to Samuel Nakasian's speech, she sees the United States as offering opportunities, but not without great struggle and hardship. As you read, think of people you know who have emigrated to the United States. Do you feel their experience is more similar to that of Nakasian or Siwik?*

In "An American Success Story," Samuel Nakasian showed a very idealistic picture of America. I don't agree with him. Of course, everybody has his or her own American Dream, but I think people think more realistically about this country. If everything Nakasian says in his speech were true, there would be many more successful people, not just a few individuals. However, I know that living in America is the hope for a better tomorrow for a lot of people.   1

In one statement, Nakasian says that America provides equal opportunities for everyone. I can only agree on the point that this country gives a lot of opportunities to everyone. But I would never say that they are equal. It depends on what   2 country you are from, at what age you came to America, and if you are a legal or illegal immigrant. I know that those people who are illegal are exploited by Americans. Employers take advantage, knowing those immigrants will work for the lowest salaries. A legal immigrant or citizen would never agree to work for this kind of money. It should not be this way.

Also the age of a person who comes to America has a big meaning. The younger you are when you come, the bigger the chances of success. Mr. Nakasian came to the United States when he was a child, so he learned English very fast, and it made everything easier for him. But it is very difficult for older people with families to learn how to speak English. Those people not only don't have enough time for study, but their language-learning abilities are not as good as young kids'.

My mother is an example. She wants to speak English at least as well as my brothers and I do and she tries hard, but it is not easy for her. And not knowing English well enough to be able to communicate makes everything complicated. So there are opportunities, as Nakasian says, but they are not equal.

Mr. Nakasian also mentioned that everybody has the right to a good education up to the highest level. That is true. But is everybody able to go to school and then go on to college? Education is very expensive. There are many people who are not poor and not rich either. Based on their income, they can't get financial aid, but they can't afford to pay the tuition by themselves either. Then what use are the educational rights for them? Of course, there are many people in situations like this, and some of them do get a college education, but these are only exceptions.

I agree with Nakasian that the American Constitution stands up for religious rights, personal freedom, democratic law. But does it really work all the time in real life? Discrimination is, always was, and will continue to be a big problem. There always will be people who try to put down others because of nationality, skin color, or religious beliefs. It is harder for non-Americans to find a job, especially if they have accents. Also, democratic law is not always just, because some people take advantage of it.

A lot of things in American society are not that great. But we all know there is no perfect country in the real world. Even so, as far as I know and think, America provides many more opportunities than any other country does, and I hope that living here will bring a change in my life, and a better future. I just don't agree with Samuel Nakasian that the United States is an ideal country.

Personal Connections

1. In paragraph 2, Siwik states that she does not agree with Nakasian that America provides *equal* opportunities for everyone: "It depends on what country you are from, at what age you came to America, and if you are a legal or illegal immigrant." What are your thoughts on this subject? How equal are the opportunities that America provides?

2. In paragraph 6, Siwik talks about discrimination, which she feels is a big problem in this country. Do you agree with her about this? If so, try to think of reasons that discrimination might occur even though it goes against the principles stated in the U.S. Constitution.

Content and Writing Techniques

1. Siwik mentions that the age at which immigrants arrive in the new country is important to their success in learning the language, and she uses the example of her mother to illustrate this point. What is effective about this example? How could the example be made even stronger?

2. In paragraph 3, Siwik says, "The younger you are when you come [to the United States], the bigger the chances of success." Write down three reasons why this statement *might be* true. Write down three reasons why it *might not be* true. Discuss these reasons with a partner or small group.

My American Dream
by Rose-Laure Lamothe

In this essay a student from Haiti tells of her unsuccessful struggle to achieve political power in her native country. For this student, the American Dream means freedom to speak out and to work for the betterment of her people. Before you read, think about what the American Dream means to you.

Freedom of speech in America is different from the situation in my native country, Haiti, where the right of anyone to speak is denied, or you are intimidated by the government authorities.   1

I left because of the lack of free speech, and emigrated to the United States on June 16, 1990. The night that my plane landed, I said to myself, "My dream has come true." I said that because my native country hadn't given me any opportunity to prove myself, even after having gone through fourteen years of school and three years of university. This lack of freedom is caused not only by the government but also by the race problems between people of different skin colors, although family background makes these problems much worse. There is even discrimination against those from different towns or countries of origin.   2

I am a woman who has fought my entire life for my values. My mother is a hard-working woman who did everything to make me accomplish something in my life because I am the only survivor of her eight children. I left my little town when I was fourteen years old for a better education in the capital of Haiti. My school was supposedly one of the best ones there. Whatever my efforts in school, however, I was still humiliated and frustrated by my teachers and fellow students. I was one of the brilliant students, but no one appreciated that. The one thing I always thought about was to be someone who was respected. I always dreamed of being in Congress as a woman representative from the middle class, as a person   3 who was proud of her family and where she came from. It was something unusual to have any women from the middle class in Congress. I dreamed of making a difference and being a good example for all suffering women like me.

After my pre-university education, I took business and economics courses. And three years after that, I went back to my little town to try to help illiterate people. I wanted them to know their rights and how to sign their names because an estimated 65 to 80 percent of the Haitian people are illiterate.

4

The idea to go back to my home town and do this occurred to me as I worked on an assignment my teacher of philosophy once gave me for homework. When I got home, I sat in my bedroom to do the assignment, but nothing came, and I didn't know what to write down or where to begin. After fifteen minutes, I said to myself, "Let me make believe that I am the president or the prime minister of this country. Now, I have to write something because tomorrow I will have a great meeting with all my people." Then the words poured out as if I was drawing out some water. This was the inspiration that led me to go back to teach illiterates.

5

Later I decided to run for the Congress in Haiti, but it is very difficult to do something positive in my country without money and power. Those in power thought that an idea like mine would never work in Haiti because the capitalists don't want anything like my ideas to be put into practice. Those rich people who have the monopoly on the coffee and cotton didn't care because this program would never really be their primary interest. For me, however, helping my people was my only concern. Because of my popularity and my interest in the community, I decided to run for the Congress to make sure my idea would become a reality. I was defeated, of course, for the reason that I was a woman from the middle class, without the necessary power and influence.

6

Since that time, I began to have problems with the government. I was threatened by the army. I received terrible, upsetting, anonymous phone calls, and for more than four hours I was asked questions by the secret police.

7

Then, I dreamed about coming to America. I knew that this is a free democratic country with a community that makes immigrants welcome, and that it is an example for so many other countries.

8

The sociological problems of Haiti have to be resolved as well as the attitudes of the government toward the poor and middle classes. This is the last part of the twentieth century, and it is our time now—for all of us who might have dreamed of a chance for our society, and also for those people who can't express themselves because of the power of other people. It is time for democracy and peace to be fulfilled, and there must be changes everywhere, economically, politically, and sociologically.

9

Personal Connections

1. Take a few minutes to freewrite about your personal definition of the American Dream. Share and discuss your definition with a partner or small group. Could you develop this definition into an essay?

2. In paragraph 5, Lamothe describes having trouble with a school writing assignment, but when she decided to pretend she was a high government official

writing an important letter, "the words poured out as if I was drawing out some water." Have you ever had a similar experience with writing? If so, what inspired you to write? Who were you writing for? What did you do with this writing when you were finished?

Content and Writing Techniques

1. Lamothe's biggest concern was to combat the problem of illiteracy in her native country. Do you agree with her that knowing how to read and write are important skills if people are to understand their political rights? What evidence can you give to support your position?

2. In paragraph 6, Lamothe states that she was defeated in her attempts to become a member of the Haitian Congress because she was "a woman from the middle class, without the necessary power and influence." Which of the following statements best describes your opinion about this problem? Discuss your answer with a partner or small group.

    a. She should have realized that she would never be elected. It was a mistake for her to run for Congress.

    b. She should have kept trying to work within the system. She should have run again for Congress in the next election.

    c. She should have tried to work outside the system by starting her own programs to combat illiteracy.

3. In the last paragraph, Lamothe states, "This is the last part of the twentieth century, and it is our time now." What do you think this statement means? What groups does Lamothe have in mind when she says "our time"? What evidence do you see around the world that this statement is true or false?

The Experiences of an Illegal Alien
by Helen Caguana

Like the previous essay, this one focuses on the problems of a disadvantaged group in society—in this case, illegal immigrants. Do you know any immigrants who came to this country illegally? How is their situation different from that of legal immigrants?

For many years I have seen people around me suffering for not having a legal status in this country, a status that is very necessary to be treated equally. As illegal aliens, these people are unable to fulfill their dreams and achieve their goals. By living in this environment I have become aware of their problems, their feelings and hopes. But most of all I have become very interested in their lives. For this reason, it came to my mind that I should interview someone who had lived as an illegal alien and who would be able to describe his life with all the necessary details. I decided to interview my friend Carlos (not his real name), a forty-five-year-old man who experienced this social inequality for many years.

Carlos was born in Bogotá, Colombia. He lived there for twenty-four years in   2
a very small village with his mother, two brothers, his wife, and two children. He described his life in Bogotá as unbearable. He said they were not able to survive in so much poverty. So, at the age of twenty-four, Carlos decided to seek a better future for himself and his family. He was tired of living in poor conditions. I asked him what kind of conditions he meant. But I noticed that all of a sudden, his mood changed, his enthusiasm disappeared, and I thought for a moment that he wanted to conclude the interview. To my surprise, after a pause, he looked up and responded: "The misery, the injustice, the dirt, the ignorance of the people. These are some of the conditions poor people must confront and deal with."

He seemed like he didn't want to discuss the subject any further, but my cu-   3
riosity and desire to find out more about his past didn't cease at that point, and taking the risk of not being answered, I asked him to share with me a little more of his experiences in that village. He then smiled and said, "Sure, I can say things that would be very helpful to anyone who would be interested in the political systems carried out in Latin America. But that would be too broad. However, I will say that my village was not different at all from other villages throughout Colombia. Poor people are mistreated by the powerful everywhere; they have no resources to fall back on. Injustices toward the poor take place, and there's no one who can help them. And what's incredible about this is that they still consider Colombia a democratic country."

I thought he was getting too deeply into the discussion of the economic situ-   4
ation in Colombia, and I was interested in exploring other aspects of his life. So I decided to ask him how his life changed when he arrived in New York. He described the experiences he went through to cross the frontier to the United States. He said he was caught by immigration agents several times, and they sent him back to Mexico, where he would work for a couple of months, save some money, and cross the frontier again. After the third time Carlos finally arrived in New York City and settled here.

On his first day he didn't have any place to stay, and he spent the whole day   5
looking for a job. He exclaimed, "I was desperately looking for a job in restaurants, hotels where they would let me stay for the night. But everything seemed impossible—the transportation, the language. No one wanted me. It was about 1:30 A.M. when I finally found a place to stay. After three days, when I had almost no money, I found a job in a restaurant as an entertainer." Carlos played the guitar and sang during the nights in that restaurant for three years, getting a very low salary.

He also worked in other places where he was treated terribly and where he   6
couldn't do anything to defend himself. He knew that defending himself meant that he would lose his job and not be able to support his family in Colombia. He went through many experiences that made him change. He learned not to trust people. He found out that life was complicated not only in Colombia but everywhere.

During his seventh year living in New York, Carlos received the sad news   7 that his mother had died. He couldn't even attend her funeral. Carlos knew that if he left New York, he would never be able to return. And so he stayed here with the terrible feeling that he had not been with his mother during the last minutes of her life. Two months after this, when Carlos was working in a restaurant as a waiter, his employer turned him over to the immigration authorities. His boss had called immigration and had told them that he had an illegal employee. The officers came that same day and took him. He was told to leave the country immediately, that they wouldn't like to deport him.

Carlos did not leave the United States. He decided to stay and hide from   8
the immigration authorities. He kept on working illegally until finally, in 1987, he got his residence as a legal alien through the amnesty system. He is now in the process of bringing his family to New York, and he also has a better job than before.

He concluded the interview by saying, "Do you see all the things I had to go   9
through in order to survive in this country? And even now that I am a resident, I still don't consider this place my home. I am a Colombian, and I always will be. The only reason I am here and want my family to come is that here we have more opportunities than in Colombia, and that is really a shame. Every citizen should stay in his or her own country, but only if that country has enough resources for the survival of its people."

I was totally satisfied with the interview. Carlos represents the life of many   10
people in this country who, like him, have fled from poverty in their own countries to live here as illegal aliens. From this interview I have realized how hard immigrant people struggle to survive and be admitted to this country. This situation has made me reaffirm my ideas that humans should not have frontiers or limits, that they should be able to live wherever they feel most comfortable.

Personal Connections

1. In paragraph 6, Caguana says that Carlos "found out that life was complicated not only in Colombia but everywhere." Freewrite for a few minutes about your interpretation of this statement. Discuss your writing with your partner, group, or class.

2. In paragraph 9, Carlos tells the writer: "I still don't consider this place my home. I am a Colombian, and I always will be." How do you describe yourself—by your original nationality, as an American, or some combination of the two?

Content and Writing Techniques

1. According to this essay, what is the major reason that people decide to leave their native countries and immigrate to the United States? Reread the entire essay, and underline every part that supports your answer to this question.

2. Caguana ends the essay by stating her belief "that humans should not have frontiers or limits, that they should be able to live wherever they feel most comfortable." Write down three reasons why this *might be* a good idea. Write down three reasons why it *might not be.*

READINGS: THE LANGUAGE BARRIER

One problem faced by nearly all immigrants—legal and illegal alike—is the challenge of learning to survive and thrive in a country where English is the dominant language. As you read the three essays in this section, think about your own experiences in learning English. What failures and successes do you remember most clearly?

Teacher, It's Nice to Meet You, Too
by Ruby Ibañez

> *Ruby Ibañez taught English as a Second Language and trained teachers in a refugee camp in the Philippines during the early 1980s. At that time, many people from Kampuchea (formerly Cambodia) were forced to flee their homeland to escape political persecution, in which a great many people—possibly millions—lost their lives. This essay, although it was written by Ibañez, is told in the voice of a Cambodian refugee who was learning English in the camp and preparing to emigrate to the United States. Before reading, try to guess what the title of the essay means.*

Hello! I'm one of the twenty students in your class. I come every day. I sit here and smile and I laugh and I try to talk your English, which you always say will be "my" language. 1

As I sit here I wonder if you, my teacher, are able to tell when I am sinking in spirit and ready to quit this incredible task. I walked a thousand miles, dear teacher, before I met you. Sitting here, listening to you and struggling to hold this pencil seems to be my "present." I want to tell you though that I, too, am a person of the past. 2

When I say that my name is Sombath I want to tell you also that back in my village, I had a mind of my own. I could reason. I could argue. I could lead. My neighbors respected me. There was much value to my name, teacher, no matter how strange it may sound to your ears. 3

You ask, "Where are you from?" I was born in a land of fields and rivers and hills where people lived in a rich tradition of life and oneness. My heart overflows with pride and possession of that beautiful land, that place of my ancestors. Yet, with all this that I want to share with you, all I can mutter is I came from Cambodia. I'm Khmer. I'm not even sure I can say these words right or make you understand that inside, deep inside, I know what you are asking. 4

"How old are you?" I want to cry and laugh whenever you go around asking that. I want so very much to say, I'm old, older than all the dying faces I have left behind, older than the hungry hands I have pushed aside, older than the shouts of 5 fear and terror I have closed my ears to, older than the world, maybe. And certainly much older than you. Help me, my teacher, I have yet to know the days of the week or the twelve months of the year.

Now I see you smiling. I know you are thinking of my groans and sighs 6 whenever I have to say "house" and it comes out "how" instead. I think many times, that maybe I was born with the wrong tongue and the wrong set of teeth. Back in my village, I was smarter than most of my neighbors. Teacher, I tremble with fear now over words like *chicken* and *kitchen*.

Now you laugh. I know why. I do not make sense with the few English 7 words I try to say. I seem like a child because I only say childlike things in your English. But I am an adult, and I know much that I cannot yet express. This I think is funny and sad at the same time. Many times the confusion is painful. But do not feel sad, dear teacher. I wish very much to learn all the things that you are offering me, to keep them in my heart, and to make them a part of me. However, there was this life I have lived through and now the thoughts of days I have yet to face. Between my efforts to say "How are you?" and "I am fine, thank you" come uncontrollable emotions of loneliness, anger, and uncertainty. So have patience with me, my teacher, when you see me sulking and frowning, looking outside the classroom or near to crying.

Please go on with your enthusiasm, your eagerness, and your high spirit. 8 Deep inside me, I am moved that someone will still give me so much importance. Keep that smile when I keep forgetting the words you taught me yesterday and cannot remember those I learned last week.

Give me a gentle voice to ease the frustration, humiliation, and shame when 9 I just cannot communicate *refrigerator*, *emergency*, or *appointment*. For you, my teacher, they are little words, but for me they are like monsters to fight. Pat me on the shoulder once in a while and help my tense body and trembling hands to write A B C and 1 2 3.

Continue to reward me with a warm "good" or "very good" when I have fi- 10 nally pronounced *church* correctly after one hundred "shurshes." Flatter me by attempting to speak a phrase or two from my language and I will end up laughing with you.

I am one of the students in your class. I came today and tomorrow I will 11 come again. I smile and laugh and try to talk your English, which you say will become my language.

Personal Connections

1. Underline any parts of this essay that relate to your own feelings about learning English. Discuss your feelings with a partner. Then freewrite for fifteen minutes about this question: How are your feelings about learning English similar to or different from the ones described in the essay?

2. In paragraph 9, Sombath mentions several English words that "are like monsters to fight." Make a list of English words that are your own personal "monsters."

3. This essay was written both for students of English and for English teachers. Place an *S* next to any of the following messages that seem to be directed toward students. Place a *T* next to any messages that are directed toward teachers.

   a. Try not to judge people by their present circumstances.

   b. If you keep trying hard enough, you will eventually get what you want.

   c. People need encouragement in order to succeed.

   d. Be patient in everything you do.

Discuss your answers with a partner or small group.

4. Do you know anyone who survived a dangerous situation such as a war, a natural disaster, or a serious accident? If so, freewrite for fifteen minutes about that person. How was his or her life similar to Sombath's? How was it different?

Content and Writing Techniques

1. In paragraph 2, Sombath says, "I, too, am a person of the past." What do you think this means?

2. In paragraph 5, find evidence that Sombath has struggled hard to survive.

3. Which word best describes Sombath's feelings about learning English?

   a. ambivalence

   b. confusion

   c. frustration

   d. enthusiasm

4. The title of this essay has the word *too* in it. Why do you think the writer included this word in the title?

Learning English Ain't Easy
by Betty Liu Ebron

Betty Liu Ebron, a columnist for the New York Daily News, *writes about a problem shared by every recent immigrant — learning to speak and understand English. Before you read, think about your own struggle with English. What was the most difficult problem you faced in learning the language?*

Can't anyone speak English?   1

This ain't Russia; this is America.   2

They can't speak English, but they sure can count money.   3

I got lucky yesterday. My cabdriver spoke a little English.   4

That's how many New Yorkers feel about their new neighbors, who are con-   5
tinuing the immigrant tradition that makes the city so uniquely diverse. These are the same people who forget that their parents or grandparents didn't speak such good English when they arrived here.

"It's very difficult, pronunciation," sighed Edward Proklov, 33, of Staten Island by way of Russia. "I took school for English for three months. I read books. I speak after one year. I understand after two years." 6

Learning English demands patience from everyone in a city where one of three New Yorkers is foreign-born, two of five residents speak English as a second language and more than 600,000 people barely speak English at all. 7

"Other Americans, they make fun of us—'What did you say? *What did you say?* ' " said Fernando Bueno, 40, a maintenance worker who came from Colombia twenty-two years ago and became a citizen fifteen years ago. 8

"I try to speak clear," he said. "But some Americans, they only look at us and don't try to understand us. They think, 'Oh no, *no!* You're Spanish. We can't talk to you.' " 9

Here's where cultural breakdown sets in—or to be blunt, prejudice. 10

"The police, they ask me all the time for my green card," Bueno said. "I say, 'I am an American citizen. The only green card I have is American Express!' They think because I have a Spanish accent and I came from Colombia, I am a drug dealer. I never even smoke marijuana!" 11

No one is more sensitive about lacking English skills than immigrants. 12

Darnes Taveras, a writer from Queens, witnessed the suffering of her Dominican immigrant parents. 13

"They feel less empowered," said Taveras, 25. "Oh, my mother took English classes and stuff. But it just didn't pan out. She had six kids and a factory job. To learn, you have to have a certain amount of peace of mind. You can't constantly be stressed out." 14

There are other factors. 15

"I think people are a bit nicer to little foreign girls than they are to little boys who don't speak English," said Eurim Shun, 29, whose parents left Korea when she was 9. "It's easier to make friends when you're playing hopscotch. Little boys, you're called names." 16

Even immigrants who already know English can find it tough. British English, for instance, doesn't sound anything like American English. 17

"Here you can curse any way you want, but over there in India, 'bloody' is the most insulting thing, like in 'You bloody idiot!' " explained Rajesh Ranchal, 21. 18

Ranchal, a physical therapy college major who works days at a newsstand, arrived four years ago and picked up American English in months. It took a year-and-a-half for his co-worker, Manu Solanki, 49, who left India for Queens six years ago. 19

"Age makes it harder," said Solanki. So does slang: "They say prez, not president, not husband, hubby." 20

More people want to learn English than the system can handle. The Board of Education has thousands on a waiting list for its adult English classes. At the Queens Borough Public Library, people wait for hours to sign up. At the New York Public Library, they pick students for English classes by lottery. 21

In the meantime, everyone needs to be patient. After all, in the end, no matter what language you speak, we all want the same things. 22

Personal Connections

1. Have you ever had trouble communicating with Americans because of your accent or other language problems? Do you feel that Americans are prejudiced against people who speak with an accent? What good and bad experiences have you had in speaking English with Americans?

2. In paragraph 6, a man who has immigrated to the United States from Russia states that he began to speak English before he could understand it. How did the language learning process work for you? Did you speak first or understand first?

Content and Writing Techniques

1. In your opinion, what is the *main idea* of this essay? Write one sentence in which you express the main idea. Discuss these sentences with your partner, group, or class.

2. This essay was originally published in a daily newspaper. In what ways are newspaper articles different from other types of writing? Give specific examples from this essay to illustrate your ideas.

3. Do you agree that it is harder for older people to learn a new language? Give examples from your own experience to support your opinion.

4. Reread the conclusion of this essay. Do you feel it provides an effective ending for an article about language learning? Do you agree with Ebron's statement that "no matter what language you speak, we all want the same things"?

A Reaction to "Learning English Ain't Easy"
by Isana Loshinsky

A student from the former Soviet Union responds to the preceding essay about the difficulties of learning English. She focuses on the need for tolerance and coexistence in a country where almost everyone has an immigrant background.

A language is the most important means by virtue of which human beings communicate. Unfortunately, people living in different parts of the world have different languages, which undoubtedly makes such needful communication awkward. Thus, all of us who need to communicate with those who speak different languages have to be more patient and attentive to each other.

Nevertheless, being myself in a situation when I am forced to speak a language that is not my native one, I have realized that many Americans, specifically inhabitants of New York City, do not have that patience and tend to get exasperated easily and fast. On this point I absolutely agree with Betty Liu Ebron, the author of the article "Learning English Ain't Easy." These same people completely forget that their grandparents or parents didn't speak perfect English. They themselves have to thank their parents for the fact that they were born in America and had the possibility to learn English from early childhood.

Speaking of perfect English, I always ask myself what perfect English is. Is it a sum of correct pronunciation, correct grammar, and a well-developed vocabulary? In my opinion, there are very few people who possess such a skill of speaking perfect English unless we are talking about teachers and other academics. However, in a country of immigrants, there might be some people who speak with an accent but use correct grammar. I believe that there are many of them. It is impossible to demand perfect pronunciation from people who started learning English during adolescence or later. There are objective biological and psychological reasons for that matter. Besides, to prove that one is really worth something, it is sufficient to have English at a level at which you can explain and be understood.

The other aspect of the article that I agree with is that native-born Americans or people who have lived here for many years consider themselves privileged due to speaking English as a native language. Sometimes when it is beneficial for such people, they make believe they don't understand. They don't even make any attempt to understand. Hearing my accent, for instance, my landlord always asked his wife, who was kinder to me: "What? What did *she* say?" That *she* he stressed especially, emphasizing that he had no respect for me at all. With equal success he could have referred to me as *it*. It would sound the same in his exegesis.

In conclusion, I would say that prejudice against people who have trouble speaking English and following it up with hostility do not promote our coexistence. America is a country of immigrants. That means we all came here to be equal, for a better life. Some of us got lucky not to be the first generation, which always has to sacrifice its well-being for the well-being of the next ones. All of us have to remember where we came from and what the beginning was. Thus, may we have a little respect and patience with each other! It really can facilitate our coexistence.

Personal Connections

1. In paragraph 3, Loshinsky writes, "I always ask myself what perfect English is." Write out your own definition of "perfect English," and discuss it with your partner, group, or class. Do you think you will ever achieve "perfect English"? Why or why not?

2. Has an American ever been rude to you because you spoke with an accent? If so, tell this story in a piece of freewriting.

3. Have you ever had a dream in which you were speaking English? In your dream did you speak with an accent? In your opinion, what was the significance of this dream?

Content and Writing Techniques

1. In paragraph 3, Loshinsky states, "It is impossible to demand perfect pronunciation from people who started learning English during adolescence or later," and goes on to assert that there are "objective biological and psychological reasons" for this. Do you agree that people who begin to learn a language after adolescence will never achieve perfect pronunciation? What evidence do you have to support your opinion?

2. In paragraph 5, Loshinsky writes that the first generation to immigrate to a new country "always has to sacrifice its well-being for the well-being of the next ones." Do you agree with this statement? Freewrite about your opinion on this question for ten to fifteen minutes, and then discuss your writing with a partner.

3. This essay was written in class, and Loshinsky included it in her portfolio as a sample of her best in-class writing. If you were one of the teachers evaluating her portfolio, what comments would you make? What are the strengths of this essay? In what areas could it be improved?

WRITING STRATEGIES

CUBING

Cubing is a way of generating ideas by looking at a topic from six different points of view (like the six sides of a cube). It is not necessarily a way of organizing an essay. After going through the six steps, you may decide that some parts fit together while others do not. The process is similar to photography—from a roll of twenty-four pictures, you may be lucky to get a few really good shots. When you write your essay, use those parts of the cube that work best for you.

Once you know your topic for writing, you can begin cubing. Plan to spend about ten minutes on each of the six steps. Remember to take a break when you get tired.

The list that follows explains the different steps. The examples were written by Steven Haber on the theme of immigration.

Steps to Cubing

1. *Description:* What things look like, definitions, facts, figures, general characteristics, physical qualities, descriptions of places.

Example: Definition of the term *immigrant*

Immigrants are people who have left their native country to settle permanently in a new country. They often face problems such as the language barrier, culture shock, loss of social status, loneliness, and homesickness. Immigrants are often forced to take low-paying and/or dangerous jobs in order to support themselves.

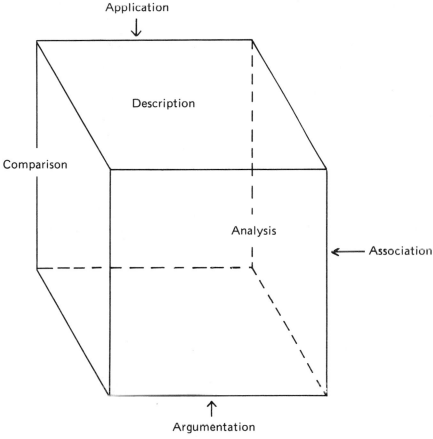

Figure 9–1   Cubing

2. *Comparison:* How is it similar to or different from. . . ? How is it different in different places or countries? If you are writing about a person, how is he or she like or unlike someone else?

Example: Legal versus illegal immigrants in the United States

Legal immigrants are those who come to the United States with visas or green cards. They can eventually apply for permanent residence or citizenship. As legal residents or citizens, they are entitled to full legal protection and benefits such as unemployment insurance, Social Security, and public education for their children.

Illegal immigrants are those who enter the country without legal papers; they may simply walk across the border or stow away on a boat. This second group receives almost no protection under the law and is often forced to accept the worst jobs at the lowest pay. They are not entitled to any benefits and must rely completely on themselves for support.

3. *Association:* Memories, thoughts, freewriting, examples, experiences, personal connections with the topic.

Example: Personal memory

My great-grandfather emigrated from Rumania to this country with his family in the late 1880s. Speaking very little English and with a wife and five children to feed, he supported himself by setting up a tailor shop. He used a heavy steam presser to press pants; this required so much force that his right arm grew to be two inches longer than his left.

Although he struggled all his life to make a living in America, he never made much money. His sons, however, opened up a chain of candy and toy stores. Eventually, they did so well that they began to import toys from Europe and Japan and sell them to stores all across the country.

4. *Analysis:* The reasons why things happen, supporting details, evidence, controversies, discussions, investigations.

Example: Reasons for immigration

Immigrants come to the United States for a variety of reasons. Some come because of political or religious persecution. Others come for the educational opportunities. However, the vast majority come for employment opportunities and the possibility of improving their standard of living.

In many countries, there are simply not enough jobs that pay well, even for those who are well-educated or trained in a profession. In the United States, even in a recession, the unemployment rate is around 7 percent. This means that most people have jobs, and as a result, they are able to own houses, cars, and enjoy a standard of living that is one of the highest in the world.

5. *Application:* What problems can be solved? What are the social/economic implications? How can . . . be used?

Example: How immigrants strengthen the economy

Immigrants strengthen the economy by taking jobs that most established American citizens do not want. For example, immigrants work as waiters, dishwashers, taxi drivers, and security guards. These are generally low-paying and/or dangerous jobs. If there were no immigrant labor force, the labor costs to businesses would be much higher, forcing many companies to fail or raise the prices they charge to their customers.

In addition, immigrants stimulate the economy by creating jobs that did not exist before. For example, Korean fruit markets and nail salons, Chinese and Indian restaurants, and Dominican grocery stores are all businesses created and maintained by immigrants.

6. *Argumentation:* Opinions, conclusions, recommendations, personal feelings, social criticism, positive suggestions.

Example: Opinion about immigration

The U.S. government should not place additional restrictions on immigration, but should maintain the number of legal immigrants at the present level. Restricting immigration will neither increase the number of jobs in the economy nor significantly reduce the expenses that governments have to pay. The vast majority of people on welfare, in public schools, in hospitals, and in prisons are not immigrants, but established American citizens.

In addition, if it becomes more difficult to enter the United States legally, there will be a greater temptation to enter illegally. It is better to allow immigrants to enter in an orderly manner so that they can become tax-paying members of society as opposed to uncontrolled, unprotected, and untaxed illegal aliens.

Steven Haber's Comments on Cubing

As I started writing this cube, I wasn't really sure what I wanted to say on the topic of immigration. But as I worked my way through the steps, a number of ideas began to develop. For example, the definition reminded me that although most people think they know what an immigrant is, they do not stop to make the distinction between legal and illegal immigrants, an important difference when we think about immigration policy. That is why, in the comparison section, I compared legal to illegal immigrants.

The association section made me think of my own personal connection to this topic, and reminded me that the situation of immigrants coming to America today has not changed much in the hundred years or so since my great-grandfather came here. Immigrants still face language and culture problems, and the first generation still seems to make tremendous sacrifices so that the second generation can do better.

Finally, I began to think about the present anti-immigrant opinions I read about in the newspapers, which seem to me both ignorant and unfair. I decided to point out the positive contributions immigrants make to the economy and to argue against cutting back on legal immigration.

TOPIC SENTENCES AND SUPPORTING EVIDENCE

American expository or argumentative writing often contains topic sentences, which state the main idea of the paragraph in which they appear. These topic sentences serve as signposts for readers, helping them follow the writer's line of reasoning. Often the topic sentence is the first sentence of the paragraph, but sometimes you have to read the whole paragraph before you can figure out the main idea. In longer or more complex paragraphs, two successive sentences may be needed to express the main idea.

Each topic sentence is usually backed up with some specific examples, facts, or statistics, which support the main idea and make the paragraph more convincing. For example, if I tell you that many people in New York are at a disadvantage because they don't speak English, you may or may not agree with me. But if I tell you that according to the latest U.S. Census, one out of three New Yorkers was born in a foreign country, you may take my opinion more seriously.

Activity

The following activity asks you to identify the topic sentences and supporting evidence in "A Reaction to 'Learning English Ain't Easy' " on pages 210–11.

1. Skim through the essay and find the topic sentence that expresses the idea that Americans are not patient with people who do not speak English well. Underline this sentence.

Now find the sentences, or parts of sentences, in the same paragraph that express each of the following supporting details:

   a. Americans do not think about the fact that many of their ancestors did not speak English well.
   b. People forget how fortunate they are to be born in this country and thus to speak English as their native language.

Place brackets [ ] around each of these sentences and in the margin identify whether the sentence explains detail *a* or *b*.

2. Find the paragraph that tries to define what is meant by "perfect English." Underline the topic sentence that expresses this main idea.

In the same paragraph, bracket the sentences that present the following supporting details, and in the margin label the sentences *a*, *b*, or *c*:

   a. Immigrants may speak correctly but still have an accent.
   b. Not many Americans, even those born in this country, speak perfect English.
   c. It is not realistic to expect people who came to the United States as adults to pronounce words as a native speaker would.

3. Underline the topic sentence that tells us that Loshinsky is introducing a second point of agreement with the author of "Learning English Ain't Easy." What was the key word that indicated that Loshinsky was introducing a new idea?

What general writing strategy does Loshinsky use to support the main point that is stated in the topic sentence of this paragraph?

4. Look at the concluding paragraph of this essay. Underline what you believe to be the topic statement of this paragraph. Has Loshinsky stated this idea elsewhere in her essay? If so, where?

Activity

The next activity asks you to formulate two different topic sentences on the general subject of the American Dream and then to add appropriate supporting evidence. When you finish, you will have written two paragraphs.

1. Work in a group of three or four students. Individually, take about three minutes to write down quickly your own definition of the American Dream.

2. Compare your definition to those of others in your group.

3. On the left side of a piece of paper, list some of the aspects of the American Dream that were mentioned. Then, on the right side, list things that sometimes challenge the Dream.

	American Dream	*What Sometimes Happens*
Example:	a. Equal opportunity	a. Discrimination
	b. A high standard of living	b. Homelessness
Your List:	a.	a.
	b.	b.
	c.	c.
	d.	d.
	e.	e.

4. Discuss the lists. Decide on one of the aspects from the left-hand list that your group would like to develop into a paragraph.

5. Working with your group, practice writing a topic sentence that expresses the main point you would like to make in your paragraph.

Example: Equal opportunity will always be an important part of the American Dream.

6. Try to come up with some general supporting evidence for this topic sentence.

Example: Equal opportunity will always be an important part of the American Dream. Today there are more women and minorities entering the professions than at any time in history.

7. After you have written down some general supporting evidence, see if your group can come up with any personal examples, statistics, or other information to further illustrate these ideas.

Example: Equal opportunity will always be an important part of the American Dream. Today there are more women and minorities entering the professions than at any time in history. For example, in my parents' generation, women were mostly housewives and hardly any of them went to college. But things are different now. In my own family, one of my sisters is a stockbroker, the other is a lawyer, and I am studying to be an accountant.

8. Now complete steps 4–7 using one of the items from the list of things that sometimes challenge the Dream.

9. When you have finished both paragraphs, have one group member read them out loud. Can you think of any ways to make the paragraphs more convincing? When all the groups have finished, share your paragraphs in a discussion with the entire class.

GRAMMAR IN CONTEXT
PRACTICE WITH THE PRESENT PERFECT TENSE

The exercise that follows gives you a chance to practice using the present perfect tense. Remember that this tense is used to refer to something that began in the past but continues into the present or is still important in the present. At times, the present perfect tense is also used for things that *always* or *never* happened. (If you need to review this tense, see the section entitled "Using the Present Perfect Tense" on page 156.)

Activity

Work with a partner. Choose words from each column to form complete sentences that are true statements about the people mentioned. Use the present perfect tense in each sentence.

Examples: I have always loved making money.

My family has always enjoyed watching TV.

I	have/has always	avoid	working hard
My partner	have/has always	enjoy	drinking beer
My friends	have/has always	dislike	watching TV
My family	have/has always	hate	making money
We	have/has always	love	dancing

Variation: In each of the sentences, change always to never.

Example: I have never avoided working hard.

PROOFREADING FOR ARTICLES

Pay special attention to the use of articles (*a*, *an*, and *the*) in the following paragraphs, adapted from an essay entitled "To Go or Not to Go" by Liliya Bomme. Correct any errors in the use of articles, and then discuss your changes with a partner or small group. (For a review of article usage, see "Coping with Articles" on pages 121–22.)

There are different reasons for emigration, but result is the same—we move   1

to other place. The emigration is not just the moving to another country, but the

leaving your native land. And this is the most important thing. Not everyone can do it although the life in the native country is unbearable. Some people are afraid to go to another place.

In fact, the life in one country is different from life in another. It depends on   2
people, on system, on traditions, friends, favorite places, hobbies, native language. So many things connect the people to their native country. And it's really difficult to leave. Just serious reasons should cause them to do it.

What happens when person finally decides to take this great step—to emi-   3
grate? This person hopes, sometimes is sure, he or she will be happy in a new place. But who knows? There are no absolutely perfect places in the world.
(See Answer Key, page 324.)

VOCABULARY PRACTICE: IMMIGRATION

Sometimes students feel that each new essay topic is like starting all over again with English. It's true that different topics tend to require different vocabulary and grammatical structures. The following exercise gives you a chance to practice vocabulary and grammar within the context of immigration.

Activity

Read through the following essay quickly to get the meaning. Then go back and fill each blank with a word that makes sense. Note that there may be more than one correct answer.

I have _____ many funny experiences since I _____ to   1
the United States because I _____ understand a lot of things when I first _____ here. I still _____ mistakes too. Sometimes I _____ after _____ mistakes, but sometimes I feel terrible.

When I first _____ to America, I usually _____ out to   2
look around. One day I went to Burger King even though I didn't know how to speak English because I _____ so hungry. I thought that in Burger King it _____ be easy to order food.

When I got inside, I _____ to a couple of people order because   3
I couldn't _____ the menu board. After I chose a name of something to order and _____ to pronounce it a couple of times,

I _____ in front of the cashier. Although I pronounced the name several times, she didn't understand me, so I _____ body language by _____ to the menu board, but it was getting worse.

She asked me something after I paid for my food, but I really couldn't 4 understand. Later I understood that she asked what kind of sauce I wanted. But I was so _____ at that time. There were so many people _____ at me.

(See Answer Key, page 324–25, for some possible answers.)

VOCABULARY PRACTICE: THE LANGUAGE BARRIER

Using a dictionary can be frustrating because a word you don't know is often defined by other words you don't know. In cases like this, trying to use the dictionary can feel like going around in circles of confusion. The following exercise asks you to figure out the meaning of words in context by matching certain words with appropriate definitions.

Activity

In this activity, you will read phrases taken from the article "Learning English Ain't Easy" on pages 208–209. After each quotation, you will see several definitions. Match the definitions with the appropriate words in the quotation.

1. From paragraph 5: ". . . continuing the immigrant tradition that makes the city so uniquely diverse."

   a. Underline the word that means <u>very special or different</u>.
   b. Put a check [✔] above the word that refers to <u>something that has gone on for a long time</u>.
   c. Circle the word that means <u>having many different types</u>.

2. From paragraph 7: "Learning English demands patience from everyone. . . ."

   a. Circle the word that implies <u>not giving up</u>.
   b. Underline the word that means <u>requires</u>.

3. From paragraph 10: "Here's where cultural breakdown sets in—or to be blunt, prejudice."

   a. Underline the words that refer to <u>a misunderstanding between people of different backgrounds</u>.
   b. Put a check above the word that refers to <u>judging people before you really know them</u>.
   c. Circle the word that means <u>strongly worded or direct</u>.

4. From paragraph 12: "No one is more sensitive about lacking English skills than immigrants."

    a. Put a check above the word that means <u>people who were not born in this country</u>.
    b. Circle the word that means <u>easily hurt</u>.
    c. Underline the word that means <u>not having something</u>.

5. From paragraphs 13–14: "Darnes Taveras, a writer from Queens, witnessed the suffering of her Dominican parents. 'They feel less empowered,' said Taveras, 25."

    a. Underline the words that mean <u>helpless</u>.
    b. Put a check above the word that means <u>great pain</u>.
    c. Draw two lines under the word that tells us Taveras's age.
    d. Circle the word that means <u>observed</u>.

(See Answer Key, page 325.)

ASSIGNMENTS

OPTION 1: CRITIQUE OF A PUBLISHED ESSAY

Write an essay in which you critique the ideas presented in "An American Success Story" by Samuel Nakasian (pages 196–98) *or* in "Learning English Ain't Easy" by Betty Liu Ebron (pages 208–209).

In a critique you are expected to "criticize" the ideas in someone else's writing. But note that the meaning of the word *criticize* in this sense is different from its usual definition. According to the *American Heritage Dictionary*, this type of criticism is "characterized by careful and exact evaluation and judgment" but is not necessarily negative.

The purpose of your essay is to present a balanced evaluation of the ideas in the essay you are critiquing, based on your own experiences and other relevant information. Consider the following readers as your audience: recent immigrants, people interested in equal rights, and students of political science.

Generating Ideas

1. If you decide to focus on the Nakasian essay, consider the following summary of some of the ideas he presents. Discuss these ideas with a group of classmates. Which ideas do you agree with? Which do you disagree with? Can you think of any specific examples to support your opinions?

- The United States provides equal opportunities for everyone.
- There is no longer discrimination based on race, nationality, or religion.

- Everyone has equal opportunities to work, go to school, and climb the economic, intellectual, and cultural ladder to the top.
- If you make an effort, you will succeed.

1a. If you decide to focus on the Ebron essay, consider the following summary of some of the ideas she presents. Discuss these ideas with a group of classmates. Which ideas do you agree with? Which do you disagree with? Can you think of any specific examples to support your own opinions?

- Many Americans are prejudiced against people who don't speak English well.
- Immigrants are very embarrassed about their problems with English.
- You have to have peace of mind to learn a language.
- All people want the same things out of life, regardless of what language they speak.

2. Outside of class, arrange to talk to two or three immigrants whom you know about the ideas raised in the essay you have chosen to critique. Then freewrite for fifteen to twenty minutes about what they told you.

Organizing Ideas

1. Divide a sheet of paper into two columns. In the left column, list the points you agree with in the essay you are critiquing. In the right column, list any points of disagreement.

2. Which of the two lists is longer? Overall, do you feel more agreement or disagreement with the ideas in the essay you are critiquing?

Working Toward a Thesis Statement

Two writing strategies that might help you to develop a thesis statement for this assignment are looping (pages 152–54) and cubing (pages 212–15). If you use looping, focus on your reaction to the ideas in the essay you are critiquing. If you use cubing, focus on your own ideas—either about the American Dream or about learning English.

Based on your own opinions, the ideas you got from class discussions, and your informal interviews with immigrants, try to write a thesis statement that sums up your main conclusion about the essay you are critiquing. Remember to write two or three possible thesis statements, until you have one you are satisfied with.

Think about how you could support this thesis. Could you cite your own experience to support your opinion? Could you include a quotation or example from your interviews with immigrants as supporting evidence?

OPTION 2: ANALYSIS OF YOUR OWN APPROACH TO LANGUAGE LEARNING

Write an essay in which you analyze your own methods for learning English and make a generalization about the approach to language learning that works best for you. Although this option is based on your personal experience as a language learner, it asks you to analyze your experience and come to a general conclusion in the same way that you might be asked to analyze a problem for a psychology or history paper. Moreover, by asking you to reflect on your own processes as a language learner, this option encourages you to step back from your experience and consider it as if you were an outside expert. This kind of "thinking about thinking" is sometimes referred to as metacognition. As a result of working on this option, you may come to understand yourself, and your language-learning processes, better.

Generating Ideas

1. In trying to analyze yourself as a language learner, begin by telling a story. Freewrite for fifteen to twenty minutes in response to this question:

Thinking back on how you learned English, describe a time when you experienced a breakthrough—sudden progress that made you feel good about yourself as a language learner. What led up to the breakthrough? What happened afterward? What did the breakthrough reveal about the best way for you to learn English?

1a. If you haven't experienced a breakthrough, write for fifteen to twenty minutes about this question:

Thinking back on your experience learning English, describe a specific situation that reveals your frustration as a language learner. What was there in this situation that caused you to feel frustrated? What are some of the biggest problems you face in learning English?

2. After you have finished the freewriting, exchange papers with a partner and read each other's stories. How are your experiences in learning English similar? How are they different?

Organizing Ideas

1. Based on your personal experience, rate each of the following statements on a scale ranging from 0 (not important) to 10 (very important).

Example: In learning English, it was important for me to memorize the dictionary. *1*_____

1. In learning English, it was important for me to study grammar rules. _____

2. It was important for me to read a lot of books and articles in English. _____

3. Writing in English was an important way for me to learn the language. _____

4. As I was learning English, it was important for me to speak English every day. _____

5. Watching television was an important way for me to learn English. _____

6. It was important for me to take formal classes in the English language. _____

7. Learning the words to American or English songs helped me to learn English. _____

8. Listening to language tapes or the radio while I slept helped me to learn English. _____

9. As I was learning English, it was important to do exercises in ESL textbooks. _____

10. List any other methods that helped you to learn English and indicate how important they were, using the scale from 0 to 10.

Method	0–10
_____	_____
_____	_____
_____	_____

2. Work with a partner to form categories that describe your general approach to learning English. Some possible categories to use in analyzing your approach to language learning include the following:

   a. With others (in classes, by speaking with friends) vs. alone (by studying books, listening to tapes)
   b. Hearing the language (from speaking and listening) vs. seeing the language (from reading and writing)
   c. Active (communicating with others) vs. passive (watching television, listening to tapes)

Try to think of one or two other categories that describe your favored approach to language learning, and discuss with your partner how your own approach to learning English fits into these categories. Look carefully at how you rated each of the ten statements above. Can you make any generalization about your preferred way of learning English?

3. At the end of the discussion with your partner, take a few minutes to write down several words that seem to accurately describe your approach to learning English.

Working toward a Thesis Statement

A writing strategy that might help you to develop a thesis statement for your essay is looping (pages 152–54). If you decide to try looping, you might begin by writing "My preferred way of learning English could best be described as. . . ."

Before you try to write your thesis statement, look back at your freewriting, your ratings of the statements about language learning, and the list of words you wrote at the end of the discussion with your partner. Can you think of a general statement (thesis) that expresses the relationship between these different things? Try writing several tentative thesis statements, and pick the one that seems to most accurately describe your approach to learning English.

Think about how you will support this thesis. Could you tell a story to illustrate your approach to language learning? Could you summarize the results of your responses to the ten statements about language learning? How is your approach to learning English different from that of other students?

SUGGESTED TECHNIQUES

In this chapter you are asked to write an essay supporting your opinion. Because this is a very common type of assignment in U.S. colleges and universities, it is helpful to become familiar with some of the accepted practices for this type of writing.

1. *If your essay refers to a printed source, identify this source by title and author's full name in the first paragraph of your essay.* Many students assume that identifying the source of their information is not necessary since their readers will most likely be people who are familiar with this source. However, you are expected to fully identify any printed sources you refer to in your own writing. Notice how Aneta Siwik identifies the title and author of the source she is writing about in the first sentence of her critique: "In 'An American Success Story,' Samuel Nakasian showed a very idealistic picture of America."

2. *Explain the ideas from the printed source that you refer to in your own essay.* It is not necessary—or desirable—to summarize all the ideas in the source. But you should explain those ideas that are important to your own essay. It may be helpful to imagine that you are writing for someone who has read the source material two or three years ago; thus, you will need to refresh the reader's memory. If you are not sure how to express another writer's ideas in your words, refer to the section "Paraphrasing and Quoting" on pages 263–68.

3. *If you quote from the source, check to make sure you have copied the quotation exactly as it appeared in the original. In the case of charts or graphs, be sure that any numbers you use are correct.* It is distracting to find grammatical errors or things that do not make sense in a quotation or numbers that do not add up correctly. Mistakes such as these will probably cause the reader to doubt the rest of your ideas as well. After you have written your first draft, be sure to check any quotations or numbers against your original source. Be sure that you have copied everything correctly.

4. *Include topic sentences in your paragraphs to help the reader follow your train of thought.* Topic sentences, as demonstrated by the activities on pages 215–18, are like signposts that help readers to anticipate what is coming next. For instance, when Isana Loshinsky writes, "The other aspect of the article that I agree with . . .", we know that she plans to introduce a second point on which she agrees with the author of the article she is writing about. We anticipate that she will go on to add her own reasons to support her agreement with this point.

After you have written your first draft, check to see whether you have included topic sentences to help the reader follow your ideas.

5. *Remember to back up general statements with supporting evidence.* In American colleges and universities, writers are expected to support their general statements with more specific evidence in the form of statistics, personal examples, or material from other published sources. For example, Betty Liu Ebron emphasizes the importance of her topic, the difficulties of learning English, by including some statistics (paragraph 7): in New York City, one out of three people was not born in the United States, two out of five people speak English as a second language, and 600,000 New Yorkers have very limited English-language abilities. Isana Loshinsky supports her point about people being prejudiced against immigrants who have difficulty speaking English by including an example from her personal experience (paragraph 4).

After you have written your first draft, look back and ask yourself if there are any paragraphs where more support is needed. Where could you find this additional material?

Working with a partner, exchange essays and complete the Peer Response Sheet located at the end of the chapter. If you decide to revise this essay, refer to Part III: Rethinking/Rewriting.

PEER RESPONSE SHEET:
WRITING TO SUPPORT AN OPINION

Writer's Name: _____

Reader's Name: _____

Date: _____

(*Note to the reader:* As you respond to the writer's draft, try to focus on the ideas rather than the grammar and spelling. Discuss only those mistakes that interfere with understanding.)

1. If the writer is critiquing the Nakasian or Ebron essay, did he or she identify the essay being discussed? If so, in which paragraph did this occur? _____

_____

_____

Did the writer explain the source material clearly enough so that a reader who had not seen the source would still understand this essay? _____

_____

If not, where do you think more explanation is needed? _____

_____

_____

2. If the writer was analyzing his or her own approach to learning English, did he or she make a general statement about the preferred approach to language learning? If so, in which paragraph did this occur? _____

_____

Did the writer analyze *why* this particular approach is the most effective one for him or her? If so, in which paragraph(s) did this analysis occur? _____

_____

_____

If you think more analysis is needed, give the writer some advice about how to do this. _____

_____

_____

_____

_____

3. Did the essay include a clear thesis statement? If so, copy it in the space below.

_____

_____

_____

_____

In which paragraph does this thesis appear? _____

4. Try to find one example of a clear topic sentence. In which paragraph did this sentence appear? Copy the sentence in the space below._____

_____

_____

_____

_____

5. Did the writer give enough supporting evidence to convince you of the validity of his or her ideas? _____

_____

_____

_____

If so, what was one example of the effective use of supporting evidence? _____

_____

If not, in which paragraphs do you feel more evidence is needed? _____

_____

_____

_____

6. Suggest *one* thing that the writer could do to improve the next draft. _____

_____

_____

_____

_____

10
Claiming the Dream:
Rights and Responsibilities

If you talk to older Americans, they will often tell you about "the good old days." In the good old days, milk cost five cents a quart, you could walk safely on the streets day or night, there were no drug problems or drive-by shootings, children respected their elders, and so on. Of course, by comparison, everything today seems to be getting worse and worse.

Was it really true that things were so much better in the old days? Probably not. It is simply that people often remember the good things about their past and forget the bad. For example, while it was true that most things were much cheaper sixty years ago in this country, we were also suffering through a terrible economic depression. Unemployment in the 1930s was as high as 25 percent as compared to 6 or 7 percent today. From 1914 to 1945, the world was thrown from war to war, with the loss of millions of lives. Racial and gender discrimination was widespread and even permitted by law in many states until the 1960s.

So when people talk about how good the old days were, we should keep in mind that they may not have been as good as they seem. It is simply that the problems we face today are different from those faced by previous generations. Young people, especially college students, are presented with the challenge of working on problems facing society when they are asked to discuss, think about, and write about social issues and to offer suggestions for change.

In this chapter we will examine two issues that are affecting society today: the problem of homelessness and the issue of gay rights. Though very different problems, both concern people who are not fully accepted in society and, as a result, suffer a kind of underground existence.

As you work through these readings, think about other social problems we face. How are they similar to the ones presented here? How are they different? The writing assignment in this chapter will ask you to choose a topic that interests you and to conduct some research of your own. Two techniques for gathering additional viewpoints and information, personal interviews and library research, will be presented.

An important thing to remember when writing about social issues is that these are complex problems that do not lend themselves to simple solutions. It is not your job to solve the problems, but to learn as much as possible about them. Becoming aware of the complexities of a problem is the first step. The more you learn, the more prepared you will be to participate in the discussions and decisions that will ultimately affect us all.

READINGS: HOMELESSNESS

For the growing number of homeless people in the United States, the American Dream may seem more like a nightmare. In recent years, the problem of homelessness has been getting a great deal of attention in the media, in political campaigns, and on university campuses, and many proposals have been suggested as to what to do about the homeless. But the problem is far from being solved.

One of Us
by Ahmet Erdogan

In this personal essay, a student from Turkey reveals how a chance en-
counter with a homeless man led to a deeper understanding of the problem of
homelessness—and of the society in which we live. Before you begin to read,
write down some possible meanings of the title, "One of Us."

When we see a filthy man in torn clothing sleeping on a street corner, we 1
look at him with contempt or with pity. These people are called "homeless." There
are very few who worry about what these people, whose bones only meet the
warmth in summer, do in winter. Although they live in a city with millions of
other people, they are forsaken and lonely. Some of them talk to themselves. Others tell their thoughts and feelings with their eyes. Nobody asks them their
thoughts. If they are interviewed by a reporter, he broadcasts or publishes dis-
torted truths. And by doing so, he reinforces the prejudice of the rest of the society
about the homeless people.

Once I had this prejudice, false-consciousness, and it isolated me from soci- 2
ety. Now, I can see that it also isolated me from myself. When I first saw him, I
wasn't aware of this fact.

It was a cold winter evening. I had pulled my hat down over my ears, cov- 3
ered my face with a scarf, and put on my thick overcoat. But I still felt the bitter
cold. I walked down into the subway. When the train came, the crowd pushed to
get inside. I knew there wouldn't be an empty seat. But I was tired, and, with
hope, my eyes looked for a place to sit. On my right there were seats for at least
four people. I sat joyfully. Not one minute had passed when I raised my head with
a feeling that all eyes were concentrated on me. I looked at my clothes. There was-
n't anything strange about them. I soon became involved with the thoughts on my
mind. This time my thoughts were broken off with a weight on my left shoulder.
He was an old man. His white beard had darkened with the grime. He looked in
my eyes with his own blue eyes, which hardly opened because of sleeplessness.
His dark, dirty face—unwashed maybe for weeks—became red for a moment. He
bit his lip, which was almost lost under his mustache and beard. Then, taking his
head between his hands, he tried to go back to sleep.

The crowd on the train walked off at the second stop. I was watching the old 4
man. His shoes were worn out. He had covered his legs up to the knees with tat-
ters. The darkened skin of his knees could be seen through a hole in his pants.
With a strange feeling, I stood up from my seat and sat just across from him. At
his left on the seat there was a big bag which was full of remnants of food and
other things. When the train stopped suddenly, he awoke and some of the food in
the bag spread over the seat. The old man put the food back in the bag with special care. Then he took the remnant of a hamburger with his right hand and
shoved his mustache away from his mouth with his left hand. Just as he had bitten
into the hamburger, he felt me watching him. That aged, wrinkled face had become red with a childish shame. After he had barely swallowed the food in his

mouth, he wiped his mustache with his hand. He tore a piece of paper, rolled it thickly like a cigarette. He took the rolled paper between his lips and started to search his pockets. After a while, he gave up the search. He took the rolled paper between two fingers, looked at it with hopeless eyes, and threw it down on the floor. And again he went back to his thoughts. I took my cigarettes and matches out of my pocket. He raised his head and started to look at my face with strange eyes. "Take, uncle," I said. "I think you want to smoke. I know how difficult it is sometimes not having a cigarette." He was just looking at me strangely. "I already have decided to quit smoking. Since I don't need this anymore. . . ." Then he smiled, took the pack, and lighted a cigarette with his shaking hands.

"Isn't it forbidden to smoke here?" I asked.   5

"Yes, but this is my home. If I go out, I freeze," he replied. And he contin-   6
ued to talk after each drag. "They call us bums. No one likes us. They look at us as if we are animals though animals don't suffer in this country. They are fed with special food. Did you ever see a dog with a nice sweater on, little boots on his feet?"

He extinguished his cigarette and continued, "They say we are lazy. We   7
are not working, not because we don't want to but because we couldn't find a job. . . ."

His head between his hands, he just stared ahead, and continued, "You   8
know, my son, many years ago we didn't have this much unemployment. Then there was no fear of being laid off. . . ." His hands fell away from his head. It was easy to see the anger in his face. For a while he forgot my being there as he stared ahead. And probably many thoughts, memories were reflecting on his mind. "You know, my son, if there are a lot of hungry people who are willing to work even for nothing, there is no need to pay you more." While he was telling this, he closed his eyes and continued. "They didn't bring those people here to save them or to help them. On the contrary, they brought them here to make both them and us slaves for them. A new slavery." He opened his eyes, but he couldn't bear the lights and closed them again. He raised his head heavily while starting to talk again, "The fear of being laid off makes us slaves. But they are not contented with this. They destroyed everything, anything good."

Then he stopped his talking. That anger appeared in his face. Suddenly he   9
opened his eyes. Sheltering his eyes with his hands, he continued to talk: "How can I take a shower? Where? If I take, I freeze. I don't have anything to put on. Look, you have a hat on your head, a coat, and for sure a nest to sleep."

My face had become red. I felt this and a pain deep inside of me. I wanted to   10
say something but I couldn't move my tongue in my mouth, as if it were swollen. Then I asked in order to change the subject, "Uncle, you are always saying 'they.' Who are 'they'?"

Fearfully he looked over his left and then his right shoulder. And again he   11
took his head between his hands and stared. His lips had sealed, as if he were troubled. After a short silence he continued slowly, "You know, in many neighbor-hoods the apartments were set on fire, purposefully. If you take a walk through these streets, you will see hundreds of such apartments." I had already missed my station, and we had come to the last stop.

On the way back he kept talking. He had been taken into a mental hospital. As he said, first he was happy about that but after living there a couple of months he couldn't stand—in his words—"the animal trainers" and he escaped. He feeds himself with the remnants of food from big hotels such as the Plaza and the Sheraton, which, according to him, in one day throw away food with which thousands of homeless people could be fed. When we came back to the stop where I was to get off, he said "We lost the loving respect and trust, my son, because they wanted it so, but now I am happy because I learned that there are still men who have not been robotized. . . ." He had not finished his words, yet I got off. As the train pulled away, he kept on talking.

On my way home and for the rest of the night, all this talk reflected on my mind. He was a man, one of us. The only difference was that he was one of the victims of "they." And the number of these victims is increasing. This means that one day I too may be a victim of "they." My mind was confused. But I had learned one thing: that he and the people like him do not deserve to be blamed, to be looked down on. It should be "they." "They" are the cause of this unprecedented hunger and suffering, so "they" should be blamed, not the homeless people.

Personal Connections

1. Look back at the writing you did before you began to read. Which of your possible definitions came closest to Erdogan's meaning for "One of Us"?

2. Both the homeless man and the writer refer to "they" throughout the essay. Who might they be talking about? Do you agree that "they" are the ones to blame for the suffering of the poor and homeless?

3. Have you ever had a similar experience in which a conversation with a stranger caused you to change your mind about something? If so, you might want to write about the experience.

Content and Writing Techniques

1. Notice how Erdogan introduces his subject in the first few paragraphs of the essay. He begins with a discussion of the general problem of homelessness and then, in paragraph 3, introduces the specific homeless man who will be the focus of most of the rest of the essay. How would the essay have been different if Erdogan had omitted the first two paragraphs?

2. Reread paragraph 4. Which of the following words best characterize the writer's feelings about the man, as described in this paragraph: (a) disgusted, (b) sympathetic, (c) curious, (d) hostile? Which words characterize your own feelings toward the man?

3. In your opinion, what was Erdogan's purpose for writing this essay? In other words, what did he want his readers to do or think after reading it? Do you feel he succeeded in achieving this purpose? Explain.

Where Will They Sleep Tonight?
by Kim Dartnell

Whereas "One of Us" was a personal essay based on the insights gained from one homeless man, this selection is a more formal essay that relies on library research and focuses on the general subject of homeless women. It was written when Dartnell was a first-year college student and previously published in The St. Martin's Guide to Writing. *Before you read, think about the problems that might cause a woman to become homeless.*

On January 21, 1982, in New York City, Rebecca Smith died of hypothermia, after living for five months in a cardboard box. Rebecca was one of a family of thirteen children from a rural town in Virginia. After graduating from high school and giving birth to a daughter, she spent ten years in mental institutions, where she underwent involuntary shock treatment for schizophrenia. It was when she was released to her sister's custody that Rebecca began wandering the streets of New York, living from day to day. Many New York City social workers tried unsuccessfully to persuade her to go into a city shelter. Rebecca died only a few hours before she was scheduled to be placed into protective custody. Rebecca Smith's story is all too typical. Rebecca herself, however, was anything but a typical homeless woman; not only did she graduate from high school, but she was the valedictorian of her class (Hombs and Snyder, 1982, p. 56). 1

Rebecca Smith is one of an increasing number of homeless women in America. Vagrant men have always been a noticeable problem in American cities, and their numbers have increased in the 1980s. Vagrancy among women is a relatively new problem of any size, however. In 1979, New York City had one public shelter for homeless women. By 1983 it had four. Los Angeles has just recently increased the number of beds available to its skid-row homeless women (Stoner, 1983, p. 571). Even smaller communities have noticed an increase in homeless women. It is impossible to know the number of homeless women or the extent of their increase in the 1980s, but everyone who has studied the problem agrees that it is serious and that it is getting worse (Hombs and Snyder, 1982, p. 10; Stoner, 1984, p. 3). 2

Who are these women? Over half of all homeless women are under the age of forty. Forty-four percent are black, forty percent white. The statistics for homeless men are about the same (Stoner, 1983, p. 570). There are several ways homeless women cope with their dangerous lifestyle. To avoid notice, especially by the police, some women will have one set of nice clothes that they wash often. They will shower in shelters of YWCA's and try to keep their hairstyle close to the latest fashions. An extreme is the small number of women who actually sleep on park benches, sitting up, to avoid wrinkling their clothes. On the other end of the spectrum is the more noticeable "bag lady," who will purposely maintain an offensive appearance and body odor to protect herself from rape or robbery. These women are almost always unemployed and poorly educated. "Homeless women do not choose their circumstances. They are victims of forces over which they have lost control" (Stoner, 1983, pp 568, 569). 3

The question is, why has there been such an increase in the number of va- 4
grant American women? There are several causes of this trend. For one thing,
more and more women are leaving their families because of abuse. It is unclear
whether this increase is due to an actual increase of abuse in American families,
or whether it results from the fact that it is easier and more socially acceptable
for a woman to be on her own today. Once on her own, however, this woman all
too often finds it difficult to support herself. A more substantial reason is the
fact that social programs for battered women have been severely cut back, leaving victims of rape, incest, and other physical abuse nowhere else to go. To take
one example, the Christian Housing Facility, a private organization in Orange
County, California, that provides food, shelter, and counseling to abused families, sheltered 1,536 people in 1981, a 300 percent increase from the year before
(Stoner, 1983, p. 573).

Evictions and illegal lockouts force some women onto the streets. Social wel- 5
fare cutbacks, unemployment, and desertion all result in a loss of income. Once a
woman cannot pay her rent, she is likely to be evicted, often without notice.

Another problem is a lack of inexpensive housing. Of today's homeless 6
women, over fifty percent lived in single rooms before they became vagrants.
Many of the buildings containing single-room dwellings or cheap apartments have
been torn down to make way for land renovation. Hotels are being offered new tax
incentives that make it economically unfeasible to maintain inexpensive single
rooms. This is obviously a serious problem, one that sends many women out onto
the streets every year.

Alcoholism has been cited as a major reason for the increase in the number 7
of homeless women. I don't feel this is a major contributing factor, however. First,
there hasn't been a significant general increase in alcoholism to parallel the rise in
homeless women; second, alcoholism occurs at all levels of financial status, from
the executive to the homeless. Rather, I would like to suggest that alcoholism is a
result of homelessness, not the cause.

Probably the biggest single factor in the rising numbers of homeless women 8
is the deinstitutionalization of the mentally ill. One study estimated that ninety
percent of all vagrant women may be mentally ill (Stoner, 1983, p. 567), as was
the case with Rebecca Smith. The last few years have seen an avalanche in the
number of mental patients released. Between 1955 and 1980 the numbers of patients in mental institutions dropped by 75 percent, from about 560,000 to about
140,000. There are several reasons for this. New psychotonic drugs can now
"cure" patients with mild disturbances. Expanded legal rights for patients lead to
early release from asylums. Government-funded services such as Medicare allow
some patients to be released into nursing or boarding homes. The problem is that
many of these women have really not known any life outside the hospital and suddenly find themselves thrust out into an unreceptive world, simply because they
present no threat to society or are "unresponsive to treatment." Very few of them
are ever referred to community mental health centers. Instead, many of them go
straight out on the streets. And once homeless, all funding stops, as someone
without an address can't receive any benefits from the government.

Although deinstitutionalization seems to have been the biggest factor in 9 the increase in vagrant women, there is some evidence that the main cause is economic. In 1981, 3,500,000 Americans were living below the poverty line. Unemployment hit 10.1 percent in 1982, the highest it has been since 1940. Yet, that same year saw $2.35 billion cut from food-stamp programs. Reductions in Aid to Families with Dependent Children (AFDC) hit women particularly hard because four out of five AFDC families are headed by women, two thirds of whom have not graduated from high school. (All data are from Hombs and Snyder, 1982.) Coupled with inflation, recession, unemployment, and loss of other welfare benefits, these cuts have effectively forced many women into homelessness, and can be expected to continue to do so at a greater rate in the years to come.

The United States may be one of the world's most prosperous nations, but for Rebecca Smith and others like her, the American Dream is far from being fulfilled. 10

REFERENCES

Stoner, M. R. (1983). The plight of homeless women. *Social Service Review, 57,* 565–581.

Stoner, M. R. (1984). An analysis of public and private sector provisions for homeless people. *The Urban and Social Change Review, 17.*

Hombs, M. E., and Snyder, M. (1982). *Homelessness in America.* Washington, D.C.: Community for Creative Non-Violence.

Personal Connections

1. In paragraph 8, Dartnell discusses the fact that more and more mentally ill people are being released from mental institutions to live on their own. Do you feel this is a good policy? Why or why not?

2. The essay concludes with this statement: "The United States may be one of the world's most prosperous nations, but for Rebecca Smith and others like her, the American Dream is far from being fulfilled." In your opinion, why is it that some Americans, such as Samuel Nakasian, author of the first selection in chapter 9, succeed while others, such as Rebecca Smith and the homeless man in "One of Us," do not?

Content and Writing Techniques

1. Compare the first three paragraphs of this essay with the first three paragraphs of the previous essay, "One of Us." Notice where the writers have decided to include statements about the *general* problem of homelessness and where they have included examples of *specific* homeless people. Write a *G* by the general statements that you find and an *S* by the specific ones. Which essay begins with a specific example? Which begins with general statements? Why do you think each writer chose to introduce the subject of homelessness in this way?

2. If you had time to read only one essay—this one or the previous one— which would you read for each of the following purposes?

    a. To study for a test on the causes of homelessness.

    b. To prepare for a speech arguing for improvements in the shelter system.

    c. For your own personal interest.

    d. To convince your friends that homeless people are sometimes not what they seem.

3. What are the different causes that Dartnell gives for the increase in the number of homeless women? Reread paragraphs 4–9, and in each paragraph find the sentence (or part of a sentence) that explains a cause most directly. Do these sentences come at the beginning, middle, or end of the paragraphs? How do these sentences help you to understand the points Dartnell is making?

4. In this essay, Dartnell writes with a voice of authority, which helps to convince readers of the validity of what she is saying. What specific techniques does she use to achieve this "voice of authority"?

Homelessness
by Anna Eliasson

> *In his essay "One of Us," Ahmet Erdogan refers to a group known as "they": "They destroyed everything, anything good." In this essay, Anna Eliasson, a student from Sweden, looks at the question of who "they" really are and at some of the causes of homelessness.*

Every morning I walk a couple of blocks to school. In this short period of time, I see a lot of different people. On my right, I see a businessman worth one million dollars—and on my left, a penniless man. Nowhere else have I seen the gap so great as in New York.   1

The homeless and the poor are lying in the streets, while people negligently pass by. Nowhere else but in New York have I seen poverty this poor and wealth this rich. The faces of the poor and the decadence of the rich expose the differences even more, to an extent where we can no longer close our eyes and shut them out.   2

There are various ways to eliminate homelessness. In the United States, there seem to be two alternatives—either to force the homeless into shelters or to convince them to go there voluntarily. These choices are an example of what is called the original dilemma in politics—i.e., freedom versus order. It is a question of what we, the people, value most. Do we want to restrict personal freedom in favor of obtaining order?   3

My conviction is that forcing someone into a shelter would be to deprive that individual of personal freedom, and would therefore be unconstitutional. The Fifth Amendment of the Constitution states that the federal government does not have the right to deprive a person of life, liberty, or property without due process of law.   4

To persuade the homeless to go to the shelters is the other option, a task   5
which could be difficult for many reasons. First of all, the shelters are known to be
inadequate—the system is not functioning as it should. Secondly, most of the
homeless are not in need of the shelters. What they need are jobs, education, or
medical (psychiatric) treatment.

I don't believe in either of these alternatives. The issue of homelessness must   6
be seen in a larger, ideological and political perspective. The homeless are just one
group among several in our society who don't live a decent life.

The Declaration of Independence states that all men are created equal and   7
have equal opportunities and rights. I argue that the political system in the United
States does not foster equality. People in the United States do not have equal opportunities. What you obtain in your life is what you can purchase. You have to
pay large sums in order to get education and medical care, which I consider to be
two basic rights. Some people are actually denied these things. Is that equality? An
individual is free to do what he wants to do in life—as long as his credit cards are
valid.

I discussed politics the other day with an American. His conviction was that   8
the government should not provide Social Security. He also believed that the people in the United States would never agree to paying higher taxes. Who are "the
people"? Is it the fifty percent of the eligible who voted in the last presidential
election, or is it maybe the two percent of the population who own half of America's industry and capital?

The problem of homelessness lies in the inequality of the people in the   9
United States. In my country, Sweden, poverty and homelessness are two concepts
that really do not exist. This is a result of a political system that provides equal opportunities for all individuals.

However, it may not be fair to compare the political system in Sweden to that   10
of the United States. First of all, Sweden is a smaller country geographically and
has a smaller and more homogeneous population. All political decisions are made
by a national government. There are no equivalents to the state governments in
the United States. These facts probably facilitate a stronger feeling of shared values
and solidarity.

Second, the interest groups[1] in Sweden tend to be integrated with the politi-   11
cal parties. For instance, the labor unions are strongly connected to the Social Democratic Party. Moreover, the six major political parties represent different groups
in the society. Every individual is able to identify him or herself with one of the six
party platforms.

In the United States, the interest groups have almost become competitors to   12
the political parties. Through effective lobbying[2] among the members of Congress,
the interest groups have been able to secure their interests, sometimes to the detri-

[1]*interest groups:* People who organize efforts to convince government leaders to vote for laws that will
benefit their group. For example, organizations opposed to abortion will try to convince their representatives to vote against laws that permit abortion.

[2]*lobbying:* The activities used by interest groups to influence government leaders, for example, demonstrations, petitions, letter writing, meetings.

ment of the political parties and the majority of the people, and, in my view, to the detriment of the democratic process.

The two major parties are also quite conservative. No real government alternatives are given, which could be one of the reasons why interest groups have become so important. If the lobbies are the real decision makers, who, for example, does the lobbying for the homeless?   13

Third, in Sweden, the whole government scope is more to the left compared to that of the United States. The majority party, the Social Democratic Party, values equality over total personal freedom, and the taxes are high in order to redistribute the income. In the United States, socialism is associated with totalitarian states, and the concept of social democracy is little known. The fear of socialism has, in my view, made it impossible to accomplish real social change in the United States.   14

To me, it appears that the problem of homelessness must be seen in a larger political perspective. It cannot be solved without changing the values and opinions of those who control the spending of taxes—those who are elected by us, the people.   15

Personal Connections

1. Do you feel that the general attitude toward the homeless in America is (a) sympathetic, (b) uncaring, or (c) hostile? You might want to take a brief survey of your friends or classmates in order to answer this question.

2. In your opinion, do people from other countries have the right to criticize social conditions in the United States? How do you feel about outsiders criticizing your own country, culture, or ethnic group?

Content and Writing Techniques

1. Eliasson begins her essay with a personal experience. How would the essay be different if it started at paragraph 3?

2. In paragraphs 9–14, underline the specific sentences that imply the following opinions:
   a. In Sweden equal opportunity is greater than in the United States.
   b. Sweden has political representation for a wide variety of interest groups.
   c. In the United States the government does not represent the interests of the homeless.
   d. A nontotalitarian form of socialism may provide the solution to homelessness.

Discuss your results with a partner.

READINGS: GAY RIGHTS

In the past most homosexual, or gay, people were forced to keep their sexual identities a secret. Gay men or lesbians who announced their homosexuality risked losing their jobs, their family relationships, and their positions in society. Some even risked going to jail, as homosexuality was, and still is, outlawed in many states.

Today, there is a gradual acceptance of homosexuality in the United States. Not only are many gay people openly declaring their sexual identities, they are also claiming the same rights and privileges that male-female (heterosexual) couples have traditionally enjoyed. These include tax benefits for gay couples, equal health care coverage, and the right to adopt children.

As you read and discuss the readings in this section, think about other groups who have struggled for acceptance by society in the past. How were their struggles similar to or different from those involving gay rights?

An Interview with a Gay Couple
by Naresh Kumar

> *In this interview, a student from India talks to a homosexual couple about their feelings toward each other and toward the society in which they live. As you read, think about the question of gay rights. Should society reject homosexuality, tolerate it to a certain extent, or fully accept it as an alternative lifestyle?*

For the first couple of days, I could not find anyone to interview on the topic of gay rights for my English class. Knowing what the professor's reaction would be, "Try again," I decided to look for a person who would not be afraid of answering all kinds of personal questions.   1

When I was looking for someone to interview, my brother, Raj, mentioned that there is a gay couple working at the hospital where he works. I asked my brother to arrange an interview for me. First Raj laughed because last Christmas, he gave one of the men, Larry, a Christmas gift. Larry asked Raj to come to the cafeteria and said, "Why did you give me this gift?" He thought that Raj was interested in him and wanted to go out with him. Larry told him frankly, "I already have a boyfriend and I cannot go out with you."   2

My brother stared at him for a while and didn't understand anything. But after Raj found out that Larry is gay, he explained that he only gave him the gift because he is a good friend, just like his other friends who work at the hospital.   3

After hearing the story, I decided to go to the hospital to talk to Larry and his partner, Mike. They did not hesitate to answer any of my questions.   4

My first question was "Do you feel as passionate toward each other as we [heterosexual men] do toward women?" Mike answered, "Of course. We are people just like you. The only difference is that the feelings you have for girls are the feelings I have for Larry."   5

I asked how they felt being surrounded by people who are not gay. Mike said he did not believe the society that surrounds them is as bad as some   6 people think. "Many of our neighbors are very cooperative and supportive when they hear about us because we are the only gay couple in the whole building."

I asked when and why they chose to live with someone of the same sex. How did they tell their parents, and what was their reaction? This time Larry answered. They first met in high school, and after a while started to have feelings for each other because neither of them was satisfied with partners of the opposite sex. When they told their parents about the relationship, their parents were furious at them, but Larry and Mike went out anyway.

When I asked whether the government should give gay people all rights, including the right to adopt children, Mike gave a snappy comeback. "Yes, we deserve all the rights there are, including the right to adopt and raise children because we work and pay taxes just like you heterosexuals."

My last question was, "Since the Bible clearly explains that a marriage partner has to be of the opposite sex, how do you respond to that?" "A lot has changed since the Bible was written," Mike answered, "and no one can live by each line of the Bible. They can only respect it to a certain point."

After my last question, it was time for Larry and Mike to go back to work. I shook their hands and wished them a happy life in the future.

In my opinion, gays should have all their rights. After talking with this couple, I learned that being a homosexual is not a disease, but a way of life. If a gay couple adopts a child, it doesn't mean that the child will be gay unless he or she wishes to be gay. Being around gays has nothing to do with sexual preferences. Homosexuals are not out to convert others. They are just human beings who have chosen another route for life. It is like the Constitution says; no one shall be denied his or her rights based on color, creed, race, or sex.

Personal Connections

1. Often, one conversation with someone who is directly involved in a social issue can change the way we see that person and that issue. After this interview, Kumar says he changed his views on the topic of gay rights. Have you ever met someone who changed the way you thought about a social issue? If so, can you explain why you changed your mind?

2. Have you ever been in a situation in which your behavior was different from that of others around you: for example, your religious customs, clothing, language, or political beliefs? How did you feel about being different?

Content and Writing Techniques

1. At the beginning of this essay Kumar includes a story, or anecdote, about a Christmas gift. Why do you think he decided to include this story in the essay? How does the story relate to Kumar's subsequent argument in favor of gay rights?

2. In this essay, the writer uses an interview to make a point about a social issue. Compare this essay to Kim Dartnell's essay (pages 236–38) which uses li-

brary research. How is Kumar's piece similar to Dartnell's? How is it different? Which piece do you find more convincing?

3. Both Kumar and the gay couple feel that homosexuals should be given all the rights and privileges currently enjoyed by heterosexual couples. These would include the right to adopt children, equal tax benefits for gay couples, health insurance for both partners, and legal recognition of gay marriages. Write down reasons why such rights have not been offered to homosexual couples. List these reasons in three categories: (a) moral reasons, (b) emotional reasons, and (c) practical reasons.

Rights of Homosexuals
by Naresh Kumar

> *Here, the author of the preceding essay, which was based on an interview, presents his opinion in a more formal, argumentative essay. He explains how his views on homosexuality have changed since coming to the United States and argues in favor of equal rights for homosexuals.*

Thinking about homosexuals makes many people frown, but as I look at it, choosing a partner is a personal decision. In my opinion, homosexual couples should receive the same rights as any other married couples. 1

When I was in India, my knowledge about homosexuals was very limited. Most of the people in the society where I lived had given them such disrespectful names and drawn such pitiful pictures in their minds that I was scared to go near them. In my country homosexuals still have no rights at all such as health care, equal taxation, or the right to adopt or raise children. In India if homosexuals want to do something like any other person—get a higher education, start a business, and so on—they can't. The society would never let them do it because nobody wants a homosexual to become a successful person. The way the society thinks shows that people are not well-educated and they are also prejudiced. When I lived there, I thought just like any other Indian. My views were not well-educated either. 2

But since I came to the United States and started getting an education, my opinions began to change. I now understand that homosexuals have the same feelings and the same qualities as others but are different in one way. Now I feel that homosexuals should receive all rights—such as health care, tax benefits, and the right to raise or adopt a child—just like other married couples. We can find homosexuals in every field of work and walk of life nowadays. 3

In my opinion, we should judge homosexuals the same way we judge anyone else. Most of them live a normal life. They work hard and pay taxes. They do not bother anyone. They just have a different lifestyle. That's why I strongly agree that homosexuals should receive the same rights as every other American citizen. 4

Personal Connections

1. The writer says that in his native country most people have given homosexuals "disrespectful names" and have "drawn pitiful pictures in their minds." Make a list of words or phrases that best describe the attitude toward homosexuality in your native country. Discuss your list with a partner or small group.

2. In paragraph 3, the author explains, "Since I came to the United States and started getting an education, my opinions began to change." Have any of your opinions begun to change since coming to this country? Discuss this question with a partner or small group.

Content and Writing Techniques

1. In this essay, Kumar uses traditional argumentation to make a point about gay rights. Compare this essay to the previous one in which he uses material from an interview to convince his readers. How are the two essays similar? How are they different? Which piece do you find more convincing?

2. In writing about his native India, Kumar states: "The way the society thinks shows that people are not well-educated and they are also prejudiced" (paragraph 2). Do you agree that there is a direct link between a society's level of education and its acceptance of people who are different? What historical evidence could you give to support this position? What evidence could you give to argue against it?

3. Write a brief response to this essay, either agreeing or disagreeing with Kumar's position that homosexuals should be given the same rights as all other Americans.

Gay Parents: Living in Fear

This article, which originally appeared as an editorial in The New York Times, *discusses the legal barriers gay couples sometimes face when they try to create families. Before you read, think of some of the reasons why a judge might order a child to be removed from the home of a gay couple. (If many of the words in this article are unfamiliar to you, turn to the section entitled "Vocabulary Practice: Gay Rights" on pages 255–56.)*

When it comes to preserving the two-parent family, some judges are pretty picky. In Virginia, a judge recently took a child from two parents who loved him and placed him with his single grandmother. In Oklahoma last week an appeals court judge upheld a ruling that took two girls away from another such family. The reason? In both cases, the parents were the same gender.

In the Virginia case, the judge said the mother's relationship with her female partner was immoral. In the Oklahoma case, the judge cited "expert" testimony from a previous case that the child of such a family "might encounter future prejudice by a disapproving society."

Neither explanation rings true.   3

Some children grow up in homes where they witness or suffer physical and   4
emotional abuse. That's immoral. A loving relationship between two adults of the same gender is not.

Many children live in families that attract prejudice. But would it be acceptable to separate a child from loving parents on such grounds because one   5
parent was black and one white? Or because they followed unusual religious practices?

As the *Times*'s Susan Chira reported last week, children of gay families may   6
have some difficulties. As adolescents, they may feel isolated from peers who exhibit anti-gay prejudice. But those problems seem pale compared to the trauma of being removed from a loving home.

Researchers who have studied children of gay parents have found no evi-   7
dence of harm. The time-worn prejudice that homosexuality is contagious has been all but disproved. Long-term studies have yet to be done; but there is no credible evidence that children in gay households are any more likely to be gay than children of heterosexual parents.

There's also no evidence, from fifteen years of social research, that children   8
growing up with homosexual partners as parents are any more likely to experience gender confusion or sexual abuse.

In fact, one study concluded that children of lesbian mothers spent more   9
time with their fathers than children of heterosexual single mothers.

There's also evidence that children who live with lesbian couples have   10
greater self-esteem and a better family life than children of single lesbian mothers; yet many judges demand, before allowing a child to remain with a lesbian mother, that the mother's partner leave the home.

Some homosexual couples are being allowed to adopt children, and same-   11
gender partners are being allowed to become legal parents of their lovers' biological children. But this official tolerance is uneven and unpredictable. Nearly half the states still ban homosexual acts, which weakens a homosexual parent's case in asking for custody of a child. And in all states, different judges may make different decisions about the children of gay families.

The number of American children nobody wants, or who grow up in abusive   12
families, is tragically high. It's almost universally recognized that two loving parents are better than one. Yet judges continue to deprive children of loving, intact families—because their parents are gay.

In deciding what's best for a child, it's fair to look at a large range of issues.   13
But the sexual orientation of parents is not one of them. Gay parents should not have to live in fear of losing their children simply because of who they are.

Personal Connections

1. According to this article, "It's almost universally recognized that two loving parents are better than one" (paragraph 12). List the advantages of growing up in a family with two parents. Which of these advantages would also apply if both parents were the same sex?

2. The article also states: "The number of American children nobody wants, or who grow up in abusive families, is tragically high" (paragraph 12). Paraphrase this sentence (express it in your own words). In your opinion, what are some factors in contemporary American society that might be partly responsible for this tragic situation?

Content and Writing Techniques

1. Underline the sections of the article that disagree with the following opinions about gay parents. In the margin, label these sections *a*, *b*, *c*, and *d*.
   a. Homosexual relationships are immoral.
   b. Children raised by gay couples will experience prejudice from society.
   c. Children of gay parents are more likely to become gay than children raised by heterosexual parents.
   d. Children of gay parents will have difficulty understanding the differences between men and women.

2. This article represents a special type of argumentative writing found on the editorial pages of newspapers. Readers often write letters to the editor, stating their agreement or disagreement with opinions contained in editorials. Look on the editorial page of your local newspaper, and read some of these letters. Then write a letter to the editor in which you respond to "Gay Parents: Living in Fear." Make it clear whether you agree or disagree with the editor's position on what is best for the children of gay couples, and state your own opinion as convincingly as possible.

Creating a Gay Family: A Test Case

The following article, which originally appeared in The New Yorker *magazine, describes a legal case in which a gay lawyer, Thomas Steel, is trying to win paternity rights to visit with his biological daughter, Ry. If he wins the court case, he will be permitted to visit his daughter regularly each year without her mother's permission or presence. If he loses the case, he will not be allowed to see his daughter unless her mother agrees to it. In order to help you keep track of all the people involved in the article and their relationships to each other, we have prepared a brief description of each person. (If many of the words used in these descriptions are unfamiliar to you, turn to the section entitled "Vocabulary Practice: Gay Rights" on pages 255–56.) As you read, think about the members of this family. Who are the real parents?*

Thomas Steel: *A gay lawyer who lives in San Francisco. He is the biological father, through artificial insemination, of Ry Russo-Young, age twelve, and is*

*seeking paternity rights—that is, the right to visit his daughter regularly with-
out her mother's permission or presence.*

*Robin Young: The biological mother of Ry Russo-Young. She is a lesbian
and has been living with her lover, Sandra Russo, in New York's Greenwich Village for more than fifteen years. She has been a partner in raising Russo's daughter, Cade, since birth and wants to legally adopt her. Thomas Steel is suing her
for paternity rights for Ry.*

*Ry Russo-Young: Age twelve, the biological daughter of Thomas Steel and
Robin Young. Between ages three and nine, she spent several vacations with Mr.
Steel along with her mother and Sandra Russo. She has grown up as the "sister"
of Sandra's daughter, Cade.*

*Sandra Russo: The lesbian lover of Robin Young for more than fifteen
years and the biological mother of Cade Russo-Young. She has served as a partner in raising and supporting her lover's daughter, Ry, since birth. She wants to
legally adopt Ry.*

*Jack Kolb: A gay physical therapist and the biological father of Cade
Russo-Young. He has met Cade but has shown no interest in getting involved in
her life.*

*Cade Russo-Young: Age fourteen, the biological daughter, through artifi-
cial insemination, of Jack Kolb and Sandra Russo. She has been raised by her
mother and Robin Young since birth and has grown up as the "sister" of Ry
Russo-Young.*

Thomas Steel, a gay man, is suing Robin Young, a lesbian, for paternity   1
rights to their biological daughter, and the gay legal community is shuddering with apprehension. The case cuts to the core question of gay family life
now: What constitutes a gay family? Beatrice Dohrn, the legal director of the
Lambda Legal Defense and Education Fund, says, "Family courts have traditionally assumed that it is in the best interests of all kids to have a mother and
a father. But the fact is that lesbians and gay men are deliberately constructing
families in numbers that are unprecedented—often by donor insemination or
surrogacy. This is the first dispute of its kind in an appellate court in New York,
and lesbians and gay men hoping to have kids are anxiously watching this
case."

In 1979, Robin Young and Sandra Russo had few anxieties. They were in   2
love and were living together in the Village, and they were eager to begin a family.
Ms. Russo, who is small and vivacious, was an attorney for the Legal Aid Society
(she now works at Legal Services for New York City), and Ms. Young, who looks
like a preppy Merle Oberon, wanted to stay home with the kids. They hoped that
each woman would bear one baby, and that the children would be reared as the
offspring of both women, like siblings in a straight family. "In some sense, we
were going to be a traditional family," Ms. Young said the other afternoon, as she
and Ms. Russo sat on a sofa in their loft downtown.

Reasoning that gay men who were "out" were likely to be sympathetic to les-   3
bians forming families—and might even be politically motivated to help create
them—Ms. Young and Ms. Russo decided to find gay donors. They wanted men
who were intelligent, and who lived far enough away so that their being a part of
the family wasn't an option. Ms. Russo was the older of the two (she was thirty-

nine at the time, and Ms. Young was twenty-four), so they decided that she should get pregnant first. When they were on vacation in San Francisco in August, 1979, a friend put them in touch with a physical therapist named Jack Kolb. "We talked to him about what we wanted — that this would be our family, that he would have no rights or responsibilities," Ms. Russo said. And he agreed to those stipulations, and also to their request that if the child ever wanted to meet him, he'd be available. Using a glass syringe, Ms. Russo inseminated herself, and the following May her daughter, Cade Russo-Young, was born in New York.

A few months later, the women (with Cade in tow) visited San Francisco again, hoping to find a donor for Ms. Young. The same friend suggested that Thomas Steel, a successful Bay Area lawyer, might assist them. Mr. Steel, Ms. Young, and Ms. Russo agreed orally that Ms. Young would inseminate herself; that Mr. Steel would have no parental rights or obligations; and that he would make himself known to the child if she asked about her biological origins. Another girl, Ry Russo-Young, was born in 1981.

For the first three years of Ry's life, Mr. Steel had virtually no contact with her or with Ms. Young or Ms. Russo. Then, sometime in 1985, Ry's older sister began to ask about her genetic history, so her parents arranged for the four of them to travel to San Francisco to meet, as Ms. Young and Ms. Russo put it to the girls, "the men who helped make you." Mr. Steel rented a house at Stinson Beach, about an hour north of the city, for a few days, and invited the friends to join them there. Everyone had a good time. "There was a wonderful, generous spirit about it," Ms. Russo recalled, and Ms. Young added, "We felt so thankful to these guys."

Mr. Steel began visiting the lesbian couple and the girls in Manhattan, and they, in turn, visited him on the West Coast. Together, the five spent vacations in rented houses on Long Island. Mr. Steel did not support Ry financially, but he says that he made gifts of money to the family, a claim that Ms. Young and Ms. Russo dispute. Mr. Steel also says that he developed special feelings for Ry. He maintains that he was as involved as any other noncustodial parent. Ms. Young says he was just a friend, as close as many of their other friends. What is clear is that Mr. Steel eventually began to chafe at having to see Ry only at the women's discretion. In the spring of 1991, when Ry was nine, he told Ms. Young and Ms. Russo that he wanted to take her to California that summer for a two-week stay — without Ms. Young and Ms. Russo — to meet his parents. The women refused. Mr. Steel promptly sued Ms. Young for paternity rights.

In March of 1992, the case went to trial here in family court, with Mr. Steel arguing — in what many in the gay legal community saw as surprisingly traditional language — the importance of both biological fatherhood and, to his mind, Ry's "illegitimate" status. The court denied his petition. The presiding judge, Edward Kaufmann wrote, "When Ry was almost ten years old, he [Mr. Steel] decided . . . to attempt to change the ground rules of her life. This attempt has already caused Ry . . . psychological harm. . . . For her, a declaration of paternity would be a statement that her family is other than what she knows it to be and needs it to be."

Mr. Steel immediately appealed, maintaining that he sought only to provide

Ry with additional love and financial security. The case was argued again last February in the Appellate Division of the State Supreme Court, and a decision is due shortly.

Legal experts say that the outcome is by no means certain, and Ms. Russo and Ms. Young are on tenterhooks. Meanwhile, the girls, now fourteen and twelve, are looking forward to participating in a summer Shakespeare festival upstate, where Ms. Russo and Ms. Young now own a country house. And, if Mr. Steel's paternity is again denied, Ms. Young plans to formally adopt Cade, and Ms. Russo plans to adopt Ry. As they sat together the other afternoon, the mothers sent the daughters—friendly, strapping, brown-haired girls, who actually look like sisters—out shopping for steak and artichokes for dinner. "The traffic on Seventh Avenue is lousy," Ms. Young warned the girls as they went off on their errand, and Ms. Russo added, "Stick with each other, please."

Personal Connections

1. Freewrite your own definition of the word *parent*. Consider the following categories: blood relations, emotional ties, financial support. According to this definition, which of the people described in this article are the parents of the two girls?

2. Thomas Steel claims that because he is the biological father of Ry Russo-Young, he should have the legal right to visit with his daughter just as a divorced or separated parent normally would. If you were the judge in this case, would you grant Mr. Steel visitation rights? Why or why not? After you have made your decision, turn to page 273 to read the judge's actual decision.

Content and Writing Techniques

1. Which of the following statements might explain Mr. Steel's desire to have visitation rights to see his daughter, Ry?
   a. He loves his daughter and wants to see her more often.
   b. He is jealous of the mother and wants to damage her relationship with Ry.
   c. He feels Ry needs both a mother and a father in her life.
   d. He feels lonely and wants to make Ry part of his family relationships.

2. Which of the following statements might explain why Robin Young does not want Steel to have visitation rights with Ry?
   a. She is afraid that Steel may try to take her daughter away permanently.
   b. She does not trust Steel to take good care of her daughter.
   c. Because Steel has done nothing to help raise Ry, he does not deserve any rights to see her.
   d. Ry feels her family consists of her mother, Sandra Russo, and Cade. Therefore, it would be emotionally difficult to accept Steel as a family member.

3. In paragraph 7, a judge reviewing the case made the following statement:

"When Ry was almost ten years old, he [Mr. Steel] decided . . . to attempt to change the ground rules of her life. . . . For her, a declaration of paternity would be a statement that her family is other than what she knows it to be and needs it to be."

Write a paragraph explaining what you think the judge meant by this statement.

GRAMMAR IN CONTEXT
ACTIVE AND PASSIVE VOICE OF VERBS

There is an old story about the definition of news: If the headline reads "Dog bites man," that's not news. But if it says "Man bites dog," *that's* news. The point is that who performs the action of the verb can make a big difference. And this is also the key to understanding the difference between active and passive voice.

Both of the headlines quoted in the preceding paragraph are in the active voice. Notice how they change when they are rewritten in the passive voice:

Active		*Passive*
Dog bites man.	=	The man is bitten by the dog.
Man bites dog.	=	The dog is bitten by the man.

The active voice is used much more often than the passive voice in most writing. But there are certain situations in which the passive voice is preferred, particularly if the writer does not wish to emphasize who or what performed the action. Notice the different emphases of the following sentences:

Active		*Passive*
The judge sentenced the murderer to 25 years in prison.	=	The murderer was sentenced to 25 years in prison.

The first sentence puts more emphasis on its subject, "the judge," which is not necessary because most people know that only judges can sentence criminals to prison. A newspaper article on this case would probably use the passive voice to put the emphasis on "the murderer."

Activity

The verbs in the following questions are in the active voice. Answer each question in the passive voice by filling in the missing auxiliary verb and the correct form of the main verb [the verb included in brackets in the answer].

Example: Should we legalize drugs to reduce the amount of crime.
No, drugs should not [legalize] <u>be</u> <u>legalized</u>.

1. Should we force homeless people into shelters?

    No, they should not [force] _____ _____ into shelters.

2. Should the United States build more housing for the homeless?

    Yes, a lot more housing needs to [build] _____ _____.

3. Should we provide job training programs for homeless people who want to work?

    Yes, job training programs should [provide] _____ _____ by the government.

4. Can homeless mothers work and still take care of their children?

    Yes, homeless mothers can work and care for their children if day-care programs [provide] _____ _____.

5. Should gay couples adopt children?

    Whether a gay couple [allow] _____ _____ to adopt a child should [evaluate] _____ _____ on a case-by-case basis.

6. Should gays serve in the U.S. military?

    Yes, gays should [allow] _____ _____ to serve in the military.

7. Should homosexual couples pay higher income taxes than married heterosexual couples?

    No, homosexuals and heterosexuals should [require] _____ _____ to use the same tax rates.

8. Do immigrants face many problems?

    Yes, they [face] _____ _____ with all kinds of problems.

9. It isn't easy to solve these problems, is it?

    No, the problems [solve] _____ not easily _____.

(See Answer Key, pages 325–26.)

PRACTICE WITH DIRECT AND INDIRECT QUOTATIONS

People ask us for money all the time—beggars on the street, charities, people selling things. This activity explores the question of why we give to some people and not to others and also provides an opportunity to practice using direct and indirect quotations.

Activity

1. Work with a partner who has one dollar. The goal is to try to persuade your partner to give you the dollar. Set a time limit of five minutes and keep trying until you get the dollar or the time is up. If you are the partner with the dollar, do not give the money away until your partner has convinced you that he or she really needs it or that it will be to your advantage to hand it over. Don't be cheap. Once you are persuaded by the other person's arguments, give him or her the dollar.

2. Reverse roles. The person who previously gave (or did not give) the dollar should now try to persuade his or her partner to give the money. Follow the rules stated above.

3. After you have completed the first two steps, write a report describing what happened, using a mixture of direct and indirect quotations. Tell what was said in order to get the dollar in both cases, and try to explain why these arguments were or were not effective.

> **Indirect Speech:** She asked me to give her a dollar.
> She said she was hungry.
> **Direct Speech:** She asked, "Will you give me a dollar?"
> "I'm hungry," she said.

4. Hand in your report to your teacher for comment and correction.

REVIEW OF THE PRESENT PERFECT TENSE

The activity that follows gives you a chance to check your understanding of the present perfect tense. (For a review of this tense, see the section entitled "Using the Present Perfect Tense" on page 156.)

Activity

Imagine that you are living in the year 2010. Fill the blanks in the following sentences with the present perfect form of the verb given in brackets. After you have finished, find a partner to work with, and compare your answers.

> **Example:** The world [change] _____ _____ a lot since 1985.
> The world <u>has</u> <u>changed</u> a lot since 1985.

1. Doctors [find] _____ _____ cures for many diseases.

2. The condition of air and water [improve] _____ _____ a lot.

3. The number of nuclear weapons [reduce] _____ _____
   _____ .

4. However, there are still many things that [accomplish] _____ not

   yet _____ _____.

5. For example, the problem of homelessness [solve] _____ not

   _____ _____.

6. Not all drug dealers [arrest] _____ _____ _____.

7. The population [continue] _____ _____ to grow.

8. The cost of living [double] _____ _____ in the last ten

   years.

9. But for the most part, things [get] _____ _____ better.

(See Answer Key, page 327.)

SPELLING STRATEGY: VOWEL SOUNDS

After each of the sentences below (adapted from a student essay about gay rights), you will find a list of words. One of these words will contain the same vowel sound as the underlined syllable in the sentence. Underline the syllable in the word list that contains the same vowel sound as the underlined syllable in the sentence. (For additional help with spelling, see "Improving Your Spelling," pages 300–304.)

Activity

Example: Homosexuality has always been a <u>shock</u>ing idea for many people.

joking
looking
<u>rock</u>ing
touching
moving

1. Today we see more and more homosexual <u>coup</u>les holding hands or kissing publicly.

cute

route

cup

worth

compose

2. <u>This</u> can be a signal that they want to end the discrimination they have been suffering from.

ride

yield

wish

tried

firm

3. As far as their civil rights are concerned, gay people <u>live</u> in a segregated society.

tie

drive

survive

field

river

4. I personally think that this state of <u>matt</u>ers should end.

bed

mate

and

marble

mail

(See Answer Key, page 327.)

VOCABULARY PRACTICE: GAY RIGHTS

"Creating a Gay Family: A Test Case" on pages 247–50 contains examples of specialized vocabulary you may not have encountered before. Working with a partner, try to figure out the meaning of the following words and phrases from the article by matching them with the definitions that appear below:

a. *lesbian* (from paragraph 1)
b. *paternity rights* (from paragraph 1)
c. *donor insemination* or *surrogacy* (from paragraph 1)
d. *gay men* (from paragraph 1)
e. *offspring* (from paragraph 2)
f. *"out"* (from paragraph 3)
g. *noncustodial parent* (from paragraph 6)

   h. *biological fatherhood* (from paragraph 7)
   i. *illegitimate* (from paragraph 7)

DEFINITIONS

1. The process of conceiving a child without sexual intercourse _____

2. Men who prefer sexual relationships with other men _____

3. Contributing sperm to conceive a child _____

4. The rights of a father to live with or visit with his child _____

5. Openly or publicly homosexual _____

6. A parent who does not live with his or her child _____

7. Born of parents who are not legally married _____

8. A woman who prefers sexual relationships with other women _____

9. Children _____

(See Answer Key, page 328.)

ASSIGNMENT

Of course, students go to college to learn from their professors. But they also learn by discussing ideas with peers, by reading, and by doing other types of research. For example, if you are interested in the topic of sex education, you probably have some personal experience that relates to this topic: you remember how your parents taught—or didn't teach—you about sex. But this is a very limited experience.

The assignment for this chapter suggests two ways of getting a broader view of a subject by consulting outside sources. The first technique is personal interviews. The second is library research.

After you have done the interviews and/or library research, you will be asked to write an essay. The purpose of the essay is to explain your own position on the topic; information from outside sources should be used either to illustrate your own views or to give an opposing view. As your audience, consider college professors in the field you are researching and other students who may be writing on a similar topic. After revising your essay, you might consider submitting it for publication in your college newspaper or some other student publication.

As with all the other writing you have done for this book, we encourage you to choose a topic that really interests you. The following activity will help you to do this.

Topic-Choice Activity (In Class)

1. Write down three possible topics that you might want to investigate. Think of issues that are controversial and currently being discussed. You may get some ideas from the essays in this chapter, but do not limit yourself to these topics. Subjects that other students have chosen include:

> Women's rights
> Biological engineering
> Racial and ethnic discrimination

2. Once you have listed some general topics, try to narrow each one down to a subject you could discuss adequately in a short essay (three to five typed pages). One way to do this is to ask questions about your general topics.

> Women's rights: Are female students better served by colleges that enroll only women?
> Biological engineering: Should parents have the right to choose the sex of their children?
> Racial and ethnic discrimination: How have United States history books changed their treatment of this subject in the past twenty-five years?

3. Have each student in the class suggest one topic. A student volunteer should write these topics on the board.

4. Using one of your own ideas or an idea you got from a classmate, write a one-paragraph description of a subject you would like to research.

5. Hand in the description to your teacher for comment.

TECHNIQUE 1: PERSONAL INTERVIEWS

(The essay by Naresh Kumar on pages 242–43 uses a personal interview as an important source of information.)

Personal interviews can be a good place to start looking for information on a particular subject. In fact, professional writers and researchers often begin with interviews. Wall Street reporters call up economists to get opinions about why the stock market is going up or down. Scholars talk with colleagues who might have information on a subject they are studying. Television reporters go out in the street with cameras and microphones to find out what people think about a recent news story. Interviews are a way of getting information immediately and often suggest directions for further research.

Interviewing Activity

For this activity, you and a partner from your class will go to a public place (a cafeteria or lobby, for example), find some people who are not too busy, and interview them. Later you will be asked to write an essay using some of the information from these interviews.

1. Choose a partner who is interested in working on a similar subject.

2. List as many questions as you can think of on your topic.

3. Find some people to talk to. Take about thirty minutes to an hour to conduct the interviews. Try to talk to two or three people, if possible. It is advisable to have one partner ask the questions and the other take notes. If you have access to the equipment, you may want to record your interview on audiotape or videotape. (See page 150 for suggestions on taking notes on interviews.)

Interviewing Tips

- Try to choose people who are sitting alone. They will usually be more cooperative than people who are with friends.
- Be sure to identify yourself and tell the people you approach that you are doing research for your writing class. For example, you might say: "Good morning. We're doing a research project for our English class. We're interested in finding out what you think about _____. Would you be willing to answer a few questions?"
- Most people will be happy to help, but if they do not want to talk, don't worry. Just thank them and go on to someone else.
- Try to find at least two or three people who have different opinions on your topic.

Freewriting Assignment

As soon as possible after completing the interviews, write a report (about a page and a half) that provides the following information:

- Whom did you interview? (Include name, approximate age, sex, profession, or any other relevant information.)
- What did you learn from the interview?
- What do you think about what the interviewees said?
- Describe any difficulties or successes you had in conducting the interviews.
- What do you think was the purpose of this assignment?

Reactions

At the next class meeting after your interviewing session, discuss your freewriting with a small group of classmates. How did you feel about approaching someone you did not know? Were your feelings at the end of the interview different from your feelings at the beginning?

Example: Here is how Ming Tao, a student from China, answered these questions:

As the Chinese saying goes "Everything is hard to start." At first we looked around the lounge where everybody was reading or talking. I suggested to my partner we go to interview a young guy who was the only one sitting there doing nothing. My partner said to me, "I'll laugh if I start to talk to him." I also felt that it was embarrassing to start talking to a stranger.

While we were pushing each other forward, the guy noticed us, felt uncomfortable, and left. Then we saw a lady who was reading something that didn't look like a textbook. This time we didn't hesitate, and my partner started to talk to her right away. We got the right person. First of all, she was very talkative. Second, she was raised by a single parent, which was the topic we had chosen for our interview. She had so much to say about her experience and opinion.

It was sort of hard to start something new but once it gained momentum, we were almost not able to stop it.

TECHNIQUE 2: LIBRARY RESEARCH

(Kim Dartnell's essay on pages 236–38 is an example of a research essay.)

Writers often use library research as a way of gathering information to increase the credibility of what they write. If a writer cites only her own opinion on an issue—let's say, the need for sex education in the schools—this is not very convincing. But if she uses statistics—for example, that 80 percent of all American parents are in favor of sex education in the schools—the idea assumes more validity. She might also look up the opinions of experts who have studied the issue for many years.

Learning to do library research and to write about your findings effectively are complex tasks, requiring much practice. The activities included in this chapter are intended as an introduction to your own college library and to the processes of writing about the materials you find there.

Library Activity

This activity asks you to broaden your base of knowledge by locating two articles on a topic you are interested in. Later you will use some of the information from the articles in an essay of your own. We recommend that you go to the library with a partner from your class. It's often easier to locate information when you're working as part of a team.

1. Select a topic that you feel strongly about (see the "Topic-Choice Activity" on pages 256–57). Before proceeding, make sure your teacher accepts your topic.

2. Freewrite for ten minutes, expressing your own feelings on this topic. If you have trouble writing on the subject you selected, choose another one and try again. After you have finished the freewriting, rest for a minute and then read what you have written. Try to express your main opinion on this issue in one sentence; this is a tentative thesis statement for your essay, but you may change or adapt this thesis as you continue working on the assignment.

3. Go to the library and locate two magazine or newspaper articles on your topic; choose articles that were published within the last two years. The easiest way to find articles on a particular subject is by using an index such as the *Readers' Guide to Periodical Literature* or *The New York Times Index*. Many libraries now have computerized indexes to help you locate books or articles related to your topic. If you need help in using the guides or computer indexes, ask a librarian for assistance; helping people to find information is part of the librarian's job.

4. Once you have located an article, skim through it to see whether it contains information that might be useful in writing an essay on your topic. If not, put the article back, and look for a more appropriate one. For your own convenience, it is a good idea to make copies of the two articles you have chosen.

5. Before you leave the library, be sure to record the following information for each of your articles.

Author's name: _____

Complete title of article: _____

Name of publication: _____

Date of publication: _____ _____, 19 _____

Volume number (only for magazines and journals): _____

Page numbers: p. _____ through p. _____

SUMMARIZING SOURCES

Summarizing—explaining someone else's ideas in a shortened form—is an important technique in college writing. For example, students often summarize when they are taking notes on what they have read or when they refer to this information in their own research writing. To write an effective summary, you should read the source material two or three times and then put it aside, writing down only what you remember as being the most important ideas. After you have written the summary, check the original source to make sure you have not left out any important ideas or included any ideas that are details, rather than major points. The following is a brief summary of "Where Will They Sleep Tonight?" by Kim Dartnell on pages 236–38. Review Dartnell's essay and then read the summary.

SAMPLE SUMMARY

In "Where Will They Sleep Tonight," Kim Dartnell analyzes the reasons for the recent increase in the number of homeless women in the United States. Possible causes for this increase include abusive families, economic problems resulting from unemployment and welfare reductions, alcoholism, and the deinstitutionalization of mentally ill women. Dartnell speculates that the most important of these factors during the early 1980s may have been a drastic rise in the number of American women living in poverty.

Notice that the summary is much shorter than the original essay, which consisted of ten paragraphs. Only major ideas have been included. Examples such as the homeless woman who died of exposure have been omitted. For the most part, the wording of the summary is different from that of the original essay. However, since there are no effective synonyms for some words and phrases such as "alcoholism" and "deinstitutionalization of the mentally ill," they are included without quotation marks in the summary.

Summary-Writing Activity

This activity asks you to practice summarizing the two articles you located in the previous Library Activity. Summarizing these articles will help you to examine them more closely for information you may be able to use in your research essay.

1. Reread both articles. On the copy, underline information that you think you might want to refer to in your essay, and write notes in the margin that will help you to find certain information later on. For example, if you had read an article on teenage pregnancy, you might want to write "statistics on increase in teen pregnancy" or "effects of receiving sex education in school." Remember that essay writers often cite information that conflicts with their own position and then explain why they do not accept this view.

2. Write a one-page summary of each of the articles you selected. Here are some general guidelines to follow:

- Identify the article at the beginning of the summary by including the title, author, name of the magazine or newspaper, date, and page numbers. For example, you might write: "In an article entitled 'Judge Refuses to List AIDS as a Sexual Disease' (*New York Times*, Nov. 16, 1988, p. B1), Tamar Lewin reported on a court case that involves mandatory testing for AIDS."
- Summarize only the most important ideas in the article; small details do not belong in a summary.
- Explain only the ideas contained in the article; your own opinion on the issue does not belong in a summary.
- Be sure to use quotation marks around any words you copy directly from the article, and give the page number in parentheses after the quotation.

3. When you are finished writing the two summaries, attach the copies of the articles and hand them in to your teacher for comment.

Whether you are planning to base your essay on personal interviews, library research, or a combination of the two, the following suggestions will help you to organize your ideas and, begin to develop a thesis statement.

Organizing Ideas

1. Read over all the writing you have done so far on your topic, including the notes based on the interviews or library research.

2. Using the following chart as a guide, summarize the opinions of the people you interviewed or the articles you read.

Topic: _____

First source's opinion about topic: _____

    Reasons for opinion: _____

Second source's opinion about topic: _____

    Reasons for opinion: _____

Third source's opinion about topic: _____

    Reasons for opinion: _____

Your own opinion about topic: _____

    Reasons for opinion: _____

Working toward a Thesis Statement

The thesis statement of your essay should focus on your own opinion about the issue you have chosen, not just a summary of the sources you consulted. Try to spotlight the issue you researched, and use the information from the interviews and library research as supporting material.

1. Look back at the chart you filled out in the previous section. In particular, look at what you wrote down as your own opinion. Could this serve as the thesis statement for your essay?

2. Write two or three possible thesis statements, experimenting with different ways of expressing your opinion.

3. Choose the thesis that you think would work best for your essay; of course, you can change this tentative thesis at any point in the writing process.

4. After you have written a thesis that you feel comfortable with, write a preliminary first paragraph for your essay.

5. Discuss this first paragraph with a partner or small group, and then hand it in to your teacher for comment.

Developing a Tentative Outline

1. At this stage it may be helpful to write a short outline for your essay (see pages 184–85 for outlining techniques).

2. Indicate on the outline where you plan to refer to the interviews you conducted or the articles you read.

3. After you have finished the outline, hand it in to your teacher for comment.

WRITING STRATEGIES

PARAPHRASING AND QUOTING

Whether your information comes from an interview or a written source, you will need to decide how you can best use this information to add authority and interest to your own writing. Basically, there are two ways to do this: (1) quoting the other person's exact words, or (2) paraphrasing, that is to say, expressing someone else's ideas in your own words. Direct quotations can be used to make a dramatic statement or emphasize a point. But they need to be used sparingly. The general rule is to quote only when the exact wording is especially effective. Otherwise, it is best to paraphrase. In either case, it is important to give credit to the source of the ideas.

How to Paraphrase

Paraphrasing is difficult, even for native speakers of a language. Usually, professional writers say things effectively, and it is hard for students, especially those learning a second language, to say them equally well using their own words. In Western academic writing, however, it is essential not to copy the exact wording of another text. Using another author's words in this way is considered plagiarism and can lead to serious penalties. Like most other writing techniques, the best way to learn how to paraphrase effectively is to practice doing it.

The following examples based on the first paragraph of "Creating a Gay Family: A Test Case" on pages 247–50 will give you some ideas of possible ways to paraphrase print sources and to avoid unintentional plagiarism.

ORIGINAL PARAGRAPH

Thomas Steel, a gay man, is suing Robin Young, a lesbian, for paternity rights to their biological daughter, and the gay legal community is shuddering with apprehension. The case cuts to the core question of gay family life now: What constitutes a gay family? Beatrice Dohrn, the legal director of the Lambda Legal Defense and Education Fund, says, "Family courts have traditionally assumed that it is in the best interests of all kids to have a mother and a father. But the fact is that lesbians and gay men are deliberately constructing families in numbers that are unprecedented—often by donor insemination or surrogacy. This is the first dispute of its kind in an appellate court in New York, and lesbians and gay men hoping to have kids are anxiously watching this case."

ACCEPTABLE PARAPHRASE

A recent article in *The New Yorker* describes a court case that has caused great interest and anxiety among gay people who are hoping to create families. This case, which is the first of its kind in New York State, involves a homosexual man, Thomas Steel, who is asking for paternity rights to a child born to a lesbian who was artificially inseminated with his sperm. The basic issue in this case has to do with defining what is meant by a gay family.

UNACCEPTABLE PARAPHRASE

(Note that wording plagiarized from the original source is underlined.)

A recent article in *The New Yorker* describes a court case that cuts to the core question of gay family life: What do we mean by a gay family? In this case, Thomas Steel, a homosexual, is suing a lesbian for paternity rights to their biological daughter. In the past courts have assumed that it is in the best interests of all children to have a mother and a father. But now that gays are finding ways to create their own families, the courts will have to decide what constitutes a gay family.

ACCEPTABLE PARAPHRASE

(Note that wording from the original appears within quotation marks, an acceptable practice in academic writing.)

A recent article in *The New Yorker* describes a court case that addresses a question that many in the gay community are currently asking themselves: What do we mean by a gay family? In this case, Thomas Steel, a homosexual, has asked a New York State appellate court to grant him paternity rights to a child born to a lesbian who was artificially inseminated with his sperm. According to Beatrice Dohrn, legal director of the Lambda Legal Defense and Education Fund, in the past, courts have "assumed that it is in the best interests of all kids to have a mother and a father." But now that gay people are finding ways to create their own families, the courts will have to decide on the definition of a gay family.

Activity

In this activity you are asked to look carefully at several attempted paraphrases of sentences from "Creating a Gay Family: A Test Case." Working with a partner, compare each of the paraphrases to the original sentence. Discuss whether you feel it is an acceptable paraphrase. If it is not acceptable, explain why not. Then rewrite the sentence as an acceptable paraphrase of the original. If you are unsure of your answer, consult your teacher.

1. *Original Sentence:* [Robin Young and Sandra Russo] hoped that each woman would bear one baby, and that the children would be reared as the offspring of both women. (from paragraph 2)

Attempted Paraphrase: Sandra Russo and Robin Young each wanted to bear one baby, and they hoped that the children would be reared as the off-spring of both women.

2. *Original Sentence:* Reasoning that gay men who were "out" were likely to be sympathetic to lesbians forming families—and might even be politically motivated to help create them—Ms. Young and Ms. Russo decided to find gay donors. (from paragraph 3)

Attempted Paraphrase: Young and Russo believed that gay men might want to help them in their desire to have children and, for this reason, might be appropriate donors.

3. *Original Sentence:* They wanted men who were intelligent, and who lived far enough away so that their being a part of the family wasn't an option. (from paragraph 3)

Attempted Paraphrase: In looking for potential donors, Young and Russo were hoping to find intelligent men and ones "who lived far enough away so that their being a part of the family wasn't an option."

Activity

This activity asks you to practice paraphrasing using the excerpted *New York Times* article entitled "After a Ruling, Hawaii Weighs Gay Marriages," which is reproduced below.

After a Ruling, Hawaii Weighs Gay Marriages
By Jane Gross (Special to the *New York Times*)

Honolulu, April 23—This island state, where multiculturalism is a way 1
of life and not just a slogan, could become the first to legalize marriage between people of the same sex—or at least offer marital benefits for gay couples who register as domestic partners.

Whether by sanctioning gay marriage, which no other nation has done, 2
or by passing America's first statewide domestic partnership act, Hawaii
would lead the way in this fundamental redefinition of family, which some
see as a sweeping expansion of civil rights and others see as an erosion of
traditional values.

To stand on the far shore of change is a fitting role for this state, which is 3
known for a progressive public policy, a liberal state constitution, a tolerance
for diversity, an acceptance of intermarriage and a culture of flourishing
same-sex relationships.

"Because the culture here is so intermixed, we are used to living to- 4
gether and letting people be whatever they want to be," said Hoku Akiu, a
security guard, who hopes to marry his partner, Dwight Ovitt, and has already celebrated their union in a church full of sympathetic relatives and
friends.

The stage was set for this far-reaching social change when the State 5

Supreme Court ruled last May that refusing to license the marriage of three gay couples, thus depriving them of financial and legal benefits, violated the due process clause of the Hawaii Constitution. The State Constitution is more elaborate than its Federal counterpart and explicitly prohibits sex discrimination.

(*New York Times*, Monday, April 25, 1994, p. A1)

1. Try to paraphrase the title of this article. Specifically, what other verb could you substitute for *weighs*?

2. In paraphrasing articles such as this one, certain words or phrases are used in a specific sense and really can't be paraphrased. For example, it would be impossible to paraphrase the expression domestic partnership act (paragraph 2). Underline three other expressions in the article that cannot be rephrased.

3. Reread paragraphs 1 and 2 of the article. Then notice how the information in these paragraphs has been expressed in different words in the following paraphrase:

> According to a recent article in *The New York Times,* Hawaii may soon legalize homosexual marriages or, failing that, grant marital benefits to domestic partners of homosexuals. The possible acceptance of gay partnerships by the state is in keeping with Hawaii's long tradition of multiculturalism and respect for diversity.

Note that the underlined phrase serves to remind the reader of the source of this information.

4. Working in a group of three or four students, write a paraphrase of paragraphs 3 and 4 of the article. Here are some tips that may make your work easier:

- Read the paragraph two or three times, until you are sure you understand it fully. Discuss the meaning with your group, and look up in the dictionary any words you do not know.
- Put the book aside, and write your paraphrase without looking at the original source. Of course, you can look back at the original to refresh your memory, but put it away again before you start to write.
- You may need to write two or three versions before you are satisfied with your paraphrase.

5. After your group has completed its paraphrase, meet with another group that has finished. Compare the different versions. How were the two paraphrases similar? How were they different?

Paraphrasing and Quoting to Add Support

Of course, you will usually not be paraphrasing just for the sake of paraphrasing. Whether you choose to paraphrase or to quote, you usually do so to support a point you are making. The next activity gives you a chance to practice this skill.

Activity

Remember that when you include quoted material in your writing, you need to introduce the quotations with your own words so that they fit smoothly into your essay. Ideally, you should also indicate to the reader why you have chosen a particular quotation. The following list shows some ways of introducing quotes. See if you can think of other ways.

Possible Ways of Introducing Quotes

As [author's name] states, ". . ."
According to [author], ". . ."
[Author] explains, ". . ."
In the words of [author]: ". . ."
I agree with [author] that ". . ."
[Author] states, ". . ." However, in my opinion . . .

The following activity asks you to practice incorporating the ideas of others into your writing by paraphrasing and quoting. Again, you will be using the *New York Times* article on pages 265–66 as your source material.

1. Work with a partner. Imagine that you are writing an essay in which you argue that gay marriages should be legalized. Paraphrase some of the material from the article to support your opinion. The following sample paraphrase suggests one way of using information from the article to support the legalization of gay marriages:

> According to the *New York Times*, gay marriages may soon become legal in at least one state. In Hawaii, which has a long tradition of multiculturalism and toleration for diversity, the State Supreme Court decided in May, 1993, that three homosexual couples who were not allowed to marry legally were being denied some of their basic rights (Gross, 1994, p. A1).

2. Now, practice supporting this same opinion by quoting from the article — including some of the author's exact words within quotation marks. Remember to introduce the quotation in your own words. For instance, the following example includes a brief quotation from paragraph 2:

> Based on recent legal action, Hawaii may become the first state to recognize gay marriages. If so, this could be a first step toward a "fundamental redefinition of family" (Gross, 1994, p. A1).

3. After you have completed steps 1 and 2, compare your examples with those of another pair. Your teacher may ask some students to write their paraphrases or quotations on the board for the class to discuss.

4. *Optional:* If you are planning to write an essay in which you use library research to support your opinion, practice paraphrasing and quoting from one of the sources you plan to use for your essay. Write out two examples of paraphrases

and two examples of direct quotations. Be sure to include the source of your information in parentheses; if you are quoting, you must include the page number.
Then exchange papers with your partner, and discuss. By working together, try to
improve your paraphrases and quotes. Finally, ask your teacher to comment on
your work.

GIVING CREDIT TO SOURCES

In writing for American colleges and universities, it is very important to state
where you got your information. This is to enable interested readers to go to the
sources to get more information and also to give credit to the person who first stated
the idea. (The only time that you are not expected to mention the source of information is when you are restating a commonly known fact, such as "Many homeless people use drugs or alcohol.")

The importance of acknowledging the sources of ideas may derive from the emphasis on the individual in Western culture. People's ideas are thought to "belong" to
them, like property. And if you use these ideas without acknowledging their source, it
is considered similar to stealing; the name given to this type of "theft" is plagiarism,
and the penalties can be severe, ranging from failing an assignment to being expelled
from college.

Most plagiarism is not intentional but occurs because students do not know
how to give credit properly to their sources. In order to avoid plagiarism, it is important to find out what method of documentation your instructor prefers and to
use it consistently. Two of the most commonly used methods are those of the
Modern Language Association (MLA) and the American Psychological Association (APA). The APA style is usually preferred in the social sciences—such subjects as psychology or anthropology; the MLA style is used more often in the hu-
manities—such subjects as literature or foreign language. With both methods,
you are required to mention the source of the ideas briefly within parentheses in
the text of the essay and then provide complete information in a bibliography at
the end.

Documenting Sources within Your Essay

The examples that follow show the form used for documenting sources within
the text of your essay. In all cases it is important to include the author's last name. If
you are using the APA style, you also include the date of publication, but you do not
give a page number unless you have included a direct quotation from the source. If
you are using the MLA style, you do not include the date of publication, but you do
include the page number for all references.

Examples of In-Text References, APA Style

1. Author not mentioned in text:

   Expressive language is personal and related to
   everyday conversation (Britton, 1982).

2. Author mentioned in text:

According to Britton (1982), expressive language
is personal and related to everyday
conversation.

3. Author mentioned in text, direct quotation included:

According to Britton (1982), expressive language
is "close to the self" and "relies on an
interest in the speaker as well as the topic"
(p. 96).

4. Author not mentioned in text, direct quotation included:

Expressive language is "close to the self" and
"relies on an interest in the speaker as well as
the topic"(Britton, 1982, p. 96).

Examples of In-Text References, MLA Style

1. Author not mentioned in text:

Expressive language is personal and related to
everyday conversation (Britton 96).

2. Author mentioned in text:

According to Britton, expressive language is
personal and related to everyday conversation
(96).

3. Author mentioned in text, direct quotation included:

According to Britton, expressive language is
"close to the self" and "relies on an
interest in the speaker as well as the topic"
(96).

4. Author not mentioned in text, direct quotation included:

Expressive language is "close to the self" and
"relies on an interest in the speaker as well as
the topic" (Britton 96).

Complete Bibliographic Listing at End of Essay

In addition to acknowledging all outside sources within the text of your essay, you are required to provide a complete bibliographic listing of the sources you used on a separate page at the end of your paper. In the APA style, this bibliography is entitled "References." In the MLA style, it is entitled "Works Cited." The Brief Guide to the APA Style for References on page 272 identifies the different parts of common types of bibliographic entries.

The following guide provides more detailed explanations for both styles. You do not need to memorize this information. Instead, refer to the guide when you are preparing the bibliography for a research essay.

Examples of References, APA Style

1. Book with one author:

   West, C. (1994). Race matters. New York: Vintage.

2. Book with two or more authors:

   Lakoff, G., & Johnson, M. (1980). Metaphors we
       live by. Chicago: University of Chicago
       Press.

3. Article in a magazine:

   Gibbs, N. (1995, July 3). Working harder, getting
       nowhere. Time, 146, 16-20.

4. Article in a scholarly journal:

   Krugman, P. (1994, November/December). The myth of
       Asia's miracle. Foreign Affairs, 73, 62-78.

5. Article in a newspaper:

   Kamm, H. (1995, January 26). Poland reawakens to
       its history as communism's mirror shatters.
       The New York Times, pp. A1, A10.

Examples of Works Cited, MLA Style

1. Book with one author:

   West, Cornel. Race Matters. New York: Vintage,
       1994.

2. Book with two or more authors:

   Lakoff, George, and Mark Johnson. Metaphors We

Live By. Chicago: University of Chicago
Press, 1980.

3. Article in a magazine:

Gibbs, Nancy. "Working Harder, Getting Nowhere."
Time 3 July 1995: 16-20.

4. Article in a scholarly journal:

Krugman, Paul. "The Myth of Asia's Miracle."
Foreign Affairs, 73 (Nov./Dec. 1994): 62-78.

5. Article in a newspaper:

Kamm, Henry. "Poland Reawakens to Its History as
Communism's Mirror Shatters." New York Times
26 Jan. 1995, late ed.: A1, A10.

Activity

This activity is intended for students who are using library research in their essays and is designed to provide practice with the accepted methods of acknowledging print sources.

Note that the Dartnell essay on which this activity is based uses the APA style of documentation. Before you begin, ask your teacher which style he or she prefers—APA or MLA.

1. Bring to class a copy of one of the articles you intend to use in writing your essay.

2. Working with a partner, look back at Kim Dartnell's essay (pages 236–38). Find the first place where Dartnell referred to an outside source. In which paragraph did this occur? How did she give credit to the source? Copy the exact words of the citation:

_____

3. Now look at the end of Dartnell's essay, the section entitled "References." Find the complete reference to the source noted in step 2. Copy the complete information for this source:

_____

_____

4. Get out your copy of the article on your topic. Write a sentence in which you paraphrase or quote from the article, and give credit to your source in parentheses, as Dartnell did. Compare sentences with your partner, and consult your teacher if you have any questions.

A BRIEF GUIDE TO THE APA STYLE FOR REFERENCES

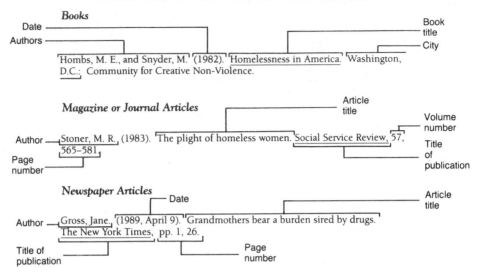

5. Using the same source, write a complete entry to be included in the bibliography at the end of the essay. Again, consult with your partner and teacher.

SUGGESTED TECHNIQUES

As you are working on your first draft, refer to these guidelines.

1. *Remember that you are the author of this essay, and you should be expressing your own opinion.* Use information from the interviews or library research to support your opinion. Do not let these other sources become the focus of your essay.

2. *Try to include some brief quotations from the interviews or articles, and remember to introduce these quotations with your own words.* Choose quotations where the wording is effective, and introduce them with your own words, explaining how they fit in with what you are saying. Be very careful not to plagiarize. Whenever you use someone else's exact words (whether they came from a personal interview or a published source), you must indicate this by using quotation marks at the beginning and end of each quote.

3. *Paraphrase (express in your own words) some of the other information from your interview or reading.* If you want to refer to certain ideas from your sources but the exact wording is not important, express it in your own words by paraphrasing. (See pages 236–38 if you are not sure how to do this.)

4. *Be sure to give credit to your sources in the essay itself, and include a list of references or works cited at the end of the essay.* After you have written your first draft, review the section on paraphrasing and quoting. Be sure you have included a reference (in parentheses) in your essay every time you refer to an idea you got from an outside source. Then, at the end of the essay, include a list of references. Check your list against the guidelines on pages 268–72 to be sure you have listed your references correctly.

When your first draft is completed, exchange essays with a classmate and fill out the Peer Response Sheet at the end of the chapter. Refer to Part III: Rethinking/Rewriting for suggestions about revising and editing your essay.

Court Decision in the Paternity Rights Case (pages 247–50)

In October 1994 the Appellate Division of the New York State Supreme Court ruled that, legally, Thomas Steel is Ry's father although the Court did not take a stand on the issue of visiting rights. This decision overturned a 1993 Family Court decision that Mr. Steel was not Ry's father. The 1994 decision is now being appealed by Robin Young to the State Court of Appeals.

PEER RESPONSE SHEET:
WRITING BASED ON RESEARCH

Writer's Name: _____

Reader's Name: _____

Date: _____

(*Note to the reader:* As you respond to the writer's draft, try to focus on the ideas rather than the grammar and spelling. Discuss only those mistakes that interfere with understanding.)

1. What was the topic of this essay? _____

_____

_____

_____

What was the writer's opinion about this topic? _____

_____

_____

_____

Where in the essay was this opinion stated? _____

_____

_____

_____

2. Did the writer use information from personal interviews or library research to support his or her opinion? Were there any places where you got confused or needed more information?

_____

_____

_____

_____

3. How would the essay have been different if the writer had not included information from outside sources?

_____

_____

_____

_____

4. If the essay involved library research, did the writer give credit to the outside sources both in the text of the essay and in a list of references at the end? Check the citations carefully, and note any places where there are problems.

_____

_____

_____

5. Make *one* suggestion for improving the next draft of this essay.

_____

_____

_____

_____

ASSESSMENT OF PROGRESS:
A CLOSING SURVEY

Instructions: As you complete your work in this course, take some time to reflect on how your writing has changed. Before you begin to answer these questions, find the surveys you filled out at the beginning and middle of the course. Read through your responses on those surveys, and then answer the following questions.

1. What new strengths have you discovered in your writing during this course? Mention a specific paper you were pleased with, and explain why.

_____

_____

_____

_____

2. What aspects of writing are still difficult for you? Explain.

_____

_____

_____

_____

3. Has your attitude toward writing changed as a result of this course? Explain.

_____

_____

_____

_____

4. Look at your answer to question 4 in the Beginning Survey. In what ways has your approach to the writing process changed? Have you discovered any new resources to help you with writing?

_____

_____

_____

_____

5. Did your writing improve in the ways that you hoped it would when you filled out the Beginning Survey?

_____

_____

_____

_____

6. Look at your answer to question 6 in the Beginning Survey. Which of the things listed were, in fact, most helpful to you? Were these the things you thought would help? Explain.

_____

_____

_____

_____

7. Do you feel that you have accomplished your own goals for this course? Are you satisfied with your progress? Why or why not?

_____

_____

_____

_____

Part III

Rethinking/ Rewriting

11
Revising

What is revising? In order to understand this term, let's first look at what revising is *not*. It is not simply a correction of grammar, spelling, or punctuation. Revising has to do with the content, ideas, development, and organization of your writing. When writers revise, they ask themselves questions such as: Is this really what I want to say? Have I included enough information? Am I repeating myself unnecessarily? Are my ideas clear? Is my paper organized so that the reader can follow the ideas easily?

The revising process is different from editing. In this book we use "editing" to mean the correction of grammar, spelling, and punctuation. We recommend that you delay editing until you have revised your essay through two or more drafts and feel satisfied with the content. It does not make sense to spend time carefully correcting the grammar and spelling of an essay if you are going to make major changes of ideas.

However, the main reason we suggest delaying the editing process is that it slows people down and stops them from concentrating on their ideas. Just imagine if, during a conversation, you had to stop and think about whether every word and sentence you said in English was correct. You would not be able to concentrate on what you were saying.

The same principle applies to writing. This does not mean that correctness is not important. We are simply suggesting that you try to develop your ideas as completely as possible before you get involved in the more mechanical process of polishing the language.

If you get into the habit of revising your writing, you will probably find that it removes some of the pressure. Knowing that you can take time later to improve and correct your essay frees you for the real work of a first draft, getting your ideas down on paper.

WHAT READERS LOOK FOR

A student in an English class once told her teacher, "I know my writing is terrible." When asked why, she said, "Because my grammar is so bad." The teacher looked her in the eye and said, "Your grammar isn't bad. It's just different."

Many students express similar feelings about their writing, that it is bad or too general or poorly organized. Perhaps this is because most of the writing we do for school has to be evaluated. If the evaluation is good, we are happy. If not, we feel frustrated or depressed. Yet a grade of *A, B, C, D,* or *F* tells us little as to why a particular paper received that grade.

The purpose of this section is to analyze what readers—teachers, writing test evaluators, and your fellow students—look for as they read your writing.

Activity 1

1. To help you get a sense of how writing is evaluated, list as many qualities as you can think of that make a piece of writing good, for example, clear ideas, good organization, and so on.

2. Discuss these qualities with a partner, small group, or the entire class.

3. Read the essay entitled "The Family in Society," on pages 166–67. How many of the qualities that you identified were you able to find in this essay?

When asked what makes writing good, most people come up with the same characteristics: clear ideas, effective organization, interesting content, appropriate vocabulary, and correct grammar, spelling, and punctuation. The problem with these categories is that without pieces of writing to connect them to, they can become meaningless.

One way of getting a clearer picture of what readers look for is to compare several writing samples. This is what many teachers do when they are trying to decide what grade to assign. The following activity will help you to see how this kind of comparison works.

Activity 2

The paragraphs that follow were taken from student essays on this topic: Do children learn violent behavior from their parents or from other sources, such as television and movies? Alone or with a partner, rate each sample as good, adequate, or poor in these categories: (1) clear ideas, (2) examples and explanations, (3) grammar, and (4) spelling. To make it easier for you to make the comparisons, we have included only the introductory paragraphs of these essays.

Sample I

It is true that children can learn violent behaviors from their parents. Just as if children could learned good things from their parents, children could also learned bad things from their parents.

I believe that children see their parents as some kind of role model. Children are more inclined to follow their parents footsteps or at least tried to imitate them which could be unfortunate if their parents abused their kids and or take drugs such as cocaine and alcohol.

Clear Ideas _____   Examples and Explanations _____

Grammar _____   Spelling _____

Sample II

It is not true to say that children learn their violent behavior just from their parents. I think children learn violent behavior not only from their parents, but from television and their environment.

Most children can not differentiate fiction from reality. This is where television comes in with its influences. Children watch movies such as Rambo, and Commando, etc. And they love these movies. They want to be like those actor in the movies so they decide to try it out, Unfortunately when there is a weapon at home they might use it and start playing with their friends. They could end up being hurt or sometimes even killed.

Clear Ideas _____   Examples and Explanations _____

Grammar _____   Spelling _____

Sample III

I disagree with this passage because children immitates all kinds older people they associate and their friends, parents, even television and movie are just few part of the tool they immitate from. For example, a kid has been raised from a loving family without any violence in the family, he could still immitate from other people he/she sees or associates. He/she still can be a violent child if he/she immitates from them. He can develop a violent behavior if he keeps on associating these violent people.

Clear Ideas _____   Examples and Explanations _____

Grammar _____   Spelling _____

Sample IV

In my country pysical panishments are viewed postiviely for the pourpous of educating children. Even in shools pysical panishments are quite common. I really hated that because children are also human-being not animals and should be treated with care and respect. Without being respected how can children be able to respect other people.

When I was little, if I didnt' do table manner properly my mother would hit me angrily. They expected us to be perfectly obidient. If I wasn't they forced me using physical violence. This tendency has not changed. I think this was the indication of immatureness. They couldn't accept the fact that I am different person and I have different view. Being forced didn't make me change my thought.

Clear Ideas _____   Examples and Explanations _____

Grammar _____   Spelling _____

Reactions

After you have finished your evaluations, discuss your reactions with the rest of the class. Which piece of writing do you think is the best? Which is the weakest? In what areas do you agree or disagree with other members of the class? You may want to compare your evaluations with the following evaluations made by Steven Haber:

Sample I

Clear Ideas   adequate_____   Examples and Explanations   poor_

Grammar   adequate_____   Spelling   good_____

The writer's opinion is fairly clear, but this idea is not developed very well. Each sentence is saying more or less the same thing, that children learn behavior from their parents. There are also some problems with *-ed* endings, which are distracting.

Sample II

Clear Ideas good	Examples and Explanations good
Grammar good	Spelling good

The opinion is clear and is better developed than in Sample I. The writer starts with the idea that children learn violence not only from parents, but also from other sources. The writer then introduces one of those sources, television, and begins to make the connection between violent television shows and movies, and violent behavior at home. Although there are a few grammar errors, these are minor and do not distract the reader too much.

Sample III

Clear Ideas poor	Examples and Explanations poor
Grammar poor	Spelling adequate

We can get the writer's idea that children learn violence from other sources besides parents, but we have to work very hard to get this idea. The first sentence seems to contain too many ideas, all run together. The last two sentences both say more or less the same thing. The grammar mistakes and missing words are more distracting than those in Samples I and II.

Sample IV

Clear Ideas good	Examples and Explanations good
Grammar adequate	Spelling poor

The writer has a clear point of view, that children should be respected and that physical punishment is wrong. The idea is developed with an example from personal experience, which seems appropriate. The misspelled words are rather distracting, especially fairly common words like "physical," "punishment," and "school."

Words of Advice on What Readers Look For

1. If you have to write an essay in class, you may want to keep it short and simple. It is difficult to develop a complex philosophical point if you have only an hour to do it.

2. Not all readers are the same. What may seem like an *A* paper to one teacher might be a *B* or even a *C* to another. This is because not all readers look for the same things. Some may emphasize ideas. Others emphasize grammar. Try to find out which aspects of writing your teacher is responding to in your grade.

3. After your teacher has handed a paper back to you, put it aside for a few days. Then take it out and look at it again. If there are comments, see if you can figure out what the teacher was referring to. If you can't, try to arrange a conference with the teacher. Or you might show the paper to a tutor or a friend whose opinion you trust.

4. Stop thinking about your writing as being good or bad. Instead, ask yourself whether you are satisfied with your work. If so, fine. If not, what can you change?

STRATEGIES FOR REVISING

As you gain experience in writing, you will discover which revision strategies work best for you. The following techniques are helpful for most writers.

---

1. Give yourself time away from your essay.
2. If possible, do your writing on a computer or word processor.
3. Share your essay with a friend or some classmates.
4. Learn from your teacher's comments.
5. Remember that it is your writing and you are in charge.

---

1. *Give yourself time away from your essay.* Before you begin to revise your first draft, it is a good idea to wait a few days after completing it. If you are like most writers, you will find it almost impossible to imagine any changes in a piece of writing you have just finished. You are too close to the essay to begin revising it. But when you come back to the draft later, you will see it with fresh eyes. You will be better able to tell which parts need improvement, and you will have more ideas about revising.

2. *If possible, do your writing on a computer or word processor.* Computers have probably done more to encourage careful revising than any other development in the history of writing. Once a piece of writing is stored in the memory of a computer or on a computer disk, you can change a word, move a paragraph from one place to another, rewrite a paragraph and change it back again without retyping or recopying the whole piece.

We believe that using a computer will benefit your writing in many ways. But the most obvious of these benefits is to take the pain out of revising and replace it with pleasure—as you improve your writing with each successive draft.

3. *Share your essay with a friend or some classmates.* One of the best sources of advice about improving your writing is other students. You can ask a friend to read your essay, or you can share your essay with a small group of classmates by reading it aloud or giving them a copy to read and comment on.

Although your friends and classmates may not be experts on the English language, they *can* help you to answer the most important question you need to ask before revising your writing: Did I get my meaning across clearly to the reader? Your meaning may seem perfectly clear to you because you have the whole story in your head. However, what seems obvious to you may not be clear to a reader who does not have this extra information. If a friend or classmate asks you to clarify or explain something, you may want to work on this section when you revise.

4. *Learn from your teacher's comments.* Some students rely only on their teachers for advice about revising. For this reason, it may be more useful to share your paper with other students *before* the teacher reads it. But certainly you can and should learn from your teacher's comments. A teacher serves the same purpose for a student that an editor does for a professional writer: to look at your writing with an experienced eye and to give suggestions based on that experience. If a certain comment confuses you or does not seem to make sense, discuss it with your teacher before you attempt to rewrite your essay.

5. *Remember that it is your writing and you are in charge.* You can get a great deal of helpful advice about revising from your classmates and teachers. When you are beginning to revise, it is a good idea to read over your essay once more, and think carefully about the feedback you have received from your readers. It may be helpful to read the essay aloud—listening to the sound of the words and how they all fit together. Some students like to tape record their writing and think about possible revisions as they listen to the tape.

After rereading your essay, ask yourself what you can do to make it better. These are some of the most common things writers do when they revise:

- Add additional details, examples, or explanations.
- Take out parts that are not relevant or that merely repeat ideas stated elsewhere.
- Change the way the essay is organized into paragraphs.
- Change the order of the sentences within a paragraph.
- Improve the introduction or the conclusion.

Sometimes, of course, writers decide to throw out the first draft and start all over again.

Since you are the only one who knows exactly what you are trying to achieve in a particular piece of writing, you are the only one who can make the final decisions about how to revise it.

ORAL PEER RESPONSE

When you ask other students to evaluate your essay, it is a good idea to give them a list of questions so that they know what kinds of comments will be useful to you. Be sure to remember these two principles for getting advice on your writing:

- Ask for some positive comments—what the reader or listener likes about your essay. Your writing will improve much more quickly if you are aware of what you do well.
- Don't ask too many questions about any piece of writing. Three or four questions will be plenty. Too much advice is sometimes worse than none at all.

(Refer to pages 21–23 for more information about peer conferences and giving constructive criticism.)

WRITTEN PEER RESPONSE

Another way to get feedback on your writing is to exchange papers with a classmate and write down your reactions. We encourage you to do this by using the Peer Response Sheets (included at the end of each chapter) for the essay assignments suggested in Part II. The following activity gives you a chance to practice filling out a Peer Response Sheet.

Activity: Responding to a First Draft

Read this first draft of a student essay describing a person, and then answer the questions on the sample Peer Response Sheet on pages 289–90.

My Friend Marek
by Andrzej Zganiacz

His name is Marek. I know him since we were 5 years old. I consider him as my best friend. He's a tall boy and likes to wear nice sport clothes. He too does much sport, he does every available for him kind of sport, but socker is his favorite. When we were in grammar school he used to be the captain of our class team. It was interesting to observe how extremaly emotionaly involved he was in the game. He didn't play socker for fun only—he played to win. If our team was loosing scores, he was getting mad, he was doing more than his best to help it; if nothing changed for better he started to cry. Sport is for him the source of fun, emotions, his inner experiences which are for him important ingredients to his spiritual life. But it isn't the only part of his spiritual life. He love to read. When he was a young boy, his mother worrying about his eyes tried to stop him from reading so much. In answer for his mother's restrictions he used to close himself in the bathroom and continued reading there. He knows much about history and it makes him a real pleasure to have such knowledge about history. The thing what the other people notice and what irritates many of them is his behavior. He always tries to make something what interfere with the environment. When all others are grave he laughs and when others laugh he is serious. He expresses his thoughts loudly and very often doesn't care about the fact that someone or a group of people can get mad with him. If he is conserned about it he says it. He likes to tell jokes and to make jokes alone or together with his friends.

Those who know Marek longer know that he is a person whom you can count on. It would be painful for him if someone got the reason to tell him: "Marek, you didn't keep your word." He is a kind of person who is not easy to know about his character much after meeting him a few times or knowing him a short period of time. His real character is hidden deep inside him behind jokes.

PRACTICE
PEER RESPONSE SHEET

Writer's Name: _____

Reader's Name: _____

Date: _____

(*Note to the reader:* As you respond to the first draft of the essay, try to focus on the ideas rather than the grammar and spelling. Discuss only those mistakes that interfere with understanding.)

1. What do you like about this essay? _____

_____

_____

_____

_____

2. What one word would you choose to describe Marek? What specific information in the draft caused you to choose this word? _____

_____

_____

_____

_____

3. List any places where you do not understand the writer's meaning. He will need to clarify these things when he rewrites. _____

_____

_____

_____

_____

_____

4. What do you notice about the organization of the essay? How many paragraphs are there? How could the writer improve the organization of the essay? _____

_____

_____

_____

_____

_____

5. What would you like to know more about? _____

_____

_____

_____

_____

6. Who do you think would be interested in reading this essay? In other words, what is the intended audience for this essay? _____

_____

_____

_____

_____

Reactions

1. Bring the completed Peer Response Sheet to class.

2. Choose a partner to work with and compare your responses. Did you like the same things about the essay? Did you share the same impression of Marek's character? Compare your suggestions for improving the organization. What did you want to know more about?

Activity: Responding to a Revised Draft

Now read the second draft of this essay, and answer the questions that follow.

Marek
by Andrzej Zganiacz

His name is Marek Kubik. I met him for the first time when we were both five years old. My father was working with his father. Once my parents took me to visit his family. Marek was taking a bath when his father introduced him to me. We spent the evening playing with the fancy toys he got from his uncle from Scotland. **1**

He was my first friend who lived on the other side of town, and I couldn't visit him too often. All my other friends lived in my neighborhood, and I could see them every day. **2**

Now he's a tall boy with a blond shock of hair. He still lives in Poland, and because of political reasons, he feels sorry that he didn't leave Poland when he had the chance to do so, a few years ago. **3**

He loves sports. Soccer is his favorite. We were in grammar school until the age of fifteen, and at that time he used to be the captain of our soccer team. It was interesting to observe how extremely emotionally involved he was in the game. I can remember one of our games on a summer afternoon. We were playing just for fun against another team from our school. Unfortunately, our team was losing. He tried to do more than his best to make things go better. When he realized that we had no chance to win, he started to cry. He didn't play soccer only for fun—he played to win. Sport was always for him a source of fun, emotions, inner experiences, which are important ingredients in his spiritual life. **4**

He also loves to read. When he was still in grammar school, his mother, worrying about his eyes, tried to stop him from reading so much. In answer to his mother's restrictions, he used to close himself in the bathroom, reading there. Henryk Sienkiewicz was his favorite author. He especially liked Sienkiewicz's "Trilogy," a set of six large books telling interesting romantic stories based on true events from Polish history of the seventeenth century. Polish high school students are supposed to know this piece of work. Marek read it twice when he was still in grammar school. Then he used to demonstrate the way Polish knights fought against the Swedish enemy. He used a wooden stick as a sword. Marek knows much about Polish history of the sixteenth, seventeenth, and eighteenth centuries, and he really enjoys possessing this knowledge. **5**

My friend loves to joke. Many people are irritated with his behavior. He always tries to be different from the majority: when all others are grave, he often starts to laugh; when others laugh, he doesn't, unless he's in the company of his good friends.   6

He always expresses his thoughts openly and doesn't care about the fact that other people may get angry at him. When we were in high school in Poland, many students were complaining about the medical care in our school. Someone said to one of our teachers that he could hardly ever get to see the doctor because when the doctor happened to be in his surgery, too many people needed to see him at the same time. The teacher was embarrassed but tried to make us not forget about the benefits of living in the "socialist paradise," where no one has to pay for medical care. Hearing this, Marek didn't hesitate to tell her that he would prefer to pay and be treated like a human being. The Communist teacher was so surprised with the answer that she didn't say anything more.   7

Those who have known Marek for a long time know that he is a person whom you can count on. It would be most painful for him if someone had a reason to tell him: "Marek, you didn't keep your word."   8

You can't know much about his character if you've known him only for a short period of time. You have to wait a long time to get the chance to talk seriously to him. When you are patient enough, you can learn about his precious values. His real character is hidden behind jokes, which for most people seem to be stupid ones. I don't belong to this group. I recognize him as my best friend.   9

Reactions

Write your answers to the following questions, and discuss your answers with a partner.

1. List three changes that the writer made in this revised essay. Explain how each of these changes affects your understanding of the essay.

2. What new material did the writer add to this draft? How does this new information affect you as a reader?

3. How did the writer change the organization of the essay in the second draft? Compare the paragraphing of the two drafts. Write a sentence expressing the main idea of each of the nine paragraphs of the revised essay. (Your list will be a sentence outline of the essay.) Are the paragraphs arranged in a logical order?

4. Compare the endings of the two drafts. Which one do you feel makes a more effective ending for the essay? Why?

5. What advice would you give to this writer if he decided to revise his essay one more time?

Activity: Giving More Helpful Peer Response

Now that more writing classes are using peer response, teachers sometimes complain that students don't do a very good job when they respond to the writing of their classmates. It is true that giving honest and constructive peer response is a skill that must be learned through practice. Like every other skill, there is sometimes a period of trial and error at the beginning. Another problem is that giving really good peer response takes time. It will probably take an hour or more for you to read your partner's paper, answer the questions on the Peer Response Sheet, and then discuss these answers thoroughly with each other. But if you keep working at it, we are convinced that the time you spend on peer response will be time well spent.

This activity asks you to compare the two student Peer Response Sheets on pages 294 and 297 and then discuss the questions in the Reactions section that follows. Both students were responding to the first draft of the essay entitled "My Friend Marek" on page 288.

SAMPLE
PEER RESPONSE SHEET A

Writer's Name: *Andrzej Zganiacz*

Reader's Name: *Student A*

Date: *September 13, 1995*

(*Note to the reader:* As you respond to the first draft of the essay, try to focus on the ideas rather than the grammar and spelling. Discuss only those mistakes that interfere with understanding.)

1. What do you like about this essay? *I liked everything. It was good.*

2. What one word would you choose to describe Marek? What specific information in the draft caused you to choose this word? *Friend. The writer says Marek is his best friend.*

3. List any places where you do not understand the writer's meaning. He will need to clarify these things when he rewrites. *I understood the essay.*

4. What do you notice about the organization of this essay? How many paragraphs are there? How could the writer improve the organization of the essay?

There are only 2 paragraphs. It needs more paragraphs because essays always have more than 2 paragraphs.

5. What would you like to know more about? *I thought the writer told enough. I liked it.*

6. Who do you think would be interested in reading this essay? In other words, what is the intended audience for this essay? *I don't know.*

SAMPLE
PEER RESPONSE SHEET B

Writer's Name: ___*Andrzej Zganiacz*___

Reader's Name: ___*Student B*___

Date: ___*September 13, 1995*___

(*Note to the reader:* As you respond to the first draft of the essay, try to focus on the ideas rather than the grammar and spelling. Discuss only those mistakes that interfere with understanding.)

1. What do you like about this essay? *I like the specific details that help us to understand Marek's character. Things like "he didn't play for fun-- he played to win." "He used to close himself in the bathroom and continued reading there." Also I like the last sentence: "His real character is hidden deep inside him behind jokes."*

2. What one word would you choose to describe Marek? What specific information in the draft caused you to choose this word? *I would choose the word "determined." Marek always pushed himself to do more than other people. He liked to win in sports. He wanted to read late at night.*

3. List any places where you do not understand the writer's meaning. He will need to clarify these things when he rewrites. *I didn't understand what the writer meant when he said that Marek "always tries to make something what interfere with the environment."*
    Also I don't understand how sports are related to "spiritual life." I thought spiritual life meant religion.

4. What do you notice about the organization of this essay? How many paragraphs are there? How could the writer improve the organization of the essay?

The essay is not very well organized. There are only two paragraphs. Many different topics are discussed in the first paragraph: what Marek looks like, his interest in sports, his love for reading, his irritating behavior. Maybe the writer could write a whole paragraph for each topic.

5. What would you like to know more about? _____

1. How did you meet Marek and where were you living at that time?

2. Like I said earlier, why do you say that sports were important in his spiritual life?

3. What kind of books did he like to read? Can you give some examples?

4. Why does he do things that irritate other people?

5. Where is Marck now? Do you still communicate with him?

6. Who do you think would be interested in reading this essay? In other words, what is the intended audience for this essay? *The intended audience is probably other ESL students. But really anyone who is interested in friendship might want to read an essay like this..*

Reactions

Discuss your answers to these questions with a small group of classmates.

1. If you were the author of "My Friend Marek," which of these Peer Response Sheets would you find more helpful in revising your essay—A or B? Why? Give an example of a comment that you would find helpful in revising. Give an example of a comment that you would not find helpful.

2. Which of the two peer responders liked the essay more? What evidence can you give to support your opinion?

3. Which peer responder gave more specific answers to the questions? Give an example of an answer that you feel is specific.

4. Did either of the peer responders give any answers that were not constructive? If so, what were they?

5. Did either of the peer responders give any answers that would embarrass or offend the writer? If so, what were they?

Like any other skill, the ability to respond to someone's writing improves with practice. If you continue to give and receive peer feedback, we think that your writing will benefit.

WHEN DOES REVISING END?
A WORD ON MEETING DEADLINES

One reason that beginning writers rarely write more than one draft is that they do not really know how to revise their work effectively. A student explains this problem: "From the first time I wrote an essay in college, the teacher told me to revise that essay. In the very beginning I didn't know what I had to do to revise my paper. So I just always copied the whole paper without changing anything."

We hope that the techniques presented in this chapter will give you some practical help in revising your writing. One student who had used some of these methods expressed it this way: "I think what helped me the most was that the draft was read by a classmate and by my teacher, and they both gave me confidence and made me see what I did right and what I was doing wrong. . . . When I revised, I tried to put myself in the reader's place; I wanted to help the reader picture what I was thinking about when I was writing."

As you become more skilled as a writer, you will probably find yourself doing more, not less, revising. But there comes a time when this process has to end—when you have to stop improving your essay and simply turn it in. Donald Murray, a successful writer and teacher of writing, concludes his essay on revising by explaining this fact of life: "A piece of writing is never finished. It is delivered to a deadline, torn out of the typewriter on demand, sent off with a sense of accomplishment and shame and pride and frustration. If only there were a couple more days, time for just another run at it, perhaps then . . ."

12
Editing

Consider this comparison: if the seats on an airplane are torn and dirty or the food trays are broken, many people might begin to wonder if the plane's engines are in a similar condition. The engines might be fine, but the impression given is that the airline does not care about proper maintenance. In the same way, if an essay is filled with errors in grammar, spelling, and punctuation, the reader may get the impression that the writer does not care very much about what he or she is saying.

This chapter deals with the last phase of the writing process—correcting grammar, spelling, and punctuation. Accuracy in these areas is important because language errors can interfere with meaning or distract the reader from the ideas presented.

The hard truth is that if you want your writing to be accepted and taken seriously, accurate language is necessary. How can you get your writing to be more correct? We admit that it is not easy, especially if English is your second language, but if you work at it, your writing will gradually become more and more correct.

STRATEGIES FOR IMPROVING GRAMMAR AND MECHANICS

The following advice is based on our observations of successful students:

1. *Take an active approach.* With your teacher's help, figure out which aspects of grammar give you the most trouble. Is it sentence errors like fragments and run-ons? Or verb endings? Or plural forms of nouns? If you know what types of errors to look for, it will be much easier to find and correct them.

2. *Learn the basic rules of grammar.* Although English is a complex language and there are quite a few exceptions, knowing the basic grammar rules will help you to eliminate many errors. We recommend that you invest in a grammar reference book that includes detailed explanations of English grammar.

3. *In your grammar work, concentrate on your own writing.* Students often complain that they can get every answer correct on a grammar exercise but continue to make the same errors in their own writing. If it is true for you, try keeping a grammar correction notebook. Divide your notebook into categories such as sentence fragments, subject-verb agreement, verb tense, and so forth. For each error, write a corrected version of the sentence *and* a new sentence to reinforce what you have learned. Figure 12–1 on page 301 shows selections from one student's correction notebook.

IMPROVING YOUR SPELLING

It is true that English spelling is difficult, especially if the spelling of your native language is phonetic as is true for Spanish or Polish. In languages with phonetic spelling, there is only one possible spelling for each word, dictated by its pronunciation. In English, however, words have been taken from many different languages and often keep their original spellings, so there are many possible spellings for every sound.

Subject-Verb Agreement

Error	Correction	New Sentence
Now Robin <u>have</u> a job in data entry.	Now Robin <u>has</u> a job in data entry.	Dave <u>has</u> a new girlfriend.
What if a storm <u>cause</u> the power in the computer room to go off?	What if a storm <u>causes</u> the power in the computer room to go off?	Drinking <u>causes</u> a lot of accidents.

Plural Forms of Nouns

Error	Correction	New Sentence
After I had taken a few <u>lesson</u>, I was one of the most annoying <u>kid</u> in the neighborhood.	After I had taken a few <u>lessons</u>, I was one of the most annoying <u>kids</u> in the neighborhood.	One of the easiest <u>things</u> I learned was how to correct a few grammar <u>errors</u> in my writing.
Two of my <u>friend</u> and I were all excited.	Two of my <u>friends</u> and I were all excited.	I helped three of my <u>friends</u> with their biology homework.

Figure 12–1

Although spelling in English is difficult, it is important to spell words correctly most of the time. If you have many spelling errors, these mistakes will distract your readers from what you are trying to say and may interfere with understanding. By following the suggestions listed below, you can greatly reduce the number of spelling errors in your writing.

1. *Make a list of words you need to learn to spell, and memorize them.* It's a good idea to write these words on small cards that you can review when you have a few extra minutes.

2. *Memorize the commonly used words that are difficult for many second language learners.* Start with the list given below. To make sure you are using these words correctly, write a sentence using each of the words, and discuss your sentences with a partner. If you and your partner disagree about a word, check with your teacher.

> bad, bed
> enough
> feel, fell, fill
> receive
> taught, though, thought
> there, their, they're
> thing, think
> this, these
> to, too, two

3. *Learn to use the spelling checker on the computer or word processor.* For students who have trouble with spelling, the spelling checker can be a godsend. Do as much of your writing as possible on a computer or word processor, and always use the spelling checker before you print. Pay attention to the words you misspell most often, and add them to your personal list of "spelling demons" to memorize.

For practice in learning how to use the spelling checker effectively, do the activities on pages 64–65 and 90–91.

4. *Learn and apply the following basic rules.* Despite the difficulties of English spelling, there are a few simple rules that apply most of the time. These rules will help you eliminate many spelling errors.

Guidelines for Adding Suffixes to Verbs

These guidelines are often related to how the word sounds when you pronounce it.

1. If a word ends in a silent *e*, drop the *e* before adding a suffix (ending) that begins with a vowel:

   smile   →   smiling
   write   →   writing
   hate   →   hated
   love   →   loving

2. If the last two letters of a word are a vowel + a consonant and the vowel

sound is short (like the *a* in hat or the *i* in hit), double the final consonant before adding the ending:

bat   →   batting
begin   →   beginning
hop   →   hopping
run   →   running
step   →   stepped

3. Sometimes the doubling of a consonant signals a change in pronunciation:

write   →   writing (long vowel sound)
write   →   written (short vowel sound)
bite   →   biting (long vowel sound)
bite   →   bitten (short vowel sound)

4. For verbs ending in *y*, you need to look at the letter just before the *y*. If the word ends in a consonant + *y*, the past tense is formed by dropping the *y* and adding *-ied*:

Base	*-ing Form*	*Past*
hurry →	hurrying →	hurried
reply →	replying →	replied
study →	studying →	studied
supply →	supplying →	supplied

If the verb ends in a vowel + y, you simply add the appropriate ending:

Base	*-ing Form*	*Past*
play →	playing →	played
pray →	praying →	prayed
stay →	staying →	stayed

Guidelines for Adding -s Endings to Nouns and Verbs

1. In most cases, you simply add *-s* to the end of the word:

house   →   houses
pencil   →   pencils
write   →   writes

2. If the word ends in a consonant + *y*, change the *y* to *i* and then add *-es*:

carry   →   carries
marry   →   marries
study   →   studies

3. If the word ends in *ch, sh, s, x,* or *z,* add *-es*:

chur*ch* ⟶ churches
ma*sh*   ⟶ mashes
hiss   ⟶ hisses
box   ⟶ boxes
fi*zz*   ⟶ fizzes

4. If a word ends in *f* or *fe,* in most cases you leave off the *f* or *fe* and add *-ves*:

kni*fe* ⟶ knives
li*fe*   ⟶ lives
wi*fe*   ⟶ wives

But notice these exceptions:

roo*f* ⟶ roofs
sa*fe* ⟶ safes

The i Before e Rule

Most children in U.S. elementary schools are taught a rhyme that helps them to know whether *i* comes before *e* in a word. The rhyme goes like this: "i before e except after c or when sounded like *ay* as in n*ei*ghbor and w*ei*gh." This rule explains the spelling of words like "bel*ie*ve" or "rel*ie*ve" (*i* before *e*) and "rec*ei*ve" or "conc*ei*ve" (except after *c*) and "v*ei*n" or "w*ei*gh" (except when sounded like *ay*). Of course, there are still a few exceptions that don't follow this rule—words like "either," "foreign," "science," and "weird."

COPING WITH IRREGULAR VERBS

Most verbs in English are *regular.* That means that in order to form the past tense, you add *-ed* to the base form. For example, the past tense of *play* is *played*; the past tense of *love* is *loved.* The past participle of regular verbs is also formed by adding *-ed.* For example, you would say, "She had played," or "I have loved."

However, some of the most commonly used verbs in the English language are *irregular.* In order to form the past tense and past participle of irregular verbs, you do not add *-ed* but change the verbs in other ways. For example, the past tense of *begin* is *began,* and its past participle is *begun.* Some irregular verbs don't change at all. For the irregular verb *cut,* as an example, the past tense and past participle are also *cut.*

You can find out whether a particular verb is regular or irregular by looking it up in the dictionary. If the past and past participle forms are *not* given, that means the verb is regular and adds *-ed.* The past and past participle forms of irregular verbs are always given in the dictionary.

Included below is a list of the most commonly used irregular verbs. Go through the list and put a check mark by the verbs you already know. Of those you don't know, you might want to choose five or so each week to memorize.

Base Form	Past	Past Participle
awake	awoke, awakened	awoken, awaked
be	was, were	been
bear	bore	borne
beat	beat	beat, beaten
become	became	become
begin	began	begun
bend	bent	bent
bet	bet	bet
bind	bound	bound
bite	bit	bit, bitten
bleed	bled	bled
blow	blew	blown
break	broke	broken
breed	bred	bred
bring	brought	brought
build	built	built
burst	burst	burst
buy	bought	bought
catch	caught	caught
choose	chose	chosen
come	came	come
cost	cost	cost
creep	crept	crept
cut	cut	cut
deal	dealt	dealt
dig	dug	dug
dive	dived, dove	dived
do	did	done
draw	drew	drawn
dream	dreamed, dreamt	dreamed, dreamt
drink	drank	drunk
drive	drove	driven
eat	ate	eaten
fall	fell	fallen
feed	fed	fed
feel	felt	felt

Base Form	Past	Past Participle
fight	fought	fought
find	found	found
fit	fit, fitted	fit, fitted
flee	fled	fled
fly	flew	flown
forbid	forbade	forbidden
forget	forgot	forgotten, forgot
freeze	froze	frozen
get	got	gotten, got
give	gave	given
go	went	gone
grind	ground	ground
grow	grew	grown
hang (an object)	hung	hung
hang (a person)	hanged	hanged
have	had	had
hear	heard	heard
hide	hid	hidden, hid
hit	hit	hit
hold	held	held
hurt	hurt	hurt
keep	kept	kept
kneel	knelt, kneeled	knelt, kneeled
knit	knitted, knit	knitted, knit
know	knew	known
lay (put)	laid	laid
lead	led	led
lean	leaned, leant	leaned, leant
leave	left	left
lend	lent	lent
let (allow)	let	let
lie (recline)	lay	lain
light	lighted, lit	lighted, lit
lose	lost	lost
make	made	made
mean	meant	meant

Base Form	Past	Past Participle
pay	paid	paid
prove	proved	proved, proven
quit	quit, quitted	quit, quitted
read	read	read
rid	rid, ridded	rid, ridded
ride	rode	ridden
ring	rang	rung
rise	rose	risen
run	ran	run
say	said	said
see	saw	seen
seek	sought	sought
sell	sold	sold
send	sent	sent
set	set	set
shake	shook	shaken
shine	shone, shined	shone, shined
shoot	shot	shot
show	showed	shown, showed
shrink	shrank	shrunk
shut	shut	shut
sing	sang	sung
sink	sank	sunk
sit	sat	sat
sleep	slept	slept
slide	slid	slid, slidden
speak	spoke	spoken
speed	sped, speeded	sped, speeded
spend	spent	spent
spin	spun	spun
split	split	split
spread	spread	spread
spring	sprang	sprung
stand	stood	stood
steal	stole	stolen
stick	stuck	stuck

Base Form	*Past*	*Past Participle*
sting	stung	stung
strike	struck	struck, stricken
swear	swore	sworn
swim	swam	swum
swing	swung	swung
take	took	taken
teach	taught	taught
tear	tore	torn
tell	told	told
think	thought	thought
throw	threw	thrown
wake	woke, waked	woken, waked
wear	wore	worn
weave	wove	woven
weep	wept	wept
win	won	won
wring	wrung	wrung
write	wrote	written

KNOWING WHEN TO CAPITALIZE

The rules for capitalization in English may differ from the ones you learned in your native language, which may cause some confusion. The following rules are intended to serve as a reference when you are not sure whether to use a lowercase (*e*) or capital (*E*) letter.

1. *Capitalize all proper nouns.* This includes names of people (Rafael), names of countries (Colombia), names of cities (Houston) and states (California), names of specific bodies of water (the Atlantic Ocean) or mountains (the Rocky Mountains), names of days (Wednesday) and months (October), names of languages (Japanese, Arabic, Spanish), names of nationalities (Korean) and religions (Judaism, Islam, Buddhism), and brand names of products (Chevrolet, Cadillac, Sony).

2. *Capitalize the first word of every sentence.*

Examples: Classes begin in September. Have you decided to register for classes?

3. *Always capitalize the pronoun* I.

Examples: I have studied at this college for two years. My friend attended the college before I did.

4. *In titles, capitalize the first and last word and each important word.* In general, you do not capitalize articles (*a, an,* and *the*) or prepositions (*for, in, of, on, with,* etc.) unless they are the first or last word in the title.

Examples:

Books: *Iron and Silk, The Woman Warrior, A Place for Us*
Magazines and newspapers: *The New York Times, Newsweek*
Movies and plays: *Nobody's Fool, Much Ado about Nothing*

LEARNING TO PROOFREAD

Proofreading is the final step in the editing process. It means reading your essay carefully and correcting as many errors as possible before you turn it in.

Students often have difficulties with proofreading because they do not realize how it differs from ordinary reading. For one thing proofreading is much, much slower. When you read for meaning, you want to keep your eyes moving so that you do not lose track of the writer's meaning. But when you proofread, you have to slow your eyes down so that you can see each letter and punctuation mark.

Besides being much slower, proofreading differs from the usual type of reading in that it focuses on correctness rather than meaning. When you have finished revising an essay, read it first for meaning. Once you are satisfied with the content, then you can begin to proofread.

The following are some strategies for effective proofreading. Experiment with the different strategies, and decide which ones work best for you.

- If you have the time, wait a few hours or days between checking your meaning and beginning to proofread.

- Hold a pencil under each word to force your eyes to see every letter, and read the essay aloud. Look carefully at the endings of words since this is where most errors occur.

- Hold a ruler or piece of white paper under the line you are reading so that you can see only one line at a time.

- Start proofreading from the end of the essay, reading the last sentence first. Some people find that this helps them to concentrate on correctness rather than on meaning.

- Be sure to proofread even if you have written your essay on a computer or word processor. The spelling checker will help you to find many—but not all—mistakes. If possible, reprint your corrected essay, but if necessary, make last-minute corrections in pen.

- Always proofread your essays more than once. Nobody catches all the errors the first time around.

Activity

Proofread the following essay, correcting all the grammar, spelling, and punctuation errors.

Writing Skill is Essential

I think that writing is an essential skill for a person in modern society because we need writing skill in jobs and for keeping records. Also writing will always be in the future and in generation ahead.

Most jobs in the world require a person to read and write. For an example a friends of mind (Robin) who is an expert in computer went to a job interview. The jobs he was looking for was data entry. When the person who interview my friend told Robin to type a sentence on the computer. What happen is that Robin knew how to work the computer, but the grammer in his sentence was wronge. Robin was dissapointed when he didn't get the job. Robin was beginning to work harder in his grammar and a year later he have a job in data entry the same job that he was turned down.

Writing is very important in the future and in generation ahead. We know the past history because there are record in writing. Now there are computer to store information and data faster than writing it. The are always a problem in computer for example what if there are a lightning storm and it cause the power in a computer room off. The computer data and memory would be erase. But if you write the data and information in paper or book it will last longer and don't have to worry about lightning storm.

Writing began when caveman are still alive. It will continue to the future. Why should we not learn to write when in past generation writing is use for communication and to store data so we can learn from our mistake that happen in the past. Also law and treaty have to be written to make the society better.

Reactions

When you have finished this proofreading activity, discuss your changes with a partner. Then check them against the Answer Key, pages 328–29. Consult with your teacher if you have any questions.

Activity

This activity gives you a chance to practice proofreading one of your own essays.

1. Bring to class a draft you have been working on, one that you feel is close to being finished.

2. Read the essay first for meaning. Make any changes that seem to be needed.

3. Now go back and proofread your essay. Remember to read the essay much more slowly, and use one or more of the proofreading techniques described on page 309.

4. When you have finished proofreading your essay, choose a partner to work with and exchange essays. Using a pencil, underline any places in your partner's essay that you think may still contain errors. Do not make corrections.

5. When both of you have finished, discuss your proofreading with each other. What was the most common type of error in each essay? Together, look carefully at the places that were underlined. Discuss them, and make corrections if necessary. Be sure to ask for your teacher's help if you need an expert opinion.

CONCLUSION

There is much more to good writing than just correctness. However, if you care about your writing and want readers to take it seriously, you will spend the extra time necessary to edit carefully and make sure your writing is as correct as possible.

PARTING WORDS FROM THE AUTHORS

We wrote this book because we were excited by our students' writing, and we felt that if more people could read stories and essays by student writers, they might be inspired to explore their own ideas for writing. We have found, and we hope you agree, that you do not need to be a professional to write well.

We would appreciate hearing about your reactions to the book. How has your writing changed as a result of using it? What activities helped you the most? Were there any that were not helpful? If you were especially pleased with any of the writing you did, we would like to read it.

Send any letters or essays to:

Rebecca Mlynarczyk and Steven Haber
c/o College Division
St. Martin's Press
175 Fifth Avenue
New York, NY 10010

Remember to include your return address so that we can write back to you.

Now you have come to the end of this book, but we hope it will mark the beginning, not the end, of your writing career.

Answer Key

page 61   *Identifying Subjects and Verbs*

1. <u>Love</u> usually <u>involves</u> people and things <u>you</u> <u>cannot</u> <u>buy</u> with money.
2. Also, <u>love</u> <u>is</u> consistent.
3. <u>It</u> <u>does</u> not <u>change</u> every day or every month.
4. <u>Things</u> <u>you</u> <u>like</u> <u>can change</u> with your mood or with the season, but not things <u>you</u> <u>love</u>.

pages 61–62   *Choosing the Right Verb Tense*

It (be) _____*is*_____ a cold and windy afternoon. When I first (get) _*get*_ ₁ to class, I (look) _*look*_____ out the window. There (be) _____*are*_____ many buses and cars crossing the road. Suddenly, I (hear) _____*hear*_____ the teacher talking in the classroom next to mine. But I (be) _____*am*_____ not sure what she (be) _____*is*_____ saying. The students in my class (be) _____*are*_____ busy writing an essay. They (do) _____*do*_____ not even know the clock (be) _____*is*_____ making a noise.

Finally, I (look) _____*look*_____ outside. There (be) _____*is*_____ a lady ₂ lying in the street. People (be) _____*are*_____ looking at her. They (seem) _____*seem*_____ like they (do) _____*do*_____ not know what (be) _____*is*_____ happening or who the murderer (be) _____*is*_____.

Later on, there (be) _____*are*_____ a couple of police cars that (come) ₃ _____*come*_____ and (take) _____*take*_____ her away.

pages 63–64   Knowing When to Use the Plural Form of Nouns

Eat Fast . . . Die Fast?

by M. K. Pun

"Good time*ˢ*, great taste . . . at McDonald's." "We do it like you do it at   1
Burger King." I don't think so. However, thousand*ˢ* of Americans do agree, and
they have been living on fast food like hamburger*ˢ* and French fry*ies* since they were
born. So, would it be possible that the more fast food you eat, the faster you will
die?

According to the Surgeon General's report on nutrition and health, what you   2
eat can kill you. The U.S. population eats altogether too much, and too much of
the wrong food*ˢ*, especially saturated fat. In fact, American*ˢ*' favorite food*ˢ*—hamburger*ˢ*, hot dog*ˢ*, and French fry*ies*—are where the saturated fat and cholesterol are
mainly from, as well as from meat and dairy product*ˢ*. That fat can increase the risk
of obesity, heart disease, and cancer.

A lot of people believe that salty food is tasty food. And usually a lot of salt is   3
put in fast food when it is being prepared. However, the Surgeon General also
stated that American*ˢ* should minimize the use of salt in cooking and at the table.

Now, imagine yourself as a balloon. Whenever you eat a hamburger, the   4
hamburger will be put in the balloon, and the balloon will explode when there are
too many hamburger*ˢ*. The more you eat, the easier the balloon explodes. The more
fast food you eat, the faster you will die. Next time, when you have a Big Mac,
won't you think twice before taking a big bite?

pages 64–65   Spelling Strategy: Using the Spelling Checker

1. Travelers, the sick, and ~~pregnent~~ *pregnant* women can defer fasting during Ramadan.
2. Of course, I was not ~~suposed~~ *supposed* to fast since most children usually start fasting
   at the age of thirteen.

3. I was very anxious and ~~curios~~ *curious* to experience the feeling of fasting.

4. After I finished my last meal, my father gave me some good ~~advize~~ *advice*.

5. The time of ~~brakeing~~ *breaking* our fast was 7:45.

pages 84–86   *Classifying Types of Sentences*

1. <u>She</u> always <u>has</u> a little smile on her face in her portraits. _____*simple*_____

2. (Although) she <u>is smiling</u>, there <u>is</u> always a <u>kind</u> of severity and dignity about her. _____*complex*_____

3. <u>She</u> <u>passed away</u> on a cold February morning eight years ago. _____*simple*_____

4. (When) my <u>father</u> <u>came</u> to wake me up, <u>I</u> already <u>sensed</u> (what) <u>had happened</u>, (and) <u>I</u> <u>was seized</u> with fear. *complex/compound*

5. My <u>grandmother</u> <u>did</u> not <u>like</u> to show the pictures of her youth to others, (but) <u>I</u> <u>liked</u> to look at them (and) always <u>tried</u> to find them. _____*compound*_____

pages 87–88   *Understanding Sentence Boundaries*

I admired her. *S* she could repeat that exercise movement over fifty times and   1 did not seem tired. I imitated it but I only could do it five times. *W* when she saw me, she went over and said, *"Y* you don't look like a youth. I'm even stronger than you."

This was the first time I met her at a park near Chinatown. *S* she was an old,   2 healthy Chinese lady. I thought she had a wealthy family and a happy life. *S* since we both spoke the same dialect, we didn't have any trouble understanding each other. *A* after we had met a couple of times, I learned that she got married when she was only fifteen. *H* her husband left his family in China for Singapore and then for the United States five months later. *T* they did not meet each other again until she came here twenty-eight years later when she was forty-three years old. *U* unfortunately, they did not have any children. *S* she is living alone in this country now.

pages 88–89   Proofreading for Sentence Boundaries

The Third Day behind the Wheel
by Wieslaw P. Zubel

When I was twenty-one, I got my first driver's license. Living in the suburbs of New Orleans, I was forced to drive a car in order to get from one place to another. At the place I lived, called Violet, nobody dared to cross the street on foot.   1

Before I took the road test, I had driven for two hours at a shopping mall parking lot. On the day after I got my license, I was already forcing my eight-year-old Ventura to fly seventy miles per hour on a two-way highway.   2

The next day I decided to check the Ventura's speed ability. I took her on a divided highway with two lanes going each direction. In the middle was neutral ground full of potholes. On both sides along the highway were ditches filled with snakes, mud, and water. In the distance, the skeletons of dead trees greeted the haunted travelers.   3

It was the beginning of dusk. When I passed the Judge Perreze Bridge and accelerated to ninety-six miles per hour. When the car wasn't going any faster, I had a glimmering thought of slowing down. Suddenly, the Ventura started bouncing from side to side and went off the road to the left. First I noticed the headlights of oncoming cars, so I was preparing myself mentally for a head-on collision. A second later, however, I had the panorama of eternal wetness and started subconsciously to press the brakes with all my might. the idea of dying in a swamp somehow didn't fit me. The Ventura was still turning. she made another cycle and a half and stopped, to my surprise. It took me a few deep breaths to recover my full awareness, but soon I was back on the highway again.   4 *pages 89–90* **Proofreading for the Plural Form of Nouns**

I Was a "Little Devil"

by Mai Ha Nguyen

In the summer of 1980 I had to attend a chemistry class because my father [1] thought I was doing poorly in it. I admired karate very much at the time, but my father always gave me good reasons not to take lesson. Therefore, instead of going to chemistry class, I skipped school and took karate at a little school nearby, without my father's permission.

After I had taken a few lesson, I became one of the most annoying kid in the [2] neighborhood. I always made plan for us (our kid gang) to fight with the other kids on the surrounding block. This was one of the game that we enjoyed most. But as you may guess, every wild start must have an end. In my case, this was how I ended my karate lesson.

One day when I got out of my karate lesson, two of my friend and I were all [3] excited because tomorrow would be the big contest to go a step higher in karate. Suddenly I bumped into somebody. When I looked up, it was a guy who was around my age, but by appearance stronger than me. However, I didn't notice that, but stood up and started a fight with him. Even though he said "Sorry" many time and asked me to forgive him, I didn't. We took off our slipper and started. The kid surrounding us were cheering, and their yelling made me even more excited. I was winning for the first several minutes, but my strength left me as the fight went on. Finally, the guy punched me so hard that he completely knocked me down. I sat on the ground with bruise on my body and a bloody nose. He came over, looked at me, and asked: "Are you okay? I didn't want to fight, but you insisted. I'm sorry." After that he left. I was sitting on the ground feeling like a total fool.

On my way home, I didn't cry out loud, but tear kept rolling down my [4] face. After crying, I began to laugh about my stupidity and decided to give up physical fighting for the rest of my life. That was the end of my karate lesson.

pages 90–91   Spelling Strategy: When the Spelling Checker Doesn't Work

1. She was surprise to seex me standing there calm and without tears.
2. Rosita build up the idea that I was a hard young girl cause she couldn't understood anything I though important.
3. In my mother's absent, she ran the house and razed us.
4. When she smiled, we could see the perfectly strait white teeth of witch she was so proud.
5. One day, when she was changing her cloths, Rosita seen me observing her.

pages 115–17   Making Subjects and Verbs Agree

Snack/Meal

by Abu Tyeb Salleh

Food is essential to our lives. We spend an average of three hours each day eating; one-eighth of our lives is spent consuming food. Therefore, we "invented" two ways of enjoying it—snacks and meals.   1

Snacks are light food we eat between meals. They satisfy our craving for food and let us eat without having to sit at the table. They help us to exercise our jaws and yet let us enjoy the taste. Snacks need little or no preparation, and we can snack almost anywhere, any time, and in any mood.   2

You munch when you are on the bus. You munch when you are in the classroom; you munch when you are hungry; you munch when you are not; you munch when you are depressed; you munch when you are glad; you munch with your bunch of friends, but often you munch solitarily.   3

Snacks bring life to parties. ~~They~~ help to make the atmosphere happy and in-   4
formal. Snacks ~~are~~ fast to eat, and you don't have to worry too much about manners. But in terms of nutritious value, your doctor and parents would advise you
to minimize your consumption of snacks because they kill your appetite when
you have to eat a meal.

Meals, on the other hand, ~~are~~ the more elaborate and serious way of eating.   5
We are accustomed to eat two or three meals a day, and meals are the most important source of energy we need for activities during the day. Their importance and
nutritional value are therefore high.

You can skip snacks, but you can't skip meals. Because of their impor-   6
tance, we tend to spend more time on meals, preparing and enjoying them.
Meals can be romantic—candlelight dinners and breakfasts in bed are favorites among lovers. Meals also bring family members and friends around the
table and create a warm, loving, cozy atmosphere. Meals ~~are~~ the more formal
type of eating, and table manners are considered important. Meals, on the
whole, should be taken seriously.

As we can see from the above, snacks and meals differ in the way of eating,   7
time consumed, emotional involvement, and nutritious value. But they both make
the intake of food enjoyable. Although meals are considered more important,
snacks are sometimes more fun.

pages 118–20   Knowing When to Add -ed to the Verb

Goodbye to the High Tatras

by Jan Kalousek

1 = past tense
2 = present perfect or past perfect tense
3 = passive voice
4 = adjective form
5 = common expressions that always end in *-ed*

It was in January 1982 when I visit*ed* [1] the High Tatras for the last [1] time. The High Tatras are mountains in Czechoslovakia. This region is one of the last pieces of wild, unspoil*ed* [4] nature in Europe. From the age of fourteen I was a member of the mountaineering club, and I us*ed* [1 or 5] to visit these mountains every month. This visit was my last farewell to the place I lov*ed* [1] so deeply, because I knew that the next month I would leave Czechoslovakia forever.

High in the mountains there is a place called "White Fall," where there is a [2] hut us*ed* [3] by mountain climbers. I had to walk eight hours to reach this place. The snow was deep, my rucksack was heavy, and I was alone and tir*ed* [4].

The weather was cold and windy, but I had expect*ed* [2] it. I examin*ed* [1] the hut [3] closely. A couple of years ago there had been a fire and the hut had partly burn*ed* [2] up. The roof had a lot of holes, and burn*ed* [4] beams hung dangerously in the air. I search*ed* [1] inside for the best place to sleep and prepar*ed* [1] my "bed" in one corner which was better protect*ed* [4] than the others. It was gloomy inside the hut and I had to strain my eyes, especially when I cook*ed* [1] the soup.

Meanwhile, outside the visibility was getting poorer because of the clouds [4] which appear*ed* [1] in the sky. It was getting colder and the first snowflakes start*ed* [1] to fall. Soon the wind chang*ed* [1] to a gale and the snowstorm began.

I went back to the hut. Snowflakes were whirling even there; rotten beams [5] were creaking and squeaking. I went to sleep afraid, and I dream*ed* [1] heavy, ugly dreams about avalanches and other disasters.

pages 121–22   *Coping with Articles*

_____*The*_____ dictionary definition of "house" is _____*a*_____ build- [1] ing to live in, and _____*the*_____ definition of "home" is _____*a*_____ place where one lives. To me, _____*a*_____ house is _____*a*_____ building made of pieces of wood and _____*a*_____ couple of bricks, but home has

_____*a*_____ lot of meanings to me.

When I am home, I feel so comfortable and relaxed. It is _____*the*_____ place   2

where I spend most of my time, and also it is _____*the*_____ place where I learn

things which build me up as _____*a*_____ human being.

It is _____*an*_____ important thing to have _____*a*_____ building in   3

which we can build _____*a*_____ home, because I think that without my

home, I wouldn't exist now. Also without _____*a*_____ home, people would be

like animals without _____*a*_____ master. They would wander.

page 155   *Using Direct and Indirect Quotations*

Crisantina Orellana is a very old woman who was born in the quiet village of   1

Chalatenango in the northern countryside of El Salvador. During my interview,

I asked her about her age. She replied, "I really don't know it. The only thing I'm

sure of is that I was born at some day in the past and I'm still alive."

One thing is notorious in Crisantina Orellana's personality. She always looks   2

happy and full of joy. When I asked her what was the secret that has kept her full

of life, she said, "*L*ife is life. The only thing we have to worry about is how to live

it. Once you learn the way of doing so, you'll see the difference."

pages 156–57   *Review of Subject-Verb Agreement*

Julia (be) _____*is*_____ an eighteen-year-old girl, who (seem)   1

____*seems*____ to be a very ordinary person. She (like) _____*likes*_____ art, and

she (take) __*is taking*__ an art course this semester in college. But I did not

suspect that she (be) _____*is*_____ so advanced, not only in drawing but also

in ceramics.

I realized how talented she (be) _____*is*_____ when I came to interview   2 her and saw her room decorated with interesting abstract pictures on the walls and some ceramic works on the shelves. Although I (be) _____*am*_____ not a professional artist and I (do) _____*do*_____ not like abstract painting, Julia's strange pictures, her perception of colors, and her free flow of imagination delighted me. Since I (do) _____*do*_____ not have any talent at all, I always (admire) _____*admire*_____ people who (be) _____*are*_____ gifted in something. Julia (be) _____*is*_____ one of those people. Therefore, I made up my mind to interview her without any doubts.

pages 185–86   Using the Modals

An American professor was rushing to the classroom where he was scheduled to give his first lecture at a Brazilian university. When he arrived, he was surprised to find Room 101 was empty. He didn't know what had [happen] _____*happened*_____. However, being a professor, his mind went to work, and he came up with some interesting theories.   1

The professor's watch might [stop] _____*have*_____ _____*stopped*_____. Or the students might [forget] _____*have*_____ _____*forgotten*_____ that a class was scheduled for that day. Or possibly, they all might [decide] _____*have*_____ _____*decided*_____ to drop the class.   2

There were other possibilities as well. The university might [close] _____*have*_____ _____*closed*_____ early that day for a strike or protest. But surely if there had been a strike, the professor would [hear] _____*have*_____ _____*heard*_____ about it from someone.   3

Maybe there was a cultural explanation. Perhaps in Brazil, it might [be] _____*be*_____ acceptable for students to come late to class, or not to come to class at all.   4

As it turned out, the answer was quite simple. As a professor, he should   5

[know] _____*have*_____ _____*known*_____ better, but he obviously <u>had</u> not [check] _____*checked*_____ the schedule of classes carefully enough. Although he had copied down the day and time correctly, he <u>must</u> [make] _____*have*_____ _____*made*_____ a mistake about the room. He <u>had</u> [go] _____*gone*_____ to Room 101 when, in fact, he <u>should</u> [go] _____*have*_____ _____*gone*_____ to Room 110, which is where all his students were waiting.

page 187 *Proofreading for Verb Endings*

    I have never live*[2 d]* in a so-call*[5 ed]* traditional family in which people live with their grandparents, uncles, aunts, and other relatives. Even though I have never live*[2 d]* in a traditional family, I still prefer to live in a modern family.   **1**

    Our family is consider*[3 ed]* average in size, my parents, my two sisters, and me. Since there are only three children, we are given a lot of attention and freedom. I remember when we were still in Hong Kong, we always ~~have~~ *[1 had]* new clothes, school supplies, etc. Everything we need*[1 ed]* was provide*[3 d]* for us.   **2**

    On the other hand, my parents were very strict about our homework, and how we ~~do~~ *[1 did]* in school. I remember every night they ~~spended~~ *[1 spent]* time to sit down with us while we were doing our homework, and they ~~have~~ *[1 had]* to sign all our test papers.   **3**

    In our family, most of the housework was done by my parents. I use to wash *[1 or 3 d]* a few dishes at night and sweep the floors. During the weekend we were allow*[3 ed]* to stay out late. Sometimes, my friends and I decide*[1 d]* to go up to the mountains and spend a few days there. My parents usually like*[1 d]* to go with us. I will never forget those times.   **4**

    Things haven't change*[2 d]* much since we came to this country, except we don't have family trips any more because our parents are busy working every day, and we kids are busy studying and going to school.   **5** *page 188*   *Vocabulary Practice: Idioms*

1. strikes a chord = seems familiar or appropriate

2. 'pick up' = absorb, learn without being taught

3. badge of success = symbol of importance

4. snapped out = said in an impatient or angry way

5. stumbling block = problem, obstacle

pages 218–19   *Proofreading for Articles*

There are different reasons for emigration, but ^the^ result is the same — we move 1
to ^an^ other place. ~~The~~ ^E^migration is not just ~~the~~ moving to another country, but ~~the~~
leaving your native land. And this is the most important thing. Not everyone can
do it although ~~the~~ life in the native country is unbearable. Some people are afraid
to go to another place.

In fact, ~~the~~ life in one country is different from life in another. It depends on 2
^the^ people, on ^the^ system, on traditions, friends, favorite places, hobbies, native language.
So many things connect ~~the~~ people to their native country. And it's really difficult
to leave. Just serious reasons should cause them to do it.

What happens when ^a^ person finally decides to take this great step — to emi- 3
grate? This person hopes, sometimes is sure, he or she will be happy in ~~a~~ ^the^ new
place. But who knows? There are no absolutely perfect places in the world.

pages 219–20   *Vocabulary Practice: Immigration*

(*Note:* The following "answers" are merely suggestions; there are many other appropriate ways to fill the blanks.)

I have ___*had*___ many funny experiences since I ___*immigrated*___ to 1
the United States because I ___*didn't*___ understand a lot of things when I
first ___*arrived*___ here. I still ___*make*___ mistakes too. Sometimes I
___*laugh*___ after ___*making*___ mistakes, but sometimes I feel terrible.

When I first _____*came*_____ to America, I usually _____*went*_____ out to   2

look around. One day I went to Burger King even though I didn't know how to

speak English because I _____*was*_____ so hungry. I thought that in Burger King

it _____*would*_____ be easy to order food.

    When I got inside, I _____*listened*_____ to a couple of people order because I   3

couldn't _____*read*_____ the menu board. After I chose a name of something

to order and _____*tried*_____ to pronounce it a couple of times, I

_____*stood*_____ in front of the cashier. Although I pronounced the name sev-

eral times, she didn't understand me, so I _____*used*_____ body language by

_____*pointing*_____ to the menu board, but it was getting worse.

    She asked me something after I paid for my food, but I really couldn't under-   4

stand. Later I understood that she asked what kind of sauce I wanted. But I was so

*embarrassed* at that time. There were so many people _____*staring*_____ at me.

pages 220–21   *Vocabulary Practice: The Language Barrier*

1. ". . . continuing the immigrant tradition that makes the city so uniquely (diverse.)"
2. "Learning English demands (patience) from everyone. . . . "
3. "Here's where cultural breakdown sets in — or to be (blunt) prejudice."
4. "No one is more (sensitive) about lacking English skills than immigrants."
5. "Darnes Taveras, a writer from Queens, (witnessed) the suffering of her Dominican parents. 'They feel less empowered,' said Taveras, 25."

pages 251–52   *Active and Passive Voice of Verbs*

1. Should we force homeless people into shelters?

   No, they should not [force] _____*be*_____ _____*forced*_____ into shel-

   ters.

2. Should the United States build more housing for the homeless?

   Yes, a lot more housing needs to [build] _____ *be* _____ *built* .

3. Should we provide job training programs for homeless people who want to work?

   Yes, job training programs should [provide] _____ *be* _____ *provided* by the government.

4. Can homeless mothers work and still take care of their children?

   Yes, homeless mothers can work and care for their children if day-care programs [provide] _____ *are* _____ *provided* .

5. Should gay couples adopt children?

   Whether a gay couple [allow] _____ *is* _____ *allowed* to adopt a child should [evaluate] _____ *be* _____ *evaluated* on a case-by-case basis.

6. Should gays serve in the U.S. military?

   Yes, gays should [allow] _____ *be* _____ *allowed* to serve in the military.

7. Should homosexual couples pay higher income taxes than married heterosexual couples?

   No, homosexuals and heterosexuals should [require] _____ *be* _____ *required* to use the same tax rates.

8. Do immigrants face many problems?

   Yes, they [face] _____ *are* _____ *faced* with all kinds of problems.

9. It isn't easy to solve these problems, is it?

   No, the problems [solve] _____ *are* not easily _____ *solved* .

pages 253–54   ***Review of the Present Perfect Tense***

1. Doctors [find] ___*have*___ ___*found*___ cures for AIDS and cancer.

2. The condition of air and water [improve] ___*has*___ ___*improved*___ a lot.

3. The number of nuclear weapons [reduce] ___*has*___ ___*been*___ ___*reduced*___ .

4. However, there are still many things that [accomplish] ___*have*___ not yet ___*been*___ ___*accomplished*___.

5. For example, the problem of homelessness [solve] ___*has*___ not ___*been*___ ___*solved*___ .

6. Not all drug dealers [arrest] ___*have*___ ___*been*___ ___*arrested*___ .

7. The population [continue] ___*has*___ ___*continued*___ to grow.

8. The cost of living [double] ___*has*___ ___*doubled*___ in the last ten years.

9. But for the most part, things [get] ___*have*___ ___*gotten*___ better.

pages 254–55   ***Spelling Strategy: Vowel Sounds***

1. <u>cou</u>ples = cup

2. th<u>i</u>s = wish

3. l<u>i</u>ve = river

4. m<u>a</u>tters = and

pages 255–56   Vocabulary Practice: Gay Rights

1. The process of conceiving a child without sexual intercourse: <u>c. donor insemination or surrogacy</u>

2. Men who prefer sexual relationships with other men: <u>d. gay men</u>

3. Contributing sperm to conceive a child: <u>h. biological fatherhood</u>

4. The rights of a father to live with or visit with his child: <u>b. paternity rights</u>

5. Openly or publicly homosexual: <u>f. "out"</u>

6. A parent who does not live with his or her child: <u>g. noncustodial parent</u>

7. Born of parents who are not legally married: <u>i. illegitimate</u>

8. A woman who prefers sexual relationships with other women: <u>a. lesbian</u>

9. Children: <u>e. offspring</u>

page 310   Learning to Proofread

There are many acceptable ways of editing this essay. What follows is only one possibility.

Writing Skill is Essential

I think that writing is an essential skill for a person in modern society be-   1
cause we need writing skill in jobs and for keeping records. Also writing will al-
continue to   important
~~ways~~ be in the future. ~~and in generation ahead.~~

Most jobs ~~in the world~~ require a person to read and write. For ~~an~~ example, a   2
e
friend of mind (Robin) who is an expert in computer went to a job interview. The
in   *ed*
jobs he was looking for was data entry. When the person who interview my friend
him
told ~~Robin~~ to type a sentence on the computer, ~~What happen is that~~ Robin knew
a
how to work the computer, but the grammer in his sentence was wrong. Robin
p   *But he began*
was dissapointed when he didn't get the job. ~~Robin was beginning~~ to work harder
on   *had*
in his grammar and a year later he ~~have~~ a job in data entry, the same job that he
for before
was turned down.

Writing ~~is~~ *will be* very important in the future. ~~and in generation ahead~~. We know ~~the~~ past history because there are record*s* in writing. Now there are computer*s* to store information and data faster than *by* writing it. ~~The~~ *However, there* are ~~always a~~ *often* problem*s* ~~in~~ *with* computer*s*. *For* example, what if there ~~are~~ *is* a lightning storm and it cause*s* the power in a computer room *to go* ~~off~~. The computer data and memory would be erase*d*. But if you write the data and information ~~in~~ *down on* paper or *in a* book, it will last longer and *you* don't have to worry about lightning storm*s*.

Writing began when caveme*n* ~~are~~ *were* still alive. It will continue ~~to~~ *into* the future. ~~Why should we not learn to write when~~ *I*n past generation*s* writing ~~is~~ *was* use*d* for communication and to store data. ~~so~~ *In this way,* we can learn from our mistake*s* that happen*ed* in the past. Also, law*s* and treat*ies* have to be written to make the society better.

Acknowledgments

Gloria Anzaludúa. Excerpt from "La conciencia de la mestiza" from *Borderlands/La Frontera: The New Mestiza* © 1987 by Gloria Anzaldúa. Reprinted with permission of Aunt Lute Books.

Russell Baker. Reprinted from *Growing Up* by Russell Baker, © 1982. Used with permission of Congdon and Weed, Inc. and Contemporary Books, Chicago.

Robert Coles. Excerpt from *Uprooted Children: The Early Life of Migrant Farm Workers* by Robert Coles. Reprinted by permission of the University of Pittsburgh Press. Copyright © 1970 by University of Pittsburgh Press.

Kim Dartnell. "Where Will They Sleep Tonight?" student essay in *The St. Martin's Guide to Writing*, first edition. Copyright © 1985, by St. Martin's Press, Inc. From *The St. Martin's Guide to Writing* by Rise Axelrod and Charles Cooper. Reprinted by permission of St. Martin's Press, Inc.

Betty Liu Ebron. "Learning English Ain't Easy," published in the *Daily News*. Copyright © 1993 New York Daily News, L.P., used with permission.

Jane Gross. "After a Ruling, Hawaii Weighs Gay Marriages" by Jane Gross in the *New York Times* (April 25, 1994). Copyright © 1994 by the New York Times Company. Reprinted by permission.

Ruby Ibañez. "Teacher, It's Nice to Meet You, Too." Reprinted by permission of the author.

R. Levine and **E. Wolff.** "Social Time: The Heartbeat of Culture" from *Psychology Today*. Reprinted by permission of *Psychology Today* magazine. Copyright © 1985 Sussex Publishers, Inc.

Samuel Nakasian. "An American Success Story," unpublished speech. Reprinted by permission of the author.

New York Times. "Gay Parents: Living in Fear," an editorial in the *New York Times* (October 4, 1993). Copyright © 1993 by the New York Times Company. Reprinted by permission.

New Yorker. "Beyond Stonewall: Gay Struggles, 25 Years On" from The Talk of the Town (June 20, 1994). Reprinted by permission; copyright © 1994 by the *New Yorker* Magazine, Inc.

Mark Salzman. Excerpt from *Iron and Silk* by Mark Salzman. Copyright © 1986 by Mark Salzman. Reprinted by permission of Random House, Inc. and Penguin Books, Ltd.

Xiao Mei Sun. "Exodus." Copyright © 1987 by St. Martin's Press, Inc. From *Student Writers at Work: The Bedford Prizes* by Nancy Sommers and Donald McQuade. Reprinted by permission of St. Martin's Press, Inc.

Deborah Tannen. Copyright © 1986 by Deborah Tannen from the book *That's Not What I Meant*. Permission granted by Rhoda Weyr Agency, New York.

Photo Credits

Chapter One opener: Clem Fiori
Chapter Two opener: Clem Fiori
Chapter Three opener: Clem Fiori
Chapter Four opener: Steven Haber
Chapter Five opener: Pan Qingfu in the motion picture *Iron and Silk*, directed and produced by Shirley Sun, based on the book by Mark Salzman

Chapter Six opener: Photo Researchers, Inc. Bill Binzen © 1991
Chapter Six text photo: Copyright © Agence France Presse
Chapter Seven opener: photograph by Ken Light from the book *To the Promised Land* by Ken Light, published by Aperture, New York, 1988
Chapter Eight opener: Thomas Holton
Chapter Nine opener: National Parks Service: Statue of Liberty National Monument
Chapter Ten opener: David Grossman
Chapter Eleven opener: Clem Fiori
Chapter Twelve opener: Clem Fiori

Index